Times Square Rabbi

Times Square Rabbi

Finding the Hope in Lost Kids' Lives

YEHUDAH FINE

Hazelden
Center City, Minnesota 55012-0176
1-800-328-0094
1-612-257-1331 (24-hour FAX)
http://www.hazelden.org (World Wide Web site on Internet)

Library of Congress Cataloging-in-Publication Data
Fine, Yehudah, 1947–
Times Square rabbi : finding the hope in lost kids' lives / Yehudah Fine.
p. cm.
Includes bibliographical references and index.
ISBN 1-56838-145-X
1. Pastoral counseling (Judaism) 2. Socially handicapped youth—Rehabilitation—New York (State)—New York. 3. Jewish youth—Pastoral counseling of—New York (State)—New York. 4. Fine, Yehudah, 1947– . 5. Rabbis—New York (State)—New York—Biography. I. Title.
BM652.5.F56 1997
296.7'09747'1—dc21 96-53665
CIP

Book design by Will H. Powers
Typesetting by Stanton Publication Services, Inc.
Cover design by David Spohn

Editor's note
Hazelden offers a variety of information on chemical dependency and related areas. Our publications do not necessarily represent Hazelden's programs, nor do they officially speak for any Twelve Step organization.

All the stories in this book are based on actual experiences. The names and details have been changed to protect the privacy of the people involved. In some cases, composites have been created.

There is no road without twists and turns.
No road without pitfalls and snares.
And there is no road without explanation.
Sifri D'varim 20

Contents

Author's Notes

Writing this book has been an emotional and cathartic experience. It put a good deal of my lifetime of working with hundreds of people into some kind of order and spiritual perspective. The reader should be keenly aware that all these stories are composites of people and images I have encountered. The dialogues are reconstructed from my internal reservoir of countless conversations I've had with people over the years. They reflect my style, direction, and tone, but certainly are not actual dialogues. The stories then are fictionalized, because I certainly would never put on display the story of a child's life. I also chose to leave many sad and gruesome details of the kids' lives out of the book. Nevertheless, while these are fictionalized stories and composite characters, anyone who knows the street and the struggles young people encounter will recognize the reality expressed in these tales.

The reader should also be aware that all translations of Hebrew texts were done through my hand from the original. Any errors in the translations can only reflect an oversight on my part, and I offer my sincerest apology for any oversight committed. It can only be laid at my feet and certainly wasn't intentional.

Acknowledgments

I WOULD LIKE TO EXPRESS MY HEARTFELT THANKS: To my wife, Elliesheva, whose love, vision, sharing, and caring are the invisible hands behind my work. For her continual conversation with me about the needs of children and her endless hours of working with me on the book—and for her smile. Without her computer skills and dedication to me and our children, the work and this book never would have become a reality. She is my woman of valor. To Dorah, Benny, and Rafi, for their endless patience with me and for the grace and warmth they have shown to the endless stream of guests who have graced our home. Kids, I'm proud of who you are and of who you are becoming. And special thanks for the thousand times you asked, "How's the book going, Abs?" To my father, of blessed memory, whose vision, care, and love for his patients as a physician propelled me into a life of helping others. He was always there to encourage me. To my mother, whose support, dignity, and strong values I carry with me in my life. To my sister, Susan, whose enthusiasm and support for the book never let up. Even when I stumbled, she didn't. To my father-in-law, Morrie, whose steadfast encouragement at the very early stages of the manuscript was so important to me. And to my mother-in-law, Rheta, who has supported me in every endeavor. To my sister-in-law, Rae Ann, for her wonderful cheerleading and continual upbeat e-mail and phone calls in support of the book. To Betty Christiansen, my editor at Hazelden, whose grace, insight, craft, and laser-like writing skill helped shape the outcome of the book. Her commitment to the stories made her a true partner in my work. Her technical skill at being able to pinpoint the subtle changes needed in the text made me not only marvel at her abilities as a writer, but also made me thankful she took the book under her wing. It is true what authors say about their editors. They are wonderful. To Steve Lehman, acquisitions editor at Hazelden, for his warmth, sensitivity, and professionalism. He helped nurture the book and gave me confidence from our first phone call. His accessibility and personal style made me so very happy my book found a home at Hazelden. To Cathy Broberg, senior manuscript editor at Hazelden, whose skill guided the final details of the book. To Judith Appelbaum and the entire staff of Sensible Solutions, Inc., for their professional advice, belief in the importance of this book, and, most of all, for helping me find my publisher, Hazelden.

To all my teachers along the way: To my rebbes at Kollel Gur Aryeh who, years ago, showed great patience and warmth in opening the doors of Torah learning. Without their support, I would have truly been impoverished in spirit. To Reb Gedalia, of blessed memory, whose compassion all those years ago embraced my heart and touches me to this day. To Reb Zalman, whose patience, laughter, and time spent with me in learning complex spiritual matters has been invaluable. To my mentors at the Ackerman Institute of Family Therapy in New York, Fran Ackerman and Connie Scharff as well as the entire staff who trained me in seeing the ecology of family systems and who understood how closely I needed to work with families. Their training has contributed greatly in my helping others.

To all my friends: To Effie Nulman, whose humor serves as a constant reminder to have fun and whose skills as a family therapist have been a reservoir of guidance. To Billy and Patty whose family and deep friendship are an anchor for my heart. To David Rubenstein, whose friendship and advice have been so appreciated. Everybody needs such a friend. To Stephen, who has been with me in heart since the Great Highway. To Homes, who never quits; to Hills, who loves the work as much as I do; and to Beans and Jayce for their commitment to goodness. To the supporters of the Jewish Family Institute who have supported the dream of hope because they know the dream must be reality. To Coddington, Terri, and Claude from Off the Streets, for all the nighttime rides and for your heroic caring and compassion—you are an inspiration to me. To Covenant House and all the runaway and homeless shelters whose hearts for kids are bigger than the sky. To Arlene, wherever you are—I have not forgotten. And to Sinai and Ira.

To the late Andy Wood, too soon gone from this world, whose innocence is sorely missed; and to Jeff and Stone who played with him. And to everyone who played the Fillmore and Avalon in San Francisco for more than the music—the vision continues to this day. And to all the kids struggling to make sense out of their lives. There is goodness in the world and in your hearts.

Introduction

The Wondrous Way Out

How can we find meaning and hope in suffering? How do we live in order to uncover purpose and find understanding in our daily lives?

Over the past quarter of a century, many people have come to me searching for an answer to these questions. Their struggles brought them to my doorstep. My work has been to help them embark on a journey toward healing themselves.

If I were to sum up the jobs I've had in my life, my titles might read rabbi, family therapist, and educator. Magazines have called me the Times Square Rabbi. But the individuals and families who have come to my doorstep have always called me Yehudah. I've never wanted to be a title in someone's life, and furthermore, the people I've worked with have had their fill of folks with titles.

I used to complain that people always came to me at the eleventh hour. After falling through every crack in the system, they'd find out about me and get my number. Their needs were enormous and their requests outrageous.

I grew within that chaos, and in time, my complaints turned into gratitude. I've been privileged to watch the vulnerable toughen and grow. As dangerous as a physical, emotional, or spiritual emergency may be, I've witnessed how an individual can create a new life filled with love, goodness, and compassion.

My professional choices in life dovetail with my spiritual need to be on the edge lending a hand. Those choices began long ago when I created a school for the children of migrant farmworkers in the Sacramento Valley and continued with the creation of an alternative high school on the coast of northern California. When I moved to Brooklyn fifteen years ago, I founded the Jewish Family Institute and began to work with adolescents in crisis on the streets of New York City.

Word of mouth traveled fast in New York as spiritual seekers and runaways found their way to my door. In response, I began to provide counseling and respite to dozens of young people. I networked with many runaway and homeless youth shelters, centers, and agencies in the five boroughs of New York. The referrals to my institute increased and I began to work in conjunction with Covenant House's Off the Streets program. Based out of Times Square, I would ride the outreach van every Thursday night, reaching out to kids on the edge. I spent a good deal of time at the Covenant House center, as well as in a host of other small agencies' centers which provided shelter and protection for runaway and homeless youth.

But it hasn't only been the hands-on services I've provided that have helped these young people pull themselves off the streets and turn their lives around. My own inner work has immersed me in a world filled with spiritual guidebooks and maps, which, in turn, I've passed along to help others on their way.

Years ago, I began working with one such guide in the writings of the twelfth-century luminary Rabbi Moshe Ben Maimon, best known as Maimonides or the Rambam. In his fourteen-volume *Mishneh Torah*, Maimonides codified the oral teachings of Judaism and the writings of great sages. There, I stumbled onto a powerful guide to spiritual reawakening. It is called *Hilchos Teshuvah,* or in my free translation, the Path to Meaning and Hope. Indeed, when we reawaken and discover the direction of our life's journey, we truly discover meaning and hope.

The text focuses on helping us face our stumblings, pain, personal failure, and diminution of self. It shows us how to turn inward to discover that contained within each of us are the keys to inspiration, hope, and the ability to change.

In Hebrew, *Hilchos* literally means a path or the way we walk. It is often translated as "laws" or rules for living a more meaningful life. And *Teshuvah* literally means "return," but more appropriately, "spiritual reawakening." Teshuvah implies a change in our state of being, a new awareness of an inner yearning to connect with the sacred. I took license in calling *Hilchos Teshuvah* "The Path to Meaning and Hope" because I have observed that when people have profound reawakenings, their lives become filled with meaning and hope.

Teshuvah presupposes that we feel estranged or distant from God. And it's precisely that distance that propels us on our spiritual quest. You might say the principle is this: The greater the distance, the greater the tension, and the greater the tension, the greater the move toward the sacred.

A simple rubber band illustrates the paradox. The precise moment when the rubber band is pulled taut is also the precise point of maximum recoil. So the farther away we may be from God, the greater the possibility we have of coming close to God. Either you let the rubber band fly or it snaps.

When people do let it fly, when they let go of all the tension, failure, abuse, pain, and confusion, they invariably report that something wonderful happens. They say things such as, "I'm a changed person" or, "I feel I've been given another chance" or, "God turned my life around" or, "I feel so grateful." In my work with young people, I have had the honor to witness many such transformations. I marveled at their transformations and wondered if it was possible to write about them in a way that truly conveyed the wondrous ability we have to change our lives.

Shortly thereafter, I found my answer. Down in the polluted backwaters of Manhattan, where life endlessly churns up sorrow, I met Darby. Darby was on a quest to turn his life around. Even if his turning was only a small increment on the wheel, it was there. He was chasing it.

One hot summer night, while I was working the outreach van on Manhattan's Lower West Side, I had an encounter with him that put everything I was learning into focus.

I vividly remember sitting in the outreach van with Darby. He was wearing a jet-black satin dress cut tight to his body. He had a blue-green shawl draped over his shoulders and a wide silver bracelet on his left wrist. Gold bangle earrings hung from three pierces in each of his ears. He was trying to look beautiful and fit, but his darting eyes told of desperation.

Darby was quiet as he sat drinking Kool-Aid in the van. When no one else was with us, I asked what was troubling him.

I could see tears forming in his eyes as he looked out the van's window.

"Yehudah, I just tested positive for HIV. I feel real bad. I've got to stop turning tricks out here. I could really mess somebody up like I got all messed up."

Taking another sip of Kool-Aid, with tears dripping down his face, he whispered, "The hardest thing is, I got to tell my grandma. She's all I got. I'm so scared she won't understand. She'll throw me out or something. But I have to do it. I owe it to her and I owe it to myself."

I understood, right then, that I'd been witness to an extraordinary act of courage. A turning point. Darby's life had reached crisis. Before that moment, he had been racing down the road with hundreds of others like himself who thought little of consequence. But now, facing the possibility of his death, Darby knew he had to come clean. By turning his direction around, he could release himself from all the painful secrets he was carrying. By sharing his story with someone he loved, he could rip away the veils of self-deception and finally accept himself with all his imperfections. There is no timetable for healing and forgiveness. Even in a short life torn from the street, Darby still had his shot at reclaiming his dignity. By finally accepting his broken heart he could, in some measure, become whole. He could come closer to God. Sadly, I never saw or heard of Darby again. I hope and pray he did tell his grandma. Our time together haunts me to this day.

Darby's courage brought me to this book, for in Darby's life I saw how his inner turning point was reflected in Maimonides' teaching. No matter who or where we are, each of us has the capacity to turn our lives around and touch the sky.

While change at a profound level is rare on the street, nevertheless it does happen. And when you witness such a change, you can't help but remember the eternal spiritual truth that *first was darkness and then came the light*. Some of the deepest secrets of life can be discovered in the heart of darkness.

I was new to the street when I met Darby. Yet that early experience taught me something I would never forget. Day by day and year by year I kept encountering the same great lesson: Crisis can produce profound transformation. I have been privileged to see it over and over again, not only in the lives of runaways, drug addicts, and transvestites, but also in the lives of parents, spiritual seekers, and families whose stories appear in these pages.

If we choose to realize that the only way out is up, then it's possible to find the ladder that God has thrown us in the pit. We can begin to climb out.

The Path to Meaning and Hope

In teaching and counseling, I apply my observations of transformations born of crisis by using and amplifying Maimonides' text. Although it was written more than 700 years ago, Maimonides' *Hilchos Teshuvah*, which I have translated freely as the Path to Meaning and Hope, provides a powerful framework for inner growth. This ancient stream of wisdom helps us face our imperfections and take concrete action to illuminate our lives. The Rambam's words can, I found, be translated into a format that is useful to people today who are working through their own spiritual emergencies.

Using the principle of Teshuvah—which in English means "return" or "reawakening"—I designed an eight-step process that lets the seeker know precisely where he or she is and what work is needed to transform his or her life.

The eight steps take us on a journey of self-discovery. This is the secret contained in the process of Teshuvah: We experience continual rebirth of the self, the exaltation of each day of our life.

It's important to note that the inspiration offered here is not a substitute for therapy or for an established Twelve Step program. Rather, these steps can help you take the risk to discover who you are and where you are going. They can unlock the still small voice calling out to you from deep within your heart. They can help you see that crisis doesn't have to lead to despair, that it can lead, instead, to understanding the specialness of your own life.

It is by turning to face the darkness and the pain that we begin to understand our imperfections, accept them, and then make use of the tremendous potential and possibilities each of us uniquely possesses. It is through the lens of crisis that each of us can begin to truly appreciate our precious uniqueness.

And it is through our uniqueness that we can appreciate and honor the uniqueness of others. The path of Teshuvah inevitably turns life into a wonder, and that wondrous realization becomes the door to unlocking the great mystery and sacredness of each of our lives.

This eight-step guide served as an inspiration and tool for the people whose stories appear in this book. The stories are, therefore, organized around the eight steps—segments of each story demonstrate how one or more of the steps were used in helping someone climb out of pain, face a profound turning point, and make positive life changes.

STEP ONE: *Hurling Out the Pain*

An individual must confess, own up to the iniquities he or she committed whether willingly or inadvertently. This is a verbal confession. This confession is a positive commandment. How do you confess? The individual says, "I beseech You, God; I sinned, I transgressed, I was careless. Before You I did the following. . . . Behold, I regret and am embarrassed by my deeds and/or actions and I will never repeat this deed again."

(MAIMONIDES, *Hilchos Teshuvah*, Chapter One, Section One)

When we suffer, there comes a time when the pain becomes unbearable. We spiral down and down until we stop with a thud. It then becomes clear that our lives cannot continue as they were. The first step is to get it all out.

Realizing that we have to change is not enough. An action is required in order to make a stand against whatever we did. When we hurl it out, we tell someone specifically what we did and how we are now committed to putting a stop to it. This becomes a positive force propelling us toward the next step.

STEP TWO: ***Recognizing That You've Changed***

What is the essence of Teshuvah? An individual forsakes his or her misdeeds and removes them from his or her thoughts. There is finality in one's heart that there is no returning to those misdeeds. . . . And the said person knows and is witness in the hiddenness [of one's heart] that he or she will never return to this [said misdeed] again. As it is written (Hoshea 14:4), "We no longer say to the work of our hands: 'You are our gods.' " An individual needs to acknowledge this with one's lips and to say these matters that are finished in one's heart.

(MAIMONIDES, *Hilchos Teshuvah*, Chapter Two, Section Two)

Once we have laid out the cards of our pain on the table, we see that we don't want to have anything to do with them anymore. There is no doubt in our minds and hearts. We will not allow the things that led us downward to influence us again. From this day forward, we leave the struggle behind.

STEP THREE: ***Standing Up for Yourself***

Keep yourself far away from the things that caused you to sin. Change your name, which is to say, "I am a different individual, and I'm not the person who did all those things." Change your actions and deeds, all of them, to the good and straight path. And go into exile from your current place.

(MAIMONIDES, *Hilchos Teshuvah*, Chapter Two, Section Four)

We realize that in order to have nothing to do with what caused our pain, we have to separate ourselves from many things. It is as if we had a previous self who did those things or acted that way. Staying far away from that previous life is now a steadfast commitment.

Our confession has brought us to a new awareness. We become aware of a part of our personality that had been hidden in our pain. This new sense of self is like a new name. And our new name is bringing us forward to begin a new life.

STEP FOUR: ***Moving Forward with Life***

"Remember your Creator in the days of your youth" (Ecc. 12:1). [Because your life has changed, you no longer have desire in your former life.] Who attains complete Teshuvah? An individual who is challenged, who faces and confronts the same situation in which he or she stumbled and has at hand the possibility to commit that misdeed again, and who refrains and doesn't do it because of his or her individual Teshuvah. And this refraining is not out of fear nor lack of strength.

(MAIMONIDES, *Hilchos Teshuvah*, Chapter Two, Section One)

No matter how carefully we may have separated ourselves from our previous situation, something or someone will pop up and challenge us. This is a great opportunity because by meeting and overcoming the challenge, we feel strong and sure that we have moved forward with our lives.

As a result, we feel renewed, almost young again. This youthful feeling is a signal that it is time to get our lives back on track.

We have moved ourselves so completely away from our former difficulties that we stop looking back. What lies ahead of us is a wide-open world ready for our new sense of vitality.

STEP FIVE: ***Straightening Out Personal Business***

Transgressions between an individual and another are never forgiven until you reconcile your debt and appease your friend. Even if you return said individual's money that you owe, you need to reconcile and ask to be forgiven. Even if you upset someone by saying certain [hurtful] things, you must appease this person until you are forgiven. If the individual doesn't forgive, go back to that person two or three times. [But] if the individual doesn't want [to forgive you], you may leave the matter and go. The person who refuses to be forgiving is considered a sinner.

(MAIMONIDES, *Hilchos Teshuvah*, Chapter Two, Section Nine)

Before our lives can move ahead smoothly, before we can be ready for that wide-open world, we have to ask for forgiveness from the people we hurt. We are now emotionally strong enough to endure the discomfort of repairing the damage.

It's not enough to say we're sorry. We have to do everything possible to find satisfactory resolutions. There are two parts involved: paying back and seeking forgiveness. Both are necessary. To do this, it's important to go the extra mile.

STEP SIX: *Confessing Your Actions in Public*

It is exceedingly praiseworthy for an individual to do Teshuvah by confessing in public and acknowledging and making his or her sins known to others, and revealing the transgressions that occurred between the individual and his or her friends. The individual should say to them, "I sinned against so-and-so and I did such-and-such. . . . Behold, I am this day doing Teshuvah and express my regret.

(MAIMONIDES, *Hilchos Teshuvah*, Chapter Two, Section Five)

Once we've set things from the past straight, we move forward by sharing with others what we have learned. We strengthen ourselves tremendously by talking about how far we fell, how we hurt ourselves, how we hurt others, and how we struggled to climb back to where we stand with them now.

This accomplishes two powerful things. First, there is a great lesson in humility that accompanies a public admission. Second, by baring our souls publicly, we help those we've wronged recognize that our regret is sincere.

STEP SEVEN: *Living Your Forgiveness*

An individual should not wonder and say, "How is it possible for us to do what we want and thus be responsible for all our actions?" The Creator desires that individuals have free choice and be responsible for their actions without being forced or pulled. It's forbidden for a person to be cruel and not be appeased. Rather, a person ought to be easily appeased and difficult to anger. When someone who sinned against you asks you for forgiveness, you should forgive with a complete heart and a

> *willing spirit. Even if that person caused you pain and wronged you many times, don't seek revenge and don't bear a grudge.*
>
> (MAIMONIDES, *Hilchos Teshuvah*, Chapter Two, Section Ten, and Chapter Five, Section Four)

After speaking to others about our struggle, we continue onward through life, conscious of our great responsibility to make wise decisions. We must look around in the world and find ways to make positive choices for our lives.

We are now keenly aware of how we are responsible for every move we make. No one is forcing us to choose one way or the other, but we no longer consider choices that could take us in the wrong direction.

Being unforgiving in any way keeps us from making positive decisions. When we forgive someone, particularly someone who caused us pain, we pave new paths upon which others will travel the road of forgiveness.

We previously sought forgiveness from those we hurt, but memories of how others hurt *us* tend to linger. Our willingness to forgive is a sign that we have truly been transformed. Without holdouts and grudges, we are free to touch the sky.

STEP EIGHT: *Falling in Love with Life*

> *The one who serves God out of Love . . . and walks in the pathway of wisdom—not because of anything in this world; not because of fear that evil will happen; not in order to get something good from it; but rather the person does what is true because it is true—in the end, goodness will come from it. . . . What is the proper amount of love? A person should love God with a great and powerful love until that person's soul is bound up in the love of God. . . . One cannot love God except through the knowledge that one knows God. According to the amount of one's knowledge will be the amount of one's love.*
>
> (MAIMONIDES, *Hilchos Teshuvah*, Chapter Ten, Sections Two, Three, and Six)

We didn't know it, but when we first hurled out the pain, we were making room for love. We continued to evolve and be transformed by working on ourselves. Through the work of Teshuvah, we roused our minds and spirits and found within us our love of God.

We are heartsick for more knowledge of the Spirit. We let go and let love embrace our lives.

STEP ONE

Hurling Out the Pain

DANNY'S STORY

Everything has its season,
and there is a time for everything
under the heaven:

A time to be born and a time to die
Koheles; Chapter 3

STEP ONE: ***Hurling Out the Pain***

> *An individual must confess, own up to the iniquities he or she committed whether willingly or inadvertently. This is a verbal confession. This confession is a positive commandment. How do you confess? The individual says, "I beseech You, God; I sinned, I transgressed, I was careless. Before You I did the following. . . . Behold, I regret and am embarrassed by my deeds and/or actions and I will never repeat this deed again."*
>
> (MAIMONIDES, *Hilchos Teshuvah*, Chapter One, Section One)

When we suffer, there comes a time when the pain becomes unbearable. We finally become sick and tired of how we are treating ourselves—the self-abuse, the lies we tell ourselves, and the harmful compromises we have made. The feelings that bubble up in our chests are not quieted by our rationalizing and avoiding minds. We know we must change our way of living.

When we hit that point, we are ready to break free. We are now on the way to an encounter with ourselves. We are about to make contact with an urgent message: *It's time to move toward living an authentic life.*

The whys and hows of this compelling event differ for each and every one of us. Most of the time we simply rely on our defenses to avoid changing. But when we finally decide to break free from the bondage of our lies, abuse, and pain, we get busy.

There is a powerful word for the first step in this busyness. It's called *confession,* or in Hebrew, *vidui.* Its root comes from the verb *to hurl;* therefore, a confession implies the hurling out of something. A vidui is a defining spoken event that confesses, or lets out, what has happened to us, what precisely we did or what was done to us, and how that diminished the essence of who we are.

Vidui, then, is the first step to straightening out our personal crisis. It's the first step to hurling away our mistakes and our failings. If we are not willing to label our emotional shortcomings in words, how are we going to resolve our crisis? Not confessing is like being lost in the wilderness, being offered a compass and map, and refusing them, saying, "Hey, I'd rather stay lost."

Inner pain becomes the main focus of our attention. With it comes a dawning recognition that if we find perspective in our suffering, we can discover our purpose in life. If we can divest ourselves of anger and pain, we can find forgiveness and free ourselves from the demons of hurt and retribution that have left us in a seemingly endless spiral of self-destruction.

Thus, the first step out comes through hurling out the pain.

Manhattan Nights

The lower level of Penn Station smells impossibly bad. I wonder if I'll ever get used to the smell of urine and burnt subway rubber, the smell that so pervades the New York subway system that it almost identifies the city.

The landscape down in the subway tunnels is dismal, dusky, and depressing. Sunlight never slants its way down into those gloomy passageways. I call it *The Way Beyond;* a place of darkness and hope, of death and dreams. Those tunnels are haunted by the mad and the hermits, the homeless and the lost; our refugees hiding out in urban America.

It was a Thursday evening in the kingdom of the night: New York City from 8:00 P.M. to 5:30 A.M. I was working outreach with two co-workers from a runaway and homeless youth shelter. Our beat was the dark streets of Manhattan, Queens, and the Bronx. Part of the night we cruised the backwaters of the city in our outreach van. The rest of the night was spent working the streets on foot patrol and descending into dirty concrete tunnels inhabited by moaning, snoring homeless people. The passageways were cluttered with the cardboard boxes they lived in. The underground of Manhattan on winter nights was a barren outpost of desperation. Our goal was to find kids in need and to get them off the streets. If they sought shelter, we could eventually help them rebuild their lives. Life in a runaway and homeless youth shelter is not only a safe haven, but also a place to find a job, get some counseling, or even complete a high school education. But the first step was building trust with these kids. To do that, we went to them, offered our caring, and gave them some hot chocolate and a sandwich. Then, like clockwork, we came back every night to give them the message that we cared.

When I first went out on the streets into *The Way Beyond*, I was scared. In time the fear simply sharpened my senses. What I saw was a war zone: Everything was stripped down to bare essentials. People were dying and disappearing. I saw kids' bodies become ravaged by sickness in just six months. I sat and talked with kids under tunnels of garbage. Rats jumped in front of my flashlight.

Everyone was used or abused. Boys were girls and girls were selling parts of themselves. AIDS and TB ate their way through young people. Night was day, and nobody went home. No one had a home. This was a place rife with grisly rumors. Kids simply vanished. Other kids ended up in medical examiners' autopsy reports. Suicide, OD's, and murder were these kids' endgames. Crack was king and cocaine was the snow queen. This was science fiction gone real, where *beaming up* meant a blue-smoke crack journey into unreality. Everyone lied because the truth was too raw to share.

The Way Beyond taught me hard lessons. There were no norms here, only deviations and aberrations. It was in *The Way Beyond* that I began to understand the path of destruction that pain can take in a young person's life. The kids I met here all had endured devastation of one form or another. Everyone had become tough because they were so vulnerable. When I touched that vulnerability, I became aware of my own vulnerability.

That Thursday night, we were looking for a nineteen-year-old pregnant girl. She gave the underground of Grand Central Terminal as her street address. Her home. She had just tested positive for HIV, and we needed to find her. We never did, but then again, most nights we never found the kids we were looking for. However, we always managed to find kids who were looking for us.

By 2:30 in the morning, we had taken the outreach van over to the docks on the West Side Highway, moving across 5th and 6th Avenues on 47th Street. Except for the occasional all-night bodega or Korean market, most of Manhattan was asleep. Unless, of course, you knew where to look. Like at the docks.

The docks were the place to hustle when you didn't look so pretty anymore. If you couldn't sell yourself up on the Loop on Lexington because you'd been out on the street too long, you could still go to the docks; lots of easy access and commuter traffic cut through there.

The traffic was always the first thing I noticed as we approached the West Side. Even at 2:30 in the morning the docks were one big parking lot with bumper-to-bumper traffic: men in limos, low riders, station wagons, and pickups, all cruising for young boys. This was a dark slipstream world of predators feasting on kids. It was the place demons went to fulfill the nameless desires that dominated their thoughts.

Whenever we'd park at the docks, I liked to get out of the van, walk around, talk to the kids, share a cup of hot chocolate. Somehow, a rabbi was never out of place in the night world. I've never completely understood why, but I suspect that once you're willing to cross over into the netherworld of the night, you have made it through an invisible gate. Stepping out into that world was like a strange initiation into a place without rules. If you could handle being there, you were accepted.

Out on the streets, I developed senses I'd never known existed, senses that let me know what was going on around me. My body taught my mind about things. My intuition bristled up my neck and sent waves of chills down my spine. I was being let in on life's secrets and pain. That intuition is essential. Without it, I could never have touched another heart.

I learned early on that the street kids have their own code. Ironically, caring is a high virtue according to that code. I found new definitions for unconditional love within these kids. This place was the great test of love, compassion, and caring. When life is stripped down to the bare wires, every action has the possibility of being pure and real.

The Way Beyond is a hostile place. Kids instinctively protect and look out for each other. They bond in small groups and freely love and care for each other. Intense emotional attachments form quickly. After all, what else do kids have out there except life and death, love and hate, anger and violence? They seek refuge in the few values left to them. Protecting a friend is worth dying for. Their bodies might be assaulted, but no one can take away their love.

Although most of the kids I met still had their kindness and ability to give, they usually didn't know they had these gifts. But I knew that if I could consistently give those things out to them, those kids could rediscover a little bit of goodness in their own hearts. Maybe, in those brief moments, something eternal caressed them. I believed that in a short lifetime, they certainly deserved to experience the good in this world.

That was the paradox. If everything was so real, so virtuous, why was everyone dying? Why did everyone hurt so much?

Street Connections

A mustard-yellow BMW pulled to a stop about 100 feet from our van. Two young men came rolling out of the trick's car. Even from that distance in the amber street light, I could tell those guys were crackling with energy and feeling hot—on fire. My intuition instantly told me what these two guys were up to. They headed straight to the van.

They dressed in baggy denim, fancy Filas, and T-shirts honoring some nameless metal band. I knew what would happen: We were going to have a one-way conversation. Every thought, every sensation was going to pour out of their mouths like a neurological freeway firing off every circuit at random intervals. I hoped we would connect somehow. Experience had taught me how to translate and sift through a big drug barrage. It's like listening to John Coltrane. After a while you hear the melody and discover the meaning in there.

"Hey, who are you, man?" one of the young men called. He was looking at every trick's car as it slowly cruised by. "What are you doing down here? Are you the rabbi out here? I haven't seen a rabbi up close since I was in third grade. What about you, Steve? What do you think? What's he doing here?"

"Why don't you ask him?" Steve spun on his heel, smiling and laughing. "God bless America, we are rolling in it tonight. You know what I'm saying, Danny? We're getting major green tonight. First night back out of Riker's. We're gonna pull down $800. Do a nice hotel later. Drink some Chivas. Take care of our nose."

The boys were turning fast tricks, tripping fast through their minds, blowing a lot of cocaine up their noses, and pulling in a lot of cash. They were talking too fast to stop, distracted every millisecond. Drugs mixed with a lot of childhood abuse produces this phenomenon. This lifestyle begins as a means of escape for these kids; the trouble is, living on the fast chemical highway doesn't last long. The crash, which is always around the corner, arrives quickly with its lethal companions of disease and death.

The average person walking in Greenwich Village probably wouldn't notice Danny and Steve. In fact, other than at a place like the docks, kids who work the streets are invisible. They blend into the landscape, or maybe it's just that no one really wants to see them. It's easier that way. There's less discomfort. In *The Way Beyond* at night, there are lots of these kids. The action is hot, heavy, and dangerous.

Danny and Steve had just been released from Rikers Island prison for pandering and were eager to get back to "work."

I offered them some hot chocolate and peanut butter sandwiches. Over the years I've made thousands of those sandwiches. When my own kids came home from school, they always knew if it was my night out in the van. The whole downstairs smelled of peanut butter.

It may seem odd that these kids would come over to our van for a sandwich and hot chocolate. With cash to burn and speed or coke accelerating up their noses, why sit down and talk to a rabbi?

Kids on the street are covered in layers of pain, thick like mud. A lot of the mud has gotten hard, like adobe, but not all of it. It's got chinks in it. Through those chinks the light still seeps through. Then come the tears, which can wash off some of the mud. It's those tears and rays of light that bring the kids out of the darkness to bathe in the warmth for a while.

It's somehow reassuring to discover that underneath all the pain and suffering, underneath the carefully crafted exteriors they've developed, these kids want to be held. They want to change; they want to grow; they still believe there's hope. It gives me a rock-bottom faith in God. I've always felt that somebody had to be out there when those kids realized they didn't want to fall, so I went out there to catch some falls.

By the time I met Danny and Steve, I was known on the streets. The kids knew I was a rabbi, but I always introduced myself as Yehudah. They needed to know me as Yehudah. Titles would only create more distance.

Danny and Steve and I sat that night. We talked a lot about music and not much else, but we began to learn things about each other—little building blocks of trust. Danny was an accomplished blues harpist, and he carried his harps with him wherever he went.

"So, Yehudah, you into music? Who do you like?" He pulled a harp out of his front pocket and lay it beside himself.

I smiled and handed him a hot chocolate. "Good question. The best band of all time? The Allman Brothers."

"Not bad, Rabbi. Not too shabby. But give me Junior Wells or Albert Collins or Buddy Guy anytime."

"Chicago blues are a different world," I said while nodding my head. "Years ago I caught Junior Wells, Otis Rush, B.B. King, and Muddy Waters. It's a long list and a long story."

"You're kidding!" Danny looked up at me with astonishment. "Where was it? Unbelievable. Whew! I'd give anything to see them."

It was good to see that, even stoned, Danny could focus. I matched his enthusiasm. "Don't I know it? It was incredible. It was out at the Fillmore in San Francisco back in the sixties. A great venue. Who taught you to play?"

I saw Danny's eyes get a faraway look for a brief moment. I wasn't surprised when his next words were about a parent.

"My dad. He was a musician. He showed me some stuff on the harp when I was little." He gave me a momentary stare, then looked away. "I don't want to talk about it, okay?"

Next thing I knew, he was standing out on the street demonstrating the different styles of Junior Wells and the late Paul Butterfield. Lucky for me, he wasn't too stoned to play. And I'm telling you, the kid could play. If he didn't have such a hard drug habit and wasn't traveling the grim New York underworld journey, he might have made it in a band.

Digging Deeper

Steve, on the other hand, was one of those guys so beamed up that you didn't know whether he was creepy or funny. It was the same old formula again, drugs mixed with a history of child abuse. He had been running down so many wrong alleys trying to avoid his pain that he'd lost track of who he was.

Kids like Steve and Danny were out there living a lie. Then they'd end up embracing it, but the lie only led to more pain. It would get so bizarre that they would start to think that the pain could only be eased by more pain. Another paradox. It's a downward spiral until death or God steps in and lends a hand.

Steve was creepy on the outside, always trying to be impressively hot. He looked like a real character right off the page of the adults-only section: sandy-colored hair, long, perfect cut. Slender, with clothes to attract the predators. He was always preening, strutting while looking for that ultimate ride—for the right price.

He disappeared one night into a black Cadillac and vanished for days. Later he told me he had been in Jersey at some upscale home. Did unmentionable acts for some john. The price had been right.

I tried to talk to him then about STD's and HIV. He laughed and said, "Do I look like I need protection? I don't want anything on this beautiful body. I'm hot already. It would mess my shape."

He would never let his guard down, but somewhere underneath was another story. There always was another story. He just never let me see it.

Danny, however, let me see it all. At first he seemed dark, intense, and brooding. Over the months, though, we got friendly.

When he was out hustling, he liked to wear dark turtlenecks with chinos. His dark curly hair was cut short. His eyes were deep brown, liquid. Danny knew what he was doing out there. From his aftershave to his chinos, his image was all affected. Danny was an actor appearing in his own show—*The Selling of Danny.* It worked.

When a john was cruising him, trying to pick him up, Danny wouldn't pay him any attention at first. Finally, out of frustration, the john would honk his horn. Only then would Danny come closer to his car.

Danny turned it into a dramatic episode. He'd lean in and out of the shadows. Squint at the car. Turn his head away. Make the predator really hunt him. Finally he'd break into a big smile and walk right up to the car. He'd talk price and the kind of action he was willing to provide. But he'd never lean into the window. He always opened the door himself. I'd watch him step in, sit down. He did everything upscale. From the cars to the tricks, he made it clear they had to pay a lot for him.

All of this was extremely dangerous. Kids would disappear all the time. One night after I got to know Danny a bit, I asked him about it. "Aren't you scared?" I hoped I wasn't sounding too patronizing. "You don't know who you're going with. You have no backup, no protection."

He fixed me with his liquid stare, leaning back. He took a long pull on a Camel, blew it out real slow, sighed, and answered, "Yehudah, you're scared—that's it. Don't be scared for me."

His comment made the hair tingle on the back of my neck. I said, "Danny, every time you get into a car, I never know if I'm going to see you again. That scares me. Every time you disappear I think, *Damn! I'm going to lose you forever.*"

He disarmed me with the next words he said. They come out of nowhere sometimes. "My father used to come home drunk and tear up the house. Beat up my mom and then start in on me. You have any idea what it's like going to bed on a school night when you're a little kid, only to have your old man show up and beat the crap out of you? All that beating left a hole in me. Do you understand what I'm saying? Yeah, I'm one of those guys who wakes up at night sweating. Sometimes even crying. I *am* scared. I'm *always* in over my head. Hell, who isn't around here? So, I'm the guy who doesn't question my act. I don't explain myself. It's easier that way."

I later learned he came from a suburban Connecticut family. He'd had no one to protect him. He lived in the middle of that until he was sixteen, then he up and left. He'd been on the streets ever since.

I realized there was no way to measure the fear he lived with. Outside were the predators; inside was the fear. "Maybe there's a way out of that ocean of pain," I countered. "Maybe if you'd come off the street you could understand that hole in you."

Danny looked away for a moment. He stared briefly at the Korean market across the street and then back at me. He shrugged, then turned and walked away to contract business with a john.

The johns cruised from the suburbs, the Jersey shore, and the East Side condos. They were the insurance brokers, the husbands, the business execs. They were real scary types. The trouble was, no one knew by looking at them how deep their sleaze went. By day they'd be at the office or on weekends at a Sunday barbecue with their kids. But by night they were out on the streets, and you could see it in their eyes. Feral and forbidding. Downright chilling.

When I was a rookie, I used to walk over to these cruisers thinking I'd scare them off. I found out soon enough that all I'd get were stone-cold eyes looking back at me. I never got used to it. In the beginning it made me feel like I was going to vomit. Later, I learned to carry Mylanta. It still makes me sick.

One winter night, Danny met up with me for a cup of hot chocolate. It was cold, about nine degrees outside and colder in the wind. I could tell he hadn't smoked any crack in a few hours. His mood was quiet and pensive. I thought it was a good time to get a bit closer.

I asked him a heavy question. "Danny, do you remember any good times in your life when you were growing up?"

He leaned back away from me. *Uh oh, wrong question*, I thought. Instead, he answered with a question himself. "Why do you want to know?"

Now, that question required some straightforward honesty. "I'll tell you why," I said, hoping he was ready for a little speech with some teaching. "Everybody needs a lifeline. If you can remember and feel something good that once happened, you can hold on to that. It's yours. Once you've got ahold of it, you can grab another good thing. If you can find enough of those good things in your life, you'll know it's time to get off the street. This is no place for you."

He smiled. "There goes the rabbi in you. Got to lay some preaching on me."

I laughed. "Preaching or not, it's the truth. I want to know. Do you remember?"

Danny went quiet for a moment. All I could hear was the traffic whooshing by on Lexington. Our breath mingled together in a lazy vapor cloud. He sighed, "Well, there was one time, when I was little. We were all together. My mom, dad, sister, and me. It was Chanukah. We lit the menorah together. I got some presents. A huge toy glider. It felt so good and then . . ." He broke off in mid-sentence. I thought he might cry, but I couldn't tell if the tears dammed up in his heart were filled with sadness or hot anger.

He had touched up against the pain. I saw the first crack starting to open around the wall of his heart. I knew if he shared more of his life, he would inevitably share more of his pain. Once he opened that door, it would take a herculean effort to close it again. But I knew from experience he would close it. He would reach the point of no return where he would refuse to live with his pain anymore. He would attempt to break free and hurl out his pain.

Over the next year Danny and I got to know each other better. Steve, however, simply vanished into the mist of the night. Rumor was he got involved with some very nasty people and eventually caught a plane out to Hollywood, where he worked the streets off Sunset and Western. On some of my frequent trips to L.A., I'd go out to the Sunset Strip at night and ask around. I never saw Steve again.

Don't Let Me Die

About a year later, I was up on the Loop again one night. It was around 1:30 A.M. in the dead of winter. You wouldn't think the predators would be out after kids on a night like that, but the flesh hunters never stop. It's something they *have* to do, like breathing.

It was a busy night. I poured gallons of steaming hot chocolate and got compliments on my peanut butter sandwiches. "Hey, Yehudah, gourmet sandwiches!" "Rabbi, compliments to the chef." The kids knew I had prepared those sandwiches especially for them. It was the closest they came to home cooking.

I hadn't seen Danny in about four months. I had just popped side two of the Allman Brothers' *At Fillmore East* into the tape deck when a really sick-looking kid stepped into the van. *Could that be Danny?* His chinos were gone. His wardrobe was replaced by ripped jeans, an old T-shirt, and a dirty yellow-green army surplus jacket. As he sat down in the van, his pants rode up over his calves. They were swollen and covered in sores. Silent. I blinked twice.

"Danny?"

He turned slowly, his eyes were bloodshot and caked with dried mucus. "Yeah."

I was in shock. "Whoa! What's been going down? What happened?"

In a whisper, he said, "Lots of bad mistakes, Yehudah. I'm so sick I think I bought it this time."

I barely recognized him. This was my friend! He was bloated, wheezing, and feverish, leaking out stinky gas. Not pretty. Any substance abuse expert would tell you: King Crack had taken Danny on its ride to hell.

I felt like picking him up in my arms, taking him home, and tucking him into a warm bed. If only love and chicken soup could heal all wounds. If only the answers were easy. Danny was experiencing reality at the bottom. If he was going to come through this, the next stop on his elevator would have to be detox and rehab. The only floor remaining on the way down was death.

Danny leaned over. He began to bawl like a baby. Loud, messy tears. He hugged me with desperation. "Yehudah, all my stash is gone. I'm dying. Don't let me die, man. Don't let me die." He shuddered. "I gotta change. I got nothing to hold on to anymore. Nothing's right. Nothing's ever been right."

I looked right at him. "What brought you back out here tonight?

For the first time, his eyes made contact with mine. "Damn, I don't know. All I know is I hurt. I've been so beamed out, I can't even take care of myself. I'm so stoned, so dirty, so sick I don't even turn tricks. Nothing's good. I can't remember anything going right. I'm scared. You gotta help me."

The bad news here was the good news. A miracle was going on—a divine paradox. *He didn't want to die.* At the bottom of Danny's pit, in his darkest depth of pain and despair, God's lifeline was dangling down to him. That lifeline always waits at the bottom of a broken heart.

At that point, the only way out was up, but it wasn't going to be on an express elevator. Danny was going to have to make all the stops, and each stop would look like a new nightmare. But he had the lifeline and it was pulling him toward a new start, a new living for himself.

Danny had crossed the invisible boundary. The drugs wouldn't help him avoid himself anymore. The tricks and the cash were meaningless now when confronted with the reality that he could no longer live the lie. He had hit the turning point. The magical, painful turning stone in his heart had begun to grind directly on his pain. He didn't know it yet, but he was going to hurl out a lifetime of pain. From out of his sick broken body, he was uttering his first confession, his first attempt at vidui.

Hurling Out the Pain

We took Danny to the runaway shelter that night. He was so exhausted he slept for two days. Then, when Danny was ready to make his move and check himself into detox, I went to visit him. I walked into the lounge at the shelter that morning and was greeted by him blurting out, "Yehudah, I called and I can get in detox this afternoon. I'm doing it!"

Now I knew what he was talking about, but I like to doublecheck just the same. Affirmation gives your soul more strength to help guide your life. So I smiled and said, "How 'bout filling me in? I'm not too psychic at this hour. Where did you call and where are you going?"

"I'm going into detox, man. I lucked out. A spot is open if I show this afternoon. Can you give me a lift over?"

Without a pause I answered, "No problem, let's do it."

Inside, I was thanking the Almighty for this little miracle. Too often when someone has hit bottom and is ready for detox there isn't a bed open. Or there's a bed but the addict isn't ready to commit. Getting to that bed is like grabbing a life preserver. If you don't reach for it, you drown. It's that simple. If you grab it, you can float and eventually rescue yourself.

By his fifth day in detox I began to visit Danny. Detox in a New York City hospital is not like going to a fancy treatment center. But you've got warmth, a clean space, and competent medical and psychiatric attention.

I'd pick Danny up in his room and we'd shuffle down to the lounge, hang out, and talk. The lounge was never empty. The linoleum and plastic furniture had only one thing going for them: they were easy to clean quickly. We sat on the couch in the corner next to a sooty gray window; the couch always slid a bit and screeched on the linoleum, hissing as the foam filling let air out through the cracked plastic, accommodating our bodies.

I was there to provide support and counsel until Danny moved on and got himself into recovery. I was his bridge, friend, guide, and mentor all wrapped into one. He didn't have family he could turn to, and his "friends" were still dancing with the angel of death themselves.

During one visit, we were sitting quietly for a bit. Danny was staring out the gray window. The view was a typical upper-floor view in the city: other dark windows and dirty bricks. If you stuck your head out the window and looked down, you wouldn't catch a patch of green, just cement and rotting garbage. But if you looked up, you could see the sky.

That's what Danny was doing—looking up at the sky. He was looking up and he was crying.

He let out a long breath as he stared out the window. "I've been spending so much time thinking. It's like coming off the crack has opened a hole in me. It's full of all kinds of feelings. It's hard to stay focused, but there are times late at night when I'm feeling so bad that—I know this sounds crazy, but—for the first time I hurt so bad and it . . . I don't know . . . it makes sense. Like I take all this crap pouring out of me and I let it fall out. Then I kind of remember in bits and pieces how I got into this mess. For the first time in my life, I feel real bad and I'm okay about it. In fact, I even feel good about it. My hurtin' has a reason in it. I'm not letting myself be afraid anymore. It's like I gotta hurt in order to figure it out. Do you know what I'm talking about? I'm not sure I do. I guess I'm hurling out the pain, like you said."

I quietly replied, "Danny, you are, and I do know what you mean. If you keep working on yourself and letting those demons inside you fly away, it's going to start making a lot of sense. Right now you're letting go and getting rid of some real bad baggage that's hurt you most of your life. It's going to take time. It always does. Just keep doing what you're doing and trust yourself that you're starting to heal. Count on that. Pray and meditate on it."

Danny's Gift

Two months later, Danny was living a new life. He was out of rehab, had moved to Philly, and had gotten a job. At 9:00 one morning I was on alert, waiting for him to call.

He called a lot, just to check in. I had become one of Danny's baselines. On the road to recovery, everyone needs a supporter and Danny was no exception. I was there to remind him of his path, to encourage him to persevere, and to always support his enthusiasm. That kind of support helped make more room for good things to happen for him. It strengthened him and got him through his vulnerable times.

I was waiting for his call in my basement office, my Yankees cup filled to the brim with straight java. I began meditating on the baseball memorabilia filling the wall and display cases in my office. I take a lot of inspiration from Don Mattingly, Mickey Mantle, Thurman Munson, and Roberto Clemente. Their memorabilia clutter up my office, reminding me to keep focused, move forward, and work on fundamentals.

But it's the Yankee captain, number 15, Thurman, who has my heart and soul. I've got this old copy of the *Sporting News* from 1973 with Thurman on the cover. The headline says, "Playing for Keeps." That sums it all up. On the street, everyone's playing for keeps. Whoever doesn't know that won't make it.

Thurman used to say, "Look, I just loved baseball so much I played anywhere. I didn't care. I played every opportunity I had, right up until it got dark and I couldn't see anymore."[1] Thurman poured his heart into life—which, for him, ended in a plane crash in his early thirties. There are no guarantees on life's outcome, but Thurman connected at every opportunity.

I always try to make it to Yankee Stadium for Thurman Munson Day. It's a reminder that even a short life is a great gift. The gift of life is not how long we live, but what we attain.

Before I knew it, it was 10:15. The phone rang. It was Danny.

"Hey, Yehudah. What's going on?"

"Well, I've been sitting here and just took a break to muse on a little baseball. What's up with you, little brother? How's the work going?"

He took a deep sighing breath. "Very intense. I'm trying to get some perspective on where I've been, what I did. I'm trying to find a way to forgive myself. I'm still very angry. It's tough."

Danny was working his way out of the loop. Hurling out the pain is an exacting, ongoing process. We focus on finding some perspective and relationship to the suffering we experienced. Danny's release of anger and pain was slowly opening the door to forgiveness.

I got serious. "You ever cut yourself and it really hurt? Then you bandaged it up and it still hurt, but not as bad?"

"So this hurts, but it's part of the healing, right?" he asked.

"It's part of becoming whole."

Throughout the next year, Danny held his job and his recovery. After having burned cash at $600 a night, hanging in at minimum wage had taken a lot of courage.

Climbing out of the cesspool hadn't been easy. It was tough for Danny to move forward, and sustaining his momentum meant he had to take the risk to change. He learned that true change demanded he give things up, and doping and tricking were not easy habits to give up.

Danny realized it had been easier to hate himself than love himself. When he had been living out in *The Way Beyond,* he was so hammered that he had stopped caring. Pain had been the great anesthetic. All the dope and death around him had sucked the life out of him. He danced with the biggest lie of all. He tricked himself into thinking that his life was simply one big party. Little by little, Danny moved beyond all that and rebuilt his life.

He regularly kept me updated on his progress: "I'm feeling better. I tested negative for HIV. I'm hitting a lot of meetings. Meeting new folks. I've even started going to a class on spirituality at a synagogue near my apartment. I like what I'm doing. Got a girlfriend. I'm not poisoning myself anymore. I think I'm going to make it. I've even spoken to some high school kids about where I've been and where they don't want to end up. Looking back, I realize I had some luck. I mean, I'm alive."

Through the phone lines, I began to see Danny really smile for the first time. Not that I hadn't seen him smile before, but it had belonged to another part of himself. A doper's smile was never straight. How could it be when you couldn't trust anyone? Danny had crossed a threshold. He'd begun to care for himself and others.

At the end of that year, Danny called to tell me he was coming to New York for a few days. The band he played with in his spare time was going to be at a club in the city. He was staying clean.

It was Wednesday night, bitter cold and windy. It turned out Danny's band was playing at a second-rate club in the Village. It was too cold for much of an audience to show. They were the last group to go onstage, around 11:00, but they were smoking.

Danny's harp moaned and groaned. His music poured out his pain, hope, and aspirations. His gulping breath on that harp spoke volumes about where he'd been and dreamed of going. Junior Wells would have been proud.

Later, we met near Times Square off 10th Avenue at one of those open-twenty-four-hours joints. I thought of it as my Times Square office. Somehow, I felt right at home there. At 2:00 A.M., the customers were hookers on their breaks, a few homeless people, AA members with their sponsors, insomniacs, and street kids. We were all rubbing shoulders on a cold winter night.

Danny and I took a back booth. The diner was warm. It smelled of coffee with a slight hint of nervous sweat. After all, the clientele lived the struggle.

"How'd the gig go tonight?"

His smile summed it all up. "Fun."

Reaching into my sports jacket, I pulled out a cassette tape and slid it across the table. "I've got something for you."

A look of appreciation and excitement lit up his face. He looked like a little kid. "What's this? A present? You don't need to do this."

Seeing him like that made me feel proud of how far he'd come. "You're the front man playing the harp, so enjoy one of the best. There's nothing quite like Charlie Musselwhite. I used to catch him in San Francisco years ago. Thought you'd like it."

He shook his head with a laugh, "Cool. I appreciate it, Yehudah."

"My pleasure. So what's up?"

He took a deep breath. I could see him searching for the right words, thinking hard before answering. What he was about to tell me meant something important to him. "Good things, man. Good things. Being clean and working makes me feel reborn. I'm in love. Got a great sponsor who keeps me straight with the program, one day at a time. The band's great. The job's okay. Hey, who's to complain?"

I decided to press the healing advantage. "You've given any thought to volunteering for more serious outreach to kids? You'd be a real help. You know that."

He let out his breath slowly, "Yeah, I'm going to do it. For starters, I figure one day a week. My sponsor also thought it would be good, you know, for my soul."

One of the most poignant beauties I've had the privilege to see was Danny's broken heart becoming whole again. He had been broken and laid open by the world. Because he risked it all to stand up again, his heart became infused with spirit. With that infusion, he became something greater. He truly became himself.

Three months later the phone rang at 6:15 A.M. I rolled over and picked it up. It was Carol, Danny's girlfriend. She was in tears.

Just after midnight, Danny had been coming home from volunteering at a local youth center. He stopped into an all-night grocery to pick up some milk. Inside, a robbery was in progress. He didn't see the bullets coming. He took two shots in the chest and died at the entrance to the store.

It was a cold spring morning. I felt as if I'd been stabbed in the heart as I flashed to him lying there, dying. The cement must have been cold against his face. The cold frost of loneliness climbed its way up my back and nested in my heart.

That day, I cried. I didn't know whether I was crying because I had lost Danny or because I cared so much for him. I was in a real state of confusion. It's something I never want to get over. The pain stays alive in my heart, keeping me aware of the light that was Danny. His smile dispelled the darkness. His enthusiasm for life touched the heavens with its joy. The aching sadness I feel brings memories filled with emotions that give divine meaning to Danny's living and dying.

Bernie Siegal once wrote, "Love is the greatest healer. . . . It is the only road to immortality and a wonderful burden to our survivors. They will go on living the message and see life and its problems as a gift and a challenge."[2]

I am blessed to carry the burden of Danny's love. His gift of healing lives on forever.

STEP TWO

Recognizing That You've Changed

JESSICA'S STORY

Everything has its season,
and there is a time for everything
under the heaven:

A time to break down and a time to build up
Koheles; Chapter 3

STEP TWO: *Recognizing That You've Changed*

What is the essence of Teshuvah? An individual forsakes his or her misdeeds and removes them from his or her thoughts. There is finality in one's heart that there is no returning to those misdeeds. . . . And the said person knows and is witness in the hiddenness [of one's heart] that he or she will never return to this [said misdeed] again. As it is written (Hoshea 14:4), "We no longer say to the work of our hands: 'You are our gods.'" An individual needs to acknowledge this with one's lips and to say these matters that are finished in one's heart.

(MAIMONIDES, *Hilchos Teshuvah*, Chapter Two, Section Two)

If we accept our stumbling and failings, we slowly get a sense of where we have been and how we can give ourselves permission to change. Once we have made our confession and "hurled out the pain," we see that our confession is not simply a venting of our emotions but a statement to ourselves that we are moving on. We are struggling to go from the old person who lived so many lies to a new person trying to meet each day with clarity and honesty. Obviously, this is not an overnight process.

There is a teaching that says, "It is even possible to transform our failings into merits." I suspect that contained in that teaching is the secret of how powerful it is to learn from our mistakes.

While we shouldn't seek out pain or purposefully make mistakes, we can learn from our failures. We can find hope in our desolation. Unraveling that mystery will only make us more compassionate, sensitive, and understanding. As difficult as that mystery may be to decode, it nevertheless gives us tremendous hope for our own lives. In celestial terms, it means God's compassion is boundless if we allow ourselves to accept that we, with mindfulness and hard work, can change.

A Mother's Desperate Call

There never has been a sign over my office or a notice announcing me as the finder of lost souls. Most of the time I've had an unlisted number, but still, people have found me. I've often thought that if parents of lost kids were so good at finding me, they ought to be able to track down their own children. Looking back, I now see that getting my number was motivating for them. The fact that people worked so hard to get my number meant they were willing to work hard to change.

Back when I lived in Brooklyn, I had three phones. I kept one in my office, one in the bedroom, and one in the corner of the living room. Experience taught me that I needed to be on call twenty-four hours a day. The phone in the bedroom was for the calls that came in the midnight hours. While you might assume that the most desperate calls would come in then, they actually came in right before every holiday at anytime of the day.

Jessica's parents called on a spring afternoon right before Passover. When I picked up the phone, I knew it was trouble.

Instantly, I recognized the voice. We'd never met, but I knew the woman at the other end of the line. After all, how could I not recognize the voice of a desperate mother?

The first question I'm asked is almost always the same: "Are you the rabbi that helps families and kids in trouble?"

No matter how many times I hear that question, it always makes me take a quiet deep breath and say a little prayer. I brace myself for the pain that will inevitably flow into my chest.

After I said that I was indeed the person she was looking for, she got right to the point. Mothers in crisis always do that. I heard her take a choking swallow, and I pictured tears forming in her eyes. "You've got to help us," she said. "Our daughter is missing."

The first order of duty in these situations is to defuse the emotions for the time being in order to gather information. I usually start by running down a checklist. "Did you file a missing person report?" I always need to know if the police are involved. It shapes the direction of my work.

"No, she's not missing like that. She just won't tell us where she lives or works. She just stopped calling us. She thinks everybody hates her."

"When was the last time she was home?"

"About eight months ago. But there was continual fighting. We have two other children, and it was too much. I told her it was better to just call us rather than come home until things settled down."

"What's her name and how old is she?"

"Jessica. She's nineteen, almost twenty."

This basic information also had to be gathered to make certain this wasn't a police matter or a matter for social services.

She went on, giving me a quick history. "Rabbi, nothing's worked. We went to court and took out a PINS petition, you know, *one of those people in need of services* things, when she was sixteen. She ran away twice before that. After the PINS she stayed home long enough to get her GED. The whole time, we fought. Once she got her GED, she left. She's had three or four boyfriends. Scary guys. Tattoos, earrings—my God. One of them had a stud pierced through his tongue! She acts crazy with these boys."

Now, I realized this had gone on for a long time. I brought the conversation back to the present. "Tell me, what's happening right now? What has got you so worried?"

After a long, strained sigh, she began. "Jessica's always called in. Even after big fights on the phone, she'd always say, 'I love you' or, 'I'm sorry.' Then we had a huge fight over her coming home for the holidays. She said no, she had other plans. She wouldn't say what they were. I really blew it. I told her that if she didn't come home, that's it. Don't call again. She screamed at me and said, 'You all hate me. I'm outta here.' She hung up. She hasn't called since. It's been five weeks. I'm scared. Every time the phone rings, I fall apart because I think it's going to be the police telling me something awful has happened. I have horrible dreams. I'm full of guilt. I pushed her away. I want another chance."

I gave her a moment to catch her breath. She was like a warm soda bottle shaken up real hard on a hot summer day. When you pop it open, it foams all over the place and it's messy. In this case, the mess was all of Mom's pain and suffering. Anytime a kid drops out of touch there's a cause for concern. It can be a dark world for a kid alone. It's a short and easy fall into the snake pit.

From this first phone interview, I learned the family's basic style of doing business. I knew they had fought with Jessica and had pushed her away. They saw her as the bad child. It was also clear that they were still trying to control her as if she were a little girl. That certainly doesn't work very well for a twenty-year-old. Her transition to adulthood wasn't being accomplished with much grace—after all, they had kicked her out of the house. Now they'd woken up and were in a panic.

It certainly didn't take much to set this family off. They loved to fight, but I saw hope in that fighting. The time and energy they devoted to fighting could easily be turned around to their benefit. Imagine what would happen if they took all that fighting energy and channeled it into learning to talk with each other?

Sorting the Variables

When I met with Jessica's parents, Matt and Charlotte, at my office, I learned more about how the family operated: their rules and regulations, their laws or lack thereof. This information was essential if I was to be successful when, and if, I eventually met Jessica.

My top priority was to get them into therapy. Even though I'm a family therapist, this kind of crisis calls for tasks to be divided. I didn't have time to provide them with therapy myself. I suspected that I would have to hit the streets to look for Jessica, and searching the backwaters of Manhattan's nightlife is extremely time-consuming. I referred them to a competent, seasoned family therapist who specialized in adolescent crisis. My job was to give the family encouragement, spiritual support, and, most of all, to find their daughter. But I had to be straight with them and warn them that finding Jessica and getting the family back together could be a lengthy process. Parents have a hard time understanding that. They ask, "You mean this could take years?" I say, "Yeah—maybe a lifetime."

The case stays open. Once I get in we just keep plugging away. But I don't punch a time clock. No matter how long it takes, I'll be around until the dust settles.

Usually, when I find kids I've been looking for on the street, they can't go home right away. Their families just haven't changed enough to keep them from leaving again. Or even darker, the families don't want them back home. But I almost always connect with the kid and stay connected for a long time. Eventually, months or years later when the time is right, home becomes an option.

I had to make this clear to Jessica's parents, that everyone in the family had a lot of work to do before a reconciliation was possible. As it was right now, if the parents did meet with Jessica, everyone's need to be right would get in the way of their need to love one another.

I decided that before attempting reconciliation with her family, Jessica and I needed to have a heart-to-heart talk. The plan was this: If Jessica called, her parents would talk to her about meeting with me. If she didn't call, I would follow up on all the leads and hit the street.

I never liked going out by myself looking for lost kids. A lot of them didn't want to be found. They didn't want to go home. Home wasn't a pleasant place for them. Not that I couldn't find them, I could. Given enough leads, mixed with time and patience, I was pretty good at it. As much as I disliked the whole process, I had to go take a look in *The Way Beyond.*

What did I have to go on? Her parents gave me a photo. It was pretty recent, two years old. It sounded like she was a "club girl," and I had the name of a club she used to hang out in. Fortunately, it was still open. I also had the name of a photographer who had a small office that was actually listed in the phone book. I'm always suspicious of the photography crowd that allegedly puts together "portfolios" for girls. I've spent too many nights looking for kids in video parlors and heard too many stories about the pornography business. Even so, the photographer and the club were excellent leads.

Jessica's parents suspected she worked for an escort service, which, they said, meant she was *in the life*—hooking.

I asked them, "Why do you think she's doing that? Did she ever indicate she was selling herself?"

Her father, who came off as the silent type, leaned forward and replied, "Well, rabbi, you know how it is. She's been in so much trouble."

I love that male bonding. The *you know how it is* talk. After all, if she's in that much trouble, she's got to be hooking. She's *damaged goods.* It explains everything. I said back, "Well, Matt, I *don't* know how it is." I wanted him to know we weren't going to do the male thing. I went on, "Besides, there's no way for me to check that out. There are just too many escort services. Also, a good number of them aren't listed. Their *Fortune* 500 clientele need their privacy. All said, I have no way of knowing what she's doing. For all I know, she's flipping burgers at some fast food joint."

Matt was a trader on Wall Street. He liked things to have closure. He liked timetables and hours on the clock. Charlotte, on the other hand, unconsciously thought that she had to shield her husband from Jessica. Matt always needed his life to be ordered, structured, and controlled; therefore, Charlotte stepped in between Jessica and Matt. She thought she had to protect Matt from Jessica's unpredictable outbursts.

Being in the middle is a lousy place for a parent to be, especially when a child desperately needs to communicate with both parents. Adolescence is the period when kids need the most stability in their family life, and Charlotte and Matt were providing just the opposite.

If Jessica called home at this point, she'd find more of the same. Her mom would be pushing, and her dad would be behind the scenes operating the controls. And Jessica, well, she'd just split again. Adolescents have a lot of guts and courage. What they lack in maturity they try to make up for in daring. The difficulty is that daring can waltz right into high-risk behavior.

We needed a little discussion about attitudes. I opened,

"Charlotte, Matt, I'm going to give you some advice. Treat it like an experiment. I want you to think about what I'm going to say. But I have every confidence, because you are such *concerned parents,* that you will find a way to *understand and act* upon what I'm going to tell you."

That really got their attention. I needed them to see their actions in a different light, so I left them with something that therapists call *a paradoxical intervention.* It goes like this: If they didn't find a way to *understand and act,* then they weren't *concerned parents.* So their only option was to be *concerned parents* who will *understand and act.*

I got right to the point. "There are four essential points to remember in attempting to help your kid grow up. The problem is that you've been pushing too hard.

"The first thing to keep in mind with a teenager is that you've got to *let them move at their own pace, not yours.*

"The second point is that parents have *to provide stability, support, and encouragement.* You don't have to agree on everything, but you must provide a stable home environment for your child to grow."

I went on, "From what you've told me, I believe your actions have weakened rather than strengthened your daughter. That leads me to the third point. When we parent, it must be directed toward strengthening *our children's resolve in facing challenge and adversity.* What happens in your case is that Jessica does what kids typically do when they're scared. She acts out."

Matt looked off across my office and stared at my Wes Wilson poster featuring Otis Rush, the Grateful Dead, and Canned Heat. He looked as if he was listening. Charlotte wrapped her arms around her chest as if she were hugging herself. I took both their actions as a positive.

I continued. "And finally, *don't get too close to your child.* Getting too close means getting too involved in your kid's life. Being too enmeshed doesn't leave your kid room to grow on their own or to make their own mistakes. Parents must provide the knack and know-how in matters of substance, but leave the details to their kids. I suspect you're too close to Jessica.

Maybe you got so close that when you hurt, she hurts, and when you react, she reacts. All in all, it's not fair to both of you and it's crazy-making for Jessica, who right now needs to find her course in life."[1]

I continued to tell them what to say if she called. "Remember those points. Matt, remember that you're the one who's getting on the phone and giving her the information. Switching roles will give you a different look. It's a signal to her that things are different. There's been some change."

Matt resisted. "But . . . Charlotte's better at giving instructions. She's . . ."

I cut him off. "Let's look at the facts. Has it worked with your wife on the phone? If it has, tell me how we're going to proceed here. I don't see Jessica anywhere . . ."

I got up from my chair and walked around the office. I went over to my desk, looked at the empty chair, and said, "Jessica, you there? Are you willing to talk?" I opened the basement door that led from my office to the street and yelled, "Jessica, you there? You want to come in?"

As I turned back, Matt threw his hands up in the air. He nodded and said, "Okay, Yehudah, I get the point." Charlotte gave me a raised eyebrow and a little smile.

Matt was now prepared to tell Jessica about me and give her my phone number. He would let her know I wanted to meet her, telling her she could set the time and place. Kids almost always say yes to this kind of request. After all, they don't have to come into my office, which they could view as a negative. Also, the fact that their parents have reached out to someone like me sends a *we're willing to be different* message. While it doesn't win the ball game, it generally gets me into the on-deck circle.

They agreed to everything, although a bit pessimistically. They found it hard to believe that Jessica would agree to meet with me. I reminded them how at any moment in any crisis, the profound ability to connect is always present. It's another rule of the road, and another paradox: The moment a crisis becomes most outrageous is also the moment of greatest potential for reconciliation.

Before they left my office we went over the plan again. I reminded them, "If she calls, do the impossible. Don't interrogate her, and Matt, get the message across that I want to meet her. Tell her you miss her. Don't be outraged by anything she tells you or anything she's into. Just listen and try to understand. Get judgmental and you'll lose her. Build on the positives."

As they headed for the door, I walked over to the bookshelf and pulled out my trusty copy of Dr. Frank Pittman's *Turning Points.* I said, "Just to let you know I'm not the only guy with funny ideas, listen to this." I stuck my fingers into my yellow Post-it marker on page 177—my favorite page—and read, "It has been said that no one can grow up successfully until he realizes that his parents are stark raving mad, at least in a few areas. Parents . . . may not know that normal adolescents get drunk, get laid, get depressed, keep messy rooms, listen to barbaric music, . . . feel attracted to disgusting people and don't like to visit relatives they don't know well."[2]

I snapped the book shut, looked at them, and said, "We have perhaps a hard road ahead. Do you think we *adults* can keep it in perspective?"

Matt and Charlotte raised their eyebrows and nodded imperceptibly. I smiled and said, "Well, you called me!"

Hitting the Street

Two weeks went by from the time I met with Matt and Charlotte until I decided to go out on the streets and look for Jessica. I'd been waiting to see if she would call home. She hadn't.

I didn't want to wait any longer. There's always trouble lurking out in *The Way Beyond,* and I didn't want her disappearing on us. I called Matt and Charlotte around eight in the morning to let them know I was ready to make my move. Usually, 6:30–8:30 A.M. are my parent hours, before everyone goes to work. I want to touch base with all the folks I'm working with, review, and give them strength and encouragement. Even though I might not have the answers, I have my heart.

They were really scared. *What would I find?* I told them I would hit the street that night and track down the photographer the next day.

I decided to try the club scene first. If I could meet some of Jessica's friends, they could put out a good word on me. I had a pretty good reputation out on the street. I was counting on that.

I parked my car at the Park 'N Lock, an all-night lot near the Port Authority Bus Terminal. It was after midnight, when the real action begins in Manhattan. I took a cab down the West Side Highway. It was eighty degrees with 90 percent humidity. The heat gave the night a rhythm. The darkness throbbed with the sound of tires whooshing and bouncing on the broken, wet pavement.

The club was down on the West Side near the meat market. By day the market pulsated with the noise of the meat cutters and the packaging plants. At night the empty warehouses were home to the city's netherworld club scene. Down here, sweat leaked out onto the streets.

A crowd of kids had already gathered outside the club's door. The street was littered with cigarette butts, greasy hamburger wrappers, and french fry cups. They mixed with the oily water to form a collage of desperation. To these kids, this was the ultimate: a party with no beginning and no end.

A couple of steroid-pumped bodyguards served as doormen who controlled the pecking order in the kingdom and determined who would get in first. I was lucky. I got in right away.

Stepping inside was like stepping off the planet. I wondered what Janis or Jimi would have thought of this techno-party music. The light show, if you could call it that, was designed to splatter the atoms of your mind. Rhythmic blasts of pulsating colored light and sound set the stage for the designer drugs rumored to be circulating through the crowd. I shuddered and stepped into what looked like a dress rehearsal for the apocalypse. Two minutes in and the sweat started trickling down my back, part nerves, part humidity. I looked around for someone in charge.

Eventually, I found someone who was "part of the management." He was standing by a cigarette machine, surveying the empire and talking to one of the security guards, who glared at me as I stepped into his circle. I looked right past the guard and went to work. I eyeballed "Mr. Big" and then said, "Excuse me, I'm looking for somebody. I need some help." He snarled and said, "You smell like a cop, man."

I held my arms out to my sides. "Do I look like a cop? Haven't you ever seen a rabbi before? I mean, this is New York. Besides, if I was a cop, I'd flash a badge and you would *want* to help me."

At that he smiled. "Rabbi," he said, "just kidding. I was just checking out your reactions. We don't get rabbis in here. What can I do for you?"

I pulled out Jessica's photo and showed it to him and his tagalong black belt. "I'm a family friend," I said. "She's out of touch with her folks. She might be in trouble. I'm worried."

They didn't recognize her. It was a long shot anyway. There are so many kids out there, but my motto is, "You gotta try."

Then I got lucky.

Out under a vermilion strobe sat two girls I recognized, Alicia and Debbie. I almost missed them, with the smoke, lights, crowd, and Alicia's new look.

They belonged to a group of girls who hung out on the edge of my reach. They floated in and out of my life, spoke with me on the street, or shared an occasional cup of coffee. In more desperate moments, they'd call me on the phone.

Some of them held down jobs, and others, I suspected, supplemented their income working the streets or running scams. But there they were: Alicia with her million-dollar smile and Debbie with her sugar-sweet looks, both looking for trouble. In spite of it all, I loved them. They were terrific kids.

Alicia had gone through another wardrobe change. Tonight she'd gone from grunge to a decidedly Hollywood look. She had replaced her usual Timberland boots with a pair of shiny black boots that rode up to her knees. She was covered in plastic: a black plastic dress shimmered down to her knees, a perfect match for the boots. With her sunglasses and shiny black vinyl purse, she was a poser. She was laughing and talking nonstop to Debbie, but underneath that lighthearted exterior lurked a sadness that I worried her heart would never fill.

Debbie, on the other hand, looked like Debbie. She'd obviously changed into her grunge outfit after work. I could tell because of the big canvas bag she always carried. She told me once she had to be ready to party at any time. They were both club girls. They lived on the edge of their youthful immortality, pushing every night up next to the angel of death, usually without protection. To them, AIDS happened on the docks and to IV users. Cocaine, well, it might touch River Phoenix, but not them. Their scene was endless nights of dancing, going home with hot guys, and pushing the envelope of despair.

As I crossed the room, I thought maybe this wouldn't be such a bad day's work after all. Running down a bunch of telephone numbers, I'd gotten lucky and found the photographer's address. Now, here I was out at 1:00 A.M. in the lowdown world, looking for a lost kid who I didn't even know was alive, and bingo! I got lucky again. Alicia and Debbie popped up in my field of vision. I skirted around a dozen kids and slid right down into an open chair at their little table.

Both their heads popped incredulously in my direction. In a perfect duet they blurted, "Yehudah—whoa!"

I smiled. "Yes, girls, me in person."

Alicia leaned toward my ear and asked, "What are you doing down here?"

"Well, I'm full of surprises. You know that. Actually, you know what's up. I'm at work."

Debbie laughed and said, "So, Yehudah, who are you looking for? Did my folks send you?"

For a brief instant, my heart sank. I only wished that Debbie's folks had sent me. I only wished they even cared. But those thoughts were for another time.

"You're right, I'm looking for somebody. I've even got a

picture." Reaching into my jacket, I pulled out Jessica's photo and slid it across the table. The girls looked at the picture and bingo! I scored again.

They didn't know where she lived or worked, but they'd partied with her. That was a positive sign. She was in circulation and didn't have any dark stories trailing her in the night. I gave them my number, again telling them to put in a good word and tell her that I could be trusted. That it was important that Jessica and I talked. That if she needed any help, I was available. That I wanted to talk to her about her parents.

The bottom line here was to continue to get out a good word about me on the street in the hope that it would reach her. They might run into her and if they did, it would help. In either case, at least my name and presence would be in circulation. Eventually it would pay off with Jessica or another kid who needed help.

I made it home around 3:45 A.M. I was exhausted, but it had been a day of promise. In *The Way Beyond,* any hope could turn into salvation. I was on a roll. I decided to follow up with the photographer in the afternoon.

Fortunate Lies

The next day I was very keyed up. Good leads, like miracles, are awfully hard to come by, so I decided to get a jump on the photographer. Instead of calling ahead, I headed straight into Manhattan in the late afternoon. I've learned that surprise visits always make an impression. A little paranoia can squeeze out some drops of truth. If it worked in this case, maybe the photographer would put out the message that I needed to find Jessica.

His office was on the second floor of an old brick building on the edge of the West Village. It stood on one of the many short side streets seldom ticketed for garbage by the NYC Sanitation Department. Gentrification hadn't settled in here. Its only claim to fame was being a step up from the nearby Hell's Kitchen neighborhood. I walked down the street. It was littered with broken glass and rotting advertising circulars which created an endless paper graffiti collage. Andy Warhol might have seen it as art. To me it's garbage.

A homeless woman pushed her worldly possessions in a grocery cart up the street, mumbling to herself. When I got within her range, she said to me, "Mister, can you help me out?"

I passed her right by, avoiding eye contact. I told myself, *Stay focused, you've got work to do.* And my guilt added, *You'll help another time.* Half a block later, I popped into a Korean grocery and bought a quart of chocolate milk, a couple of bananas, and an apple. She was still standing down the street, back in conversation with her invisible friend. I hurried over and handed her my little care package. She blinked and said, "God bless you, son."

I nodded and turned back down the street. I guess I don't subscribe to the notion that *there's always another time.* If we live only by God's grace, then we ought to be graceful if we can to God's children, even if they have fallen on hard times. I thought to myself, *I may not get a miracle today, but at least I got a blessing.*

It was a typical early summer afternoon. The sky was getting dark, and thunderclouds were moving in fast from Jersey across the Hudson. My nerves were taut. This was a part of my life I've never liked. I don't like making these visits one bit. I don't like talking to drug dealers. I don't like talking to pimps. I don't like talking to johns. I don't like their jive, and I don't like their lies.

The way to the studio was poorly lit. The stairway and halls were layered with cracked paint and greasy handprints. I walked up to the photographer's door. It had some pretty calligraphy etched into the glass. He must have had a good alarm system, otherwise the door probably wouldn't have lasted a week. I walked in. The place looked reasonably on the level, but how was I to know.

The muscles corded up on my neck. I gave my spine a slow lazy stretch and took a quiet, cleansing breath. I was acutely aware that I didn't know what I was walking into, but I needed this man's help. I had to find Jessica. At the same time, I had to get a sense of what else he might be into. Sometimes after leaving a place, I've had to call in the cops. If I sensed that a place was fronting for some other dark and forbidding business, I had to make the call.

I introduced myself, and Stan, the photographer, shook my hand in earnest. His hand was sweaty, but he was smooth as a snake. His dark hair was slicked back into a ponytail. He didn't have on too much jewelry. He was all smiles and concerns. I've seen that before. It's a card to play when you want to keep your distance.

I had my game face on, too. I kept my breath slow and stayed focused, keeping good eye contact. Still, the sweat ran down my back in little streams. A little bit of me always gets scared. I don't fight it anymore; I live with it. Besides, having nearly bought the farm a couple of times has made me aware of my mortality.

Over the years I've walked into some spicy situations that made me feel like Clint Eastwood or Gary Cooper walking into a bar and having the whole place go gunfighter silent. But I'm not Clint or Gary, and my life isn't a movie. I've occasionally walked into situations in which I thought the good guy was sure to win, but instead, I got smoked. I had thought I couldn't lose, and instead was extremely fortunate to walk out alive. Those situations scared the hell out of me. I've learned to appreciate how stupid I can be, but I hope I'm a bit smarter now. Up to this point, caution has proved to be a lifesaver.

I simply asked Stan about Jessica and what his relationship was to her. He was quick to be helpful. He told me he'd only taken some basic portfolio shots of her. No, he didn't have her address or phone number. I saw a little sweat bead up on his upper lip. I couldn't read any more into it, but I filed it away. He took my number and said if she showed up, he'd try to get her to call. He said he wanted to help.

Fortunately, Stan lied to me—he did have her number. He apparently thought I was sincere. Maybe he tasted a little of the fear of heaven. Whatever it was, it made him call her. A week later she called me. We agreed to meet at my downtown "office"—the all-night diner on 10th Avenue.

Guardian Angels

Jessica and I met for coffee at 2:00 A.M. She had just gotten off work.

When I walked in, I picked her out right away. Long black hair, baseball cap backward, three pierces with assorted ornaments in each ear. No tattoos that I could see, no heavy makeup. Not smoking. Nice pair of boots. It told me she was holding up in her life in *The Way Beyond.* She hadn't changed much from her photo. Another good sign.

We small-talked. She asked most of the questions, checking me out face-to-face, trying to figure out how I fit the picture. My ace was that I *didn't* fit. I wasn't boxed into what she grew up with, and that helped open the door a bit. I needed to make it clear that I could be a resource, but before she could see me as that resource, we had to build some trust—a tricky item.

In *The Way Beyond,* trusting someone means giving them the power to hurt you. The rules become quite simple: Don't trust anyone and lie constantly to throw everyone off your trail. You won't hurt if you lie. You're safe. No one knows the truth.

The trouble is, the lies eat you like acid rain burning quietly into your soul. Then you start to hurt all the time, right in your heart. You ache with the pain of the paradox. If you're lucky, you reach inside and risk trusting again. You come out deciding to tell the truth to someone. In that act you feel pure terror, and in that terrifying moment, you start to let go of your pain and condemnation. It's frightening.

I had a long way to go toward building that trust with Jessica. She'd been out in *The Way Beyond* long enough to cast immediate suspicion on anyone new. But she wouldn't have chosen to meet me if she hadn't thought I might help. If I took the time to build a relationship, the trust would come.

So we sat in that diner booth with the jukebox playing, drinking too much coffee, and checking out the action.

Around 3:30 A.M., bubbles of noise and laughter burst through the diner. I turned around in the booth and craned my neck toward the door. It was Carlos and four friends. I looked closer and saw that James was one of them. I knew them from the back alleys of the meat market, where they strutted and plied their trade. They were regulars who came and met the van when we made our way through lower Manhattan.

The meat market—the netherworld of transvestites—is the lowest rung on the ladder. In the shadows of the market, anytime after midnight, everyone is armed and dangerous. It's the dark paradise of evil. More kids die down there than anywhere else on the street. The hustlers vamp, strut, curse, and act sexy and tough, but no broom can sweep up the broken dreams.

For Carlos, James, and their friends, it was definitely dress-up night. As they neared our booth, Carlos spotted me. He was sequined and feathered out, sashaying and strutting with a rhinestone cigarette holder. His nails were painted like a rainbow. His makeup covered up his five o'clock shadow perfectly.

"Yehudah honey, how you doing?"

"Carlos, James! You girls are dressed to kill. Where you been?"

"Voguing. It was a totally awesome evening. Who's your friend?"

"Everybody, this is Jessica. We just met. I'm letting her in on my business."

Carlos turned to Jessica and gave his *if looks could kill* smile. "Sugar, Yehudah's good. You can trust him. He delivers. Don't be afraid to ask him anything."

He turned back to me, batted his eyes, and said, "Yehudah, darling, we're simply starved." He brushed me lightly with a kiss on the cheek and added, "Bye, catch you later!"

"You can count on it, Carlos. Hey, James, did you talk with your aunt?"

James looked back with puppy-dog eyes. "Not yet. I'll do it today."

"James, do it. You'll feel better."

I was hit with the raw poignancy of it all and let out a sigh.

James was all smiles tonight, but a week before he was crying in my arms. When he told his parents he was gay, they kicked him out. The only one in his family who kept in touch with him was his aunt. But she didn't know he was dressing up and that he had just tested positive for the AIDS virus. The tension of a dual life was eating him up, but he was terrified of telling her—he might lose her too.

Guardian angels appear in all sizes, shapes, and forms. That night it had been Carlos and James. More than anything else, they showed Jessica that I had their stamp of approval. They had done a good deed. I was okay. A link was going to be forged between Jessica and me.

After they left, Jessica fixed me with the first real look of the night. I could see her deciding to check me out. She was going to tell me something private, but not too private. Personal, but not too personal. She wanted to see how I would handle something that's hurting. If I passed the test, we'd go on. If not . . . well, that would be it.

Jessica took a sip of her coffee and commented, "You know a lot of people."

I coolly replied, "It's not that I know so many people, it's that I genuinely care for the people I know."

Jessica looked me in the eye and opened her mouth. Then she squinted her eyes and just looked down, staring at her lap.

Right away I said, "Hey, you were going to tell me something."

Her head jerked straight up and she said, "Ah, it's not so important. I just wanted to give you my work number. I work a 900 line."

"That must be pretty strange." No sense being oblique.

"You know what, it is," she snorted. "It's sick and creepy."

"Kind of sad and pathetic too."

"I suppose so. It's also funny. All these weird men wasting all that money," she said.

"No doubt about that. If you don't laugh at some of that weirdness, you'd probably feel like spending the whole day in the shower. Those guys give *dirty old man* a whole new meaning."

She smiled and said, "Trouble is, they're not all that old."

I gave her a serious look and said, "I know."

Unfolding Verses

Two months later Jessica and I were sitting in my kitchen. Our relationship had moved from all-night restaurants to regular visits to my home. She still hadn't gone to her parents' home, but she had begun to call them regularly. I didn't push her. I just gave her nudges. When she was ready, she'd make her move. Her folks were happy enough that she was hanging out with me.

Jessica was beginning to move on with her life. The fact that she was even sitting in my home was a statement that her life was changing. She still wasn't aware of the change, but she had reached the point where she was talking about her life.

"You know I'm getting sick of working the phones. It's just creepy and dirty all the time," she said.

"Yeah," I chuckled, "It's got to be tough doing the uncensored, hot, nasty, exotic, hard-core talk every night."

The truth is, I hate phone sex. It's not that I'm simply down on perverse language. It has more to do with the destruction of personal intimacy and loving relationships. It speaks volumes about how far we've moved away from love. Jessica knew my opinions, but humor often works a lot better than morality lectures.

Jessica laughed. "Yeah. But what can I do? The money's okay. Where else could I work? I don't think I can waitress."

"Jessica, I'll make you a deal. You know your folks have been in counseling now for a couple of months. They feel stuff's happening there for them. If you try to join them for a few sessions, I'll start working on seeing if I can find some job openings for you."

She didn't pull away when I mentioned her parents. "Yeah, I know they're trying. I can tell by the way they talk to me on the phone. Things are a lot less tense." Then she laughed a little and looked at me with a funny face. "So you'll try to find some job for me? You mean it's kinda like blackmail. Either I go to therapy and get the job or I don't and I'm stuck on the 900 line?"

I smiled. "Naw, I don't really mean it that way. You know I'll work on the job for you whether or not you check out the counseling." Then I became more serious. "But I feel really strongly that it's time to recognize that your folks have changed and to come in a bit out of the cold with them. I haven't brought this up before, but you could add some perspective and maybe smooth some things out by going to a session with them. It might make your family's relationship better all the way around. What have you got to lose? You can always walk out. Give them a call. Go for it."

She looked away and said, "Hmm. Maybe. I gotta think about it."

The lesson here is simple. If the parents change, the child has a chance to change. If they can act differently, she can too. The problems that ignited the strife in the family are not as operative. If you don't have your parents to fight with anymore, you're stuck dealing with yourself.

"Yehudah, what kind of job could I even apply for? All I've got is a GED and this stupid job I've got now. I mean, what am I qualified for?" she asked.

"You sure could be a great receptionist. Not bad for starters, say in the fashion industry or downtown on Wall Street or a doctor's office? Hey, you're good on the phone, right? You're personable. It's a good place to start."

She laughed, "You know, you're so funny sometimes. But you're right. Maybe I am qualified."

Most change happens bit by bit, a step here and a step there. Yet sometimes, when you lean back in a chair and take a look, you see the changes are powerful, vivid, and lyrical. They paint a perfect picture. However the change comes, the moment it happens is terrifying. You feel exposed, vulnerable, and defenseless. The mystery is that even though you don't know where you will end up, you take the leap.

After that conversation, Jessica did make a move. She began visiting her parents. She even ventured into the therapist's office for a couple of sessions, or as she said, "to help them with some of their problems." She told me a month or so later, "The therapist is cool. Things are better; I mean we're talking and I go home now. I'm glad I'm in touch with my brother and sister."

I smiled and at the same time shook my head back and forth real slowly. Sometimes giving a double message makes sense. "Jess, you're still underground. You still work the 900 numbers and you haven't followed up on any of the job leads I gave you. You know what I'm saying. You haven't cleaned up your act. You've got business to take care of. I'm not telling you it's confession time, but as long as you've got secrets, you're not being straight and true to yourself."

She lowered her eyes. "I know, but not now. I need the money."

I wasn't quite ready to let go. I normally don't lean into someone unless there's a good reason and we know and trust each other. People do listen to people who care about them. "Jessica, here's something for you to file away for a rainy day. Things you avoid dealing with today will make an appointment with you at some later date. You're going to have an opportunity to deal with all this again. It's kinda like your soul giving you a reminder that says, *Are you ready to accept that you're changing?* Watch for it to come. It will be an opportunity to grow, to see you've changed. And remember, we all learn from our mistakes and failures if we pay close attention."

Recognizing That You've Changed

In late fall Manhattan twinkles, bathed in the lights of what seems like a million shop windows. It's a window-shopper's paradise. When I get the opportunity, I love to take long walks down through the Village. The sight of so many different people wending their way through the streets is, for me, transcendental.

Walking in the midst of all those people and being aware that as surely as they live, walk, and breathe, they have hopes, struggles, dreams, and aspirations makes me marvel at the depth and complexity of Creation.

On this particular fall evening, I had just finished giving a lecture at New York University. As I left the student union, I made my way over to Bleecker Street and plunged headlong into the West Village, on my way to a little store that sells sixties concert posters. I had just finished cruising Bleecker and cut over to West Houston when I spotted Jessica coming out of a cafe near the corner.

I could tell she was upset. From the distance I could see she was either crying, real angry, or both. It looked as though I had come across the grand finale of some argument. She was yelling at some guy. He didn't look much happier than Jessica, but from his body language, he seemed to be scoring more points.

It was an awkward moment. I debated whether I should cross the street and say hello. From the looks of things, that would probably have been a bit inappropriate. But on the other hand, I thought, *What are the odds of bumping into someone you know in the middle of New York City?* Since I always operate on the principle that there are no accidents, and a coincidence is really a *co-incide-ence,* I decided to say hello.

Fortunately, by the time I crossed the street, they had had a few more choice words and Jessica was now walking up the block—alone.

I caught up to her and said, "Good evening, young lady."

She turned quickly and simultaneously stepped back, getting ready for action. New Yorkers aren't known for their social graces on the street. Friendly hellos are greeted with a high degree of suspicion. Her eyes were bloodshot, and she'd been crying. "Yehudah, you scared the hell out of me. What are you doing here?"

I opened my hands and said, "Fate?"

But I could see that now was not the time for jokes. Quickly, I filled in: "I was speaking at NYU and just decided to browse around the Village. From the look of things and from the little I saw, maybe you want to grab a cup of coffee and talk." She shook her head yes.

We popped into a small coffee emporium. I got a cup of house blend and Jessica took some exotic mixture from South America. We grabbed a table in the back.

The place was quiet and subdued with a bunch of Boston fans hanging out by the windows facing the street. The owner had the radio tuned to some classic rock. I was more in the mood for George Strait or Billy Joe Shaver.

I didn't waste any time. "Okay, Jessica, what's going on? You look like you're either about ready to fall apart or have just passed through a thunderstorm and are about ready to get a dose of clearheadedness."

She took a sip of her coffee, scooted her chair forward, and sat straight up. She blinked once and fixed me in her sight. "Yehudah, I've had it. I mean, things are different with me. I'm tired and sick of what I do for a living. That creep, who I thought was my boyfriend, is a real jerk. All he wanted from me was weird sex. I'm not who he thinks I am. Yehudah, the truth is I've changed. I've moved beyond all of that. I honestly know I want something different."

Jessica had reached her turning point. She could now see her anger about the past from a different point of view. She had chosen to take action by getting angry at her so-called boyfriend. Rejecting him showed that she no longer rejected herself. It was a pure expression of her growing self-esteem, powered by the knowledge that she had changed.

Hot tears ran down her cheeks. They came down in little black streams as they washed off mascara. She was mad. She was insulted. She was ashamed. "Last night he started asking me, 'What do you say on the phone line to guys? Do you ever do some of that stuff that you talk about?' I told him, 'What do you think, I'm nuts?' He kept pushing it. I told him to shove it. He came back and said, 'Hey, it's you and me. We ought to be free and open with each other. You know, with our bodies. After all, we care for each other.' He wouldn't shut up, so I finally got up and left. God, he went from what I thought was a guy who was understanding to another weirdo that calls in on the phone."

"If you dumped him, what were you doing with him this afternoon?"

"Well, when I got home, he called me. He didn't apologize, but said it was all a misunderstanding and asked me to meet him for coffee after work."

"In other words, he sweet-talked you, appealed to your sensitive side."

She rolled her eyes, "Probably. I don't know. Yeah, you're right. Anyway, I sat up most of the night thinking about what was going on here. Like you always say, *What is the message? What am I learning here?* I took out that eight-step list of yours to see if it could help me see where I'm at. It hit me hard. I realized I've changed. I don't know how it even happened, but it did."

I wanted to get her a little more focused, "So what *are* you learning here?"

"It's weird. I was mad, sad, and in the strangest way felt good about all of this. It was confusing, but made sense. Do you know what I mean?"

I raised my eyebrows and nodded my head. "I'm pretty sure I do. But you explain it to me. It's your story."

"Okay, I was mad at the guy, but really mad at myself for getting into this mess. I was sad because I felt bad for myself, and I felt good because I was finally doing something positive for myself. For me."

"But you went to meet him . . ."

She interrupted, "Yeah, that's the point. I went to meet him to tell him where to get off. That he doesn't know me or respect me. And that it's over. Don't call me."

I slipped a couple of words in, "But he looked like he didn't take it too well or didn't hear you."

She laughed, and I saw she wasn't shedding any tears for that guy. She'd had a realization and it was moving those tears.

"*Please!* All he wanted was to get back in bed with me. He's a lowlife. He didn't know me at all. I told him to shove it. He got all pissed off and said who was I to tell him to shove it? I was the one doing phone sex. Blah, blah, blah. But you know, I tuned him out. It was over. I was crying 'cause I'm still mad at myself. I still feel bad. But I see now where I've been and how I'm going to change."

Hidden within Jessica's words was a clear message: "I have changed." Her pain and frustration were now motivators. Her taking action was a sign that she was willing to transform her failings into gifts. By taking steps to protect her dignity, new horizons began to appear in her life. When that happens, it uncoils an inner wellspring of goodness and motivation.

It came as no surprise to me that within a matter of weeks Jessica found a receptionist job on Wall Street. She became a volunteer in a day-care center. She learned to get along with her family. She moved forward and inward. She learned the language of the heart—forgiveness. She didn't forget what she learned in the shadow world—compassion. Her ability to be in a relationship improved dramatically. Her sense of herself allowed her to take honest risks to act in her own best interests. With that honesty, the door to love was opened.

She became blessed. She fell in love. Three years later she stood under a canopy of stars and was married.

Jessica gave me the greatest gift of all. You see, I was privileged to stand with her and her future husband under that canopy of stars. She had asked me to marry them.

STEP THREE

Standing Up for Yourself

SARAH'S STORY

Everything has its season,
and there is a time for everything
under the heaven:

A time to rend and a time to mend
Koheles; Chapter 3

STEP THREE: *Standing Up for Yourself*

> *Keep yourself far away from the things that caused you to sin. Change your name, which is to say, "I am a different individual, and I'm not the person who did all those things." Change your actions and deeds, all of them, to the good and straight path. And go into exile from your current place.*
>
> (MAIMONIDES, *Hilchos Teshuvah*, Chapter Two, Section Four)

We realize that in order to have nothing to do with what caused our pain, we have to separate ourselves from many things. It is as if we had a previous self who did those things or acted that way. Staying far away from that previous life is now a steadfast commitment.

Our confession has brought us to a new awareness. We become aware of a part of our personality that had been hidden in our pain. This new sense of self is like a new name. And our new name is bringing us forward to begin a new life. Standing up for and taking stock of yourself leaves you with only one conclusion: I am me. I'm trying hard to be the best me. No one can do this for me. I affirm myself even with all my imperfections.

Think about this. After we take stock of all we've gone through, all the trauma, isn't it time to take a stand for our lives? Isn't it time to fill our needs? Aren't we willing to have courage and patience to commit ourselves to not crossing the line again?

Granted, in the process of turning our lives around, we have to take great risks. Once we realize that we've changed, and that going back is too painful to endure, we begin to stand on new ground and claim our lives for ourselves.

All-Night Duty

It was a cool winter night in the city as I turned up 8th Avenue, just off 42nd Street. The street was littered with ghostly shadows. Making the rounds in Times Square, I was offered everything. I couldn't walk a block up from the Port Authority without a disembodied voice whispering in my ear, "What do you like, Rabbi? Young girls, boys, Asian, white, black? I have it."

This is New York's worst deli. The menu features the selling of the lost. Here, you can take an up-close look at evil making its living. As the air grows colder, the street smells of pretzel smoke, cigarettes, and urine. Between the taxis, buses, and the subway underneath the street, the metal and concrete vibrate and moan. The sound rises out of the subway grates, playing an eerie symphony of sadness. On the street, empty pizza boxes mix with handbills inviting you to see the all-night nudie shows. The neon flashes flesh, and behind those doors broken lives dance on display. I've never gotten used to it. I still wish it were a bad dream.

Tonight was my night out in the van. I was working the Times Square area with two other outreach workers from a local shelter. We were looking for Rachel. Rumor had it that she was sixteen and dancing in an all-girl adult review. The night before she had crashed at a local shelter for runaways. Although I hadn't met her before, some kid must have told her about me. I wasn't surprised when the shelter called at 11 A.M. to let me know that Rachel had wanted to speak with me. I made arrangements to call her half an hour later. But by then, she was gone.

I never did find Rachel that night. However, I did stumble upon Sarah. She was standing under an overhang of a long-closed movie theater in Times Square. If you were looking, you couldn't miss her. She had just enough mascara on to pass for eighteen. Her clothes looked fresh, like they'd come straight from a bedroom closet. She wore a clean winter coat that could have come from some mall only a few weeks before. Her hair was cut stylishly short. She looked too well taken care of—like a kid in a school yard, not on the street. Everything about her set off warning bells in my head that said, "Young runaway in trouble."

You develop instincts out in *The Way Beyond.* You learn to detect who's new to the street. New kids don't have a wary or hard look in their eyes. They don't survey their surroundings to check for danger. They don't want people to get too close to them. They haven't gotten the street's initiation.

A young runaway out on the streets of urban America will be violently assaulted at least once during the first week out there. Nobody looks the same after the first attack. It's a brutal passage into a dark world. The predators, sensing the vulnerability of these recent runaways, move in to take what they can from them. The pimps shower gifts and then take them down with rape. Or the street thieves arrive, deliver a vicious assault, and take their few possessions. Then there are the more violent encounters of which we don't hear the details because we never see those kids again.

Sarah was smoking hard on a cigarette, but had a difficult time inhaling. She kept rubbing her eyes as the smoke curled up by her face. Although her stone-faced expression and her new cigarette habit almost made her look tough, it only masked the terror.

It's obvious that no young girl belongs out there, especially a girl trying to look eighteen carrying two backpacks, her worldly possessions. Later, I found out that one was filled with her schoolbooks, the other with her clothes.

She was talking to three guys. They encircled her, showing great interest, like a wolf pack hunting down its prey. The young men sported big smiles and toothy grins. They were hungry. They were hunting. I immediately grew cautious. After all, they could be fronting for a pimp. I knew my presence would be cause for alarm. In their world, anyone talking to their potential merchandise is a threat to their livelihood.

But in defense of this girl, I decided to make my move. I had that one thing going for me: As a rabbi, I carried a little edge. The predators never could figure out what I was doing out there. It made them nervous. Perhaps they thought twice about messing with me. At the very least, it gave me a little room to talk. After all, how many rabbis wander around Times Square in the middle of the night?

I put on my best game face and prepared to step into their little circle. Stepping in is never fun. These situations always have the potential for explosive violence, and I'm never armed. I don't even carry pepper spray. I do this simply as an act of faith and caring.

I tried not to pay too much attention to the wolves. I made certain not to catch their eyes. Eye-to-eye contact can lead directly to a confrontation. Out on the street it can be seen as a challenge.

Out of one ear I listened to them breathe. I felt their rhythm and checked for irregular movements that could spell trouble. My heart was pounding, but outwardly I was cool, calm, and collected. Downright friendly. Whatever the outcome, I had to be sure to stay on top of the conversation. I needed to come across as warm, official, and helpful. If I could take charge of the situation, I could push the vultures off and win a small measure of this girl's trust, which, in this case, could mean getting her to shelter. It was a chance to save her life.

I stepped in, turned to the girl, and said, "Hi, I'm Yehudah. What's your name?"

She mumbled back, "Sarah." She was clearly lost and confused, which made her vulnerable and open to influence. Now, she was being given a choice: me or them. Her confusion left her off balance, so she was going to go with whoever could make her feel the safest.

I began my appeal. "You look lost. Do you need shelter? You know it's not safe out here." I handed her a card with the phone number of a local youth shelter. "I can get you over to the shelter right now. No one's going to ask you a lot of questions." I was loading her up with offers as quickly as possible. She needed to get away from this nightmare. The more warm and official I could sound, the more likely she would be to step off those mean streets.

I then turned to a pile of garbage sitting a few feet away and added, "You know *this* doesn't look like a good place to spend the night." I immediately turned to the predators, before they had a chance to respond, and said with concern, "You guys probably agree with that, right?"

There are certain basic rules I've learned from spending so much time with kids on the street. One of them is that if you get to kids in the first twenty-four hours of their arrival on the street, they have a better chance of surviving. Sarah took a chance and walked with me to the shelter's van, parked a few blocks away.

I took a deep breath as we walked away. It was cold. I checked the time on my father's watch. That watch is a link, one of my anchors. When my father left this world my mom gave it to me. I need it because the world I walk in is adrift. The Manhattan nightscape can contain the ultimate nightmare. The watch connects me to my father, to the warmth I received as a child and to the special memories of my childhood. The world back then seemed brighter, better, and full of goodness. These good memories give me warmth, strength, and a little courage at night on the street.

The watch read 11:30 P.M. As we walked up the street, I let out an audible sigh.

Sarah turned to me and said, "Did you say something?"

I smiled and said, "Nope, I was just thinking about what's coming up tonight. It's a heavy scene out here. I'll tell you about it sometime if you're curious. But for now, let's get over to the van and have some hot chocolate."

I approach the street with the same mental attitude that an athlete uses when preparing for competition. A key part of that training is visualizing the game. Seeing oneself *in* the game is a refined skill. Mental preparation is as important as physical preparation.

Out on the streets, I never know what I'm going to encounter. No angels are going to miraculously come out of the sky to execute any dramatic rescues. Extra mental preparation is needed before facing the razor's edge of reality. My reflexes depend on it.

The first order of business tonight was to take care of Sarah. She needed shelter. I needed to get her to safety. After that, I would head back out.

What Do You See?

As we approached the van Sarah asked, "You got any coffee or just the hot chocolate?"

"No coffee, but the hot chocolate is really good." Handing her a cup, I said, "Sarah, let's walk back down to where I found you. I want to show you something."

As we walked I said, "Let's play a game called, 'What do you see out here?' You go first."

"What?" She wrinkled up her brow like I was a little weird but seemed willing to go along with it anyway.

I chuckled. "Hey, believe me, it's an interesting game. It's a step up from Simon Says."

As we arrived back near the spot where I found her, she looked around with a sweep of her head. "Okay. . . . I see lots of people walking around. . . . Lots of signs, stores, taxis, buses. . . . Lots of kids, food, I don't know."

She seemed to be getting used to my apparent foolishness. Walking further and pointing, I said, "Take a closer look. What's going on by that movie theater across the street?"

She shrugged. "Some kids talking. Maybe selling, I don't know."

"Now it's my turn," I became serious. "I'll tell you what I see. There's bad stuff going on all around us. You just haven't been around enough to see it. Let me peel a little of the street back so we can see what's inside. Across the street I see suicide. Those guys with the basketball jackets and fancy shoes, baseball caps down low? They're dealing crack to those other kids. Watch, see . . . there it goes down. You know what smoking crack is? It's suicide on the installment plan. It feels good in the beginning, beams you out, then steals your life and soul. See that guy on the corner? Walking and whispering to every suit who walks by or anyone who looks like they carry a little cash? Take a look. There he goes. A whisper. What do you think he's saying? What's his big secret?"

She raised her eyebrows slightly, a sure sign I'd gotten a bit of her attention. Then she said, almost innocently, "I don't know."

"It's okay. I know you don't know. But I want to give you a fix on what's going on. He's selling girls. You know what I mean. He's selling flesh at $20 to $100 a pop. He even offered me some earlier. Watch him. There he goes again. Not a pretty sight, is it?"

She let off a little shudder. "Whoa—weird. You see a lot of stuff, don't you?"

I continued, matter-of-factly, "You haven't been out here very long, have you?"

She replied, "How'd you know?"

"You've got the look of a first-nighter. You didn't go home today, did you?"

She quietly said, "No."

I didn't push it any further, and she wasn't offering any explanations. Even though I wanted to get all the details, this was not the time or the place. My work here was saving a life, not making assessments.

Lots of kids I've met have what's called *street smarts.* When they have it, unlike Sarah, they know what's going on—who's dangerous, who straps a gravity knife, who poses with their fake Rolex, who packs a 9mm, who's psycho, and who's a whacko. In the end it doesn't really matter. Most kids on the street are still going to go down.

Sarah had been out less than twenty-four hours. Later, I learned that she had been raised in New York City and had gone to a city school. But nothing had prepared her for this.

I continued to hammer the vision home. "Sarah, take a look down the street toward the newsstand. What do you see?"

"I see the guys I was talking to. Timmy and his friend."

Out of the corner of my eye, I spied a kid I knew very well, Ramón. He was hanging out by the van, talking with some other kids. Ramón's a good kid. He has a day job now, rehabbed and clean from a nasty crack habit. But for some reason, he still hung out here at night. As much as I enjoyed hanging with him, I always prayed he'd go away. As long as his social life was caught up in Times Square, he was still at risk.

"Hey, Ramón, come over for a minute," I called. "I got to

ask you a question." Ramón had come into my field of vision at precisely the right moment.

With his best pose, Ramón strutted over. "*Qué pasa, mon!* What's going down, Yehudah?"

"I'm holding school here. Giving some education to Sarah. Sarah, this is Ramón."

"Hi, Ramón."

"Hey, Sarah, what's up? How you doing, girl?"

"Ramón, one question." My school lessons continued, and I nodded toward Timmy. "You know those guys over there? What are they up to?"

Ramón tilted his head down. Peering up as he lowered his shades to the tip of his nose, he answered, "Wolves or vultures. I can't tell who they're hanging for. Looks like they're ready to score or waiting to hit on some kid. They be Port Authority types. I've seen them around. Might work for some pimp."

I let out a slow breath and said, "Thanks, Ramón, for the backup. Catch you later."

Turning to Sarah, I asked, "What did Timmy want from you? What did he say he was going to give you, Sarah? A place to stay? A modeling job or work on a 900 line?"

"Yeah, something like that. He said he could help me."

It hurt to see her innocence. Kids don't choose to take up hustling or to be "in the life." They don't plan to grow up in such troubled families. It wasn't her fault. How could she know what was going down? The old adage *if you come from trouble you go to trouble* rang true. When you're desperate, a little offer of help from anyone seems like a gold mine. When you're desperate, the street world seems like one big family. No one is ever alone. Everyone's eager to help. Trouble is, this "help" too often leads you to the morgue. Your "family portrait" becomes a solitary chalk outline on the sidewalk, framed by a yellow ribbon that says *Police Line, Do Not Cross.* Or worse, you are never found.

The wolves and vultures, like those who were trying to prey on Sarah, pervert the gentle power of love, compassion, and caring. They turn cheap tricks into bondage. They've got

Ph.D.'s in manipulation, and they know how vulnerable kids like Sarah are. They call them *chickens,* and they're the chicken hawks.

I told it to Sarah straight. "Sarah, that guy was going to use you and sell you. He wasn't going to love you. He wasn't going to take care of you, at least not how you might have been thinking. Get some shelter, food, and protection for yourself. After a good night's sleep, you can see about getting some help in the morning."

The truth is, most of the kids I've met out in *The Way Beyond* don't come in off the mean streets. Sarah stood up and took the risk most kids never do: She decided to come off the streets. I noticed her and she noticed me. But it was Sarah who let the dialogue take hold.

Seeing Sarah take that step toward saving herself inspired me right in my heart. I was witnessing a miracle. I saw it in her eyes. In spite of the dread and desperation, she was showing me the truth: *Evil can't wipe out goodness.*

We got Sarah over to the runaway shelter around 12:45 A.M. She looked relieved, yet very tired. I got her a snack, gave her a quick hug, and told her I'd see her in the morning right after breakfast.

Way Station: The Shelter

After heading back out in the van until around five, I took the D train back to Brooklyn and caught a few hours of sleep. I pulled myself out of bed to have breakfast with my kids before they headed off to school, was back on the D by 8:15, and was in the runaway center before 9:00. Sarah had just finished breakfast. She had an appointment with the intake worker around 11:00, which gave us a couple of hours to hang out.

I grabbed a cup of coffee and we headed over to the lounge. Along the way I saw Chandra and Denise heading out. I was always bumping into them at dinner and in the early evenings in the lounge. Over time, we had become friends. I yelled across the lounge, "Chandra, Denise! How you doing? Going to work?"

Chandra said, "We're on the ten-to-six shift today. Got to run. We don't want to be late." I called after them, "Have a good one, ladies." They waved and swept out the door.

"They can get you jobs here?" Sarah asked.

I took the opportunity to drive home a few important points. "Yep, jobs—but you've got to go out and interview for them. You can get your high school equivalency diploma, too, but you've got to go to classes for it. The help's here, but you've got to work for it and earn your way. In a few months Chandra and Denise will have saved up enough money to move out of here and get their own place."

That got her attention. "That's really cool. I'd like that. How do I get into that?"

"Sarah, it's great that you want to get something going for yourself. But first things first. You know, one step at a time. How old are you?"

"I'm sixteen, almost seventeen," she replied.

"So, you're still under eighteen. We're going to help you find a more homey placement. Besides, it's the law. You have to be in state and city care until you're eighteen. Once you're in placement, you can see about a job or finishing school or figuring out what you need to do with your family."

She drew in a short breath and said, "You mean I'll have to go into foster care. That scares me."

"It all depends on your situation. But don't worry. Wherever you get settled, the runaway shelter will make sure it's checked out carefully. If, say, you're not going back home soon, then maybe you'll go into foster care or a group home for a while."

I stopped talking for a moment to see if she'd say something about herself or her family, but she didn't. I decided to be helpful by laying out the parameters of what was ahead. "Look, this much I can tell you. You're safe here, and any placement you go into, whether it's short or long term, is going to be safe. I can't tell you it's going to be paradise, but it will be secure, with good home cooking, counseling, and lots of visits from me."

I wasn't going to overstep the bounds. Sarah wasn't offering me her story, so there was no way I could guess her needs. If you push on kids, you might become the enemy. By embracing and accepting her from the outset, trust was established. With that trust, the details of her life would follow.

"You'll get a lot of questions answered at intake," I told her. "As you feel more comfortable, ask more questions. Make sure you get answers you understand and keep asking. Asking questions keeps you in charge of your life. I'm going to be around if you want to talk with me." I took out a piece of paper and wrote down my number. "Here's my number. Keep it in a good place."

She took my number and we sat for a while in silence. She had a lot to process and digest.

After a while she looked up and said, "Thanks. So what do you do here? Tell me something about you."

I was hoping we'd get to that. "Well, I'm not the stranger in the night or the mystery man. I live over in Brooklyn in a big old house with three great kids and a wonderful wife. I grew up on the West Coast and have no idea how I ended up in New York. In fact, right before our wedding, I told my wife I was going to spend my life working to help people improve their lives. That's what I've always been dedicated to. I told her we might live anywhere. I said I hoped that was all right. She said that she'd go anywhere with me, but please, let's avoid living in New York City."

With that, Sarah laughed. It was her first laugh in the eleven hours I'd known her. It was a good laugh. I could tell we were going to be friends.

She looked away and turned her head toward five kids sitting about ten feet away. She turned back, scrunched up her face, and asked, "Yehudah, what's that smell? God, it stinks. Where's it coming from?"

I laughed. "It's real foul, isn't it? Well, welcome to some more of the real world. The smell's coming from those kids. They're cutting some of the foulest gas in this galaxy. They're crack heads who are going into detox. The crack does that to you. You get the picture, it's not all roses in here. Everyone has a hard road to follow, but you can make it."

She shook her head and gave me a brief stare of recognition. "I get the picture, but I don't like the smell."

A week went by and Sarah was still living at the runaway shelter, tied up in the social service system. Her social worker and I were able to piece together quite a few details. The night I found her, she had come home from school only to be thrown out by her stepfather and her mother. Apparently, they didn't want her back. They would all be heading to family court at some point in the future to work it out.

Sarah was what's called a throwaway. Most people have the mistaken notion that the approximately one million children who end up on the streets yearly are runaways. The truth is that a good portion of them are throwaways. As the name implies, they simply aren't wanted anymore. They're thrown away, tossed out on the street along with the garbage. Sarah was going to need to find the strength to pull herself out of that garbage and stand up for herself.

After ten days at the shelter, she was finally placed in a group home. Now, the hard work would have to begin.

Group Home

I wouldn't say that Sarah's life settled down, but she did go back to high school. I visited her every other week, and little by little she shared pieces of her painful life. Her inner wounds were terrifying. They still bled in tears and nightmares. Still, Sarah had become more determined than ever to make a new life for herself.

When I would visit, we mostly talked about her classes, her dreams of a new life, or my kids. Other times she would take a risk and toss out a piece of her life story.

"My father was an alcoholic. He died. He was only around for a few years of my life. I don't remember much about him. I don't hate him. I don't know. . . ."

I never set any agendas in our conversations. I left that to her social worker. Besides, before Sarah could plunge into the healing process, she had to feel that her life had some foundation. I saw myself as one of the bridges back to finding and reclaiming her life. While there were never answers to the question "Why me?" there were answers to and insights into "What happened to me?" My role was spiritual adviser and friend. I was there to support her and let her know it was okay to trust again. In the beginning stages of recovery, life looks like one big puzzle. Before you can fit the pieces together, you've got to lay them out faceup on the table.

Sarah and I had a lot of conversations, and all of them began to count. She was beginning to understand that her life mattered. She was gaining self-esteem.

Yet Sarah still hadn't told me her whole story. Why should she? We were beginning to build a real relationship, and relationships aren't cheap. After all she'd been through, a good relationship deserved a high price tag. Trust could only be built on a foundation of goodwill.

Time moved on. Winter arrived.

One dark New York day, I drove across the Verrazano Bridge from Brooklyn to Staten Island, where Sarah's group home was. I decided to turn off at Victory Boulevard to take the long route. I needed time to think, to strengthen myself.

Today was the day I suspected Sarah was going to tell me a major piece of her story. On the telephone she had told me she wanted to have a deep talk. She told me it was part of her therapy to tell me some stuff. It was urged on by her social worker as part of her unique healing process. There isn't a formula to this process. But healing is one of the necessary steps to gaining freedom. Basically, it comes from letting another person in on your deepest, darkest secrets. First you must share your pain with someone you can trust and who cares. Then you experience it with someone who won't hurt you. Sarah was, I suspected, taking her first real try at standing up for herself.

This sharing was Sarah's gift to herself for her life. And I was going to receive her gift too. It was important that I felt prepared.

As I drove along the Island's backstreets, I flashed on an article I once read in *Sports Illustrated.* It chronicled the struggles and rehab of NBA coach John Lucas. For years he had battled with alcohol and cocaine. At a crucial point in his recovery, he was confronted by someone who said, "John, you know you're only as sick as your secrets." That statement ripped through him like a bolt of lightning and cleared the air in his life. It was one of those intimate arrows that strikes your mind, forcing it awake. With it comes a fresh perspective, the kind of freshness you sense after a good summer storm.

That statement also took my breath away. With simple clarity, it defined a cornerstone of life. How do we live an authentic life? The truth is that we can't until we unload and get straight with our secrets. Otherwise, they rot and fester and foul our inner landscape. They can destroy not only us, but also the ones we love.

Sarah stood at the threshold of realizing the need to turn her back on the past. If she could face the challenge now and stand up for herself, she could lay the necessary groundwork for making sure that no one would abuse her again.

I pulled up in front of Sarah's group home, which was situated in a typical Staten Island neighborhood. It was a big house with a front- and backyard, something you don't see much of in the other four boroughs. It even had a wooden fence. Inside there were five bedrooms and a basement garage.

I've been in a lot of group homes over the years. They have their positives and their negatives. A group home is a home, and yet it's not. But it's more than simply a refuge, and Sarah was glad to be there.

At the door Sarah gave me a hug. "I'm glad you came."

I hung up my coat, said hello to the house mother, turned, and handed Sarah a present.

I had brought her a menorah. To me, it's more than ironic that the miracle of Chanukah shines through the darkness of these kids' lives today. I always reflect on the teaching that a little light dispels darkness. It's one of the eternal truths that flows out of the Bible. Darkness comes before the light. The road of darkness and suffering leads to the road of light and love.

She took the gift quickly and held it as a prized possession, "Wow, for me? Thanks!"

"Well, save the thanks until you open it up." I smiled.

She ripped off the wrapping right there in the hallway. She obviously hadn't received any gifts in a long time. With astonishment, she gasped, "Yehudah, I can't believe you got this for me. I was praying that I might get a menorah. I haven't lit one since I was a little kid. I felt somehow that I needed it real bad. I don't know, just deep down with all that's happening, I knew I needed this. I don't even know the blessings or the whole story of Chanukah. You've got to teach me." Her eyes flashed a smile and glistened with tears. "You'll let me know what it's all about, right?"

I smiled right back and said, "Naturally. After all, spiritual things are my specialty. Whatever you want to learn, just ask me."

She sounded like an excited little kid, but her tears reflected deeper changes afoot. Suffering reveals the depth of your heart. Once the pain pierces the core, a spiritual yearning awakens. It's like coming in from a cold winter night, chilled to the bone. After you take off your boots, you want to head right to the woodstove and warm up. And once you've been warmed by that stove, you feel downright content. The same is true with the soul's struggle to break free. When you're given half a chance to get away from the cold abuse of the world, what emerges is the warmth in your heart and the light of your soul. The irony is that suffering brought you to this. The suffering uncovered a new joy and peace in your life.

It never surprises me how a little deed wrapped in the warmth of love taps into the needs of a person's heart. Trust is built in many ways, but the underpinnings are words and actions. Because Sarah and I spent time together regularly, we had slowly developed a bond. The menorah was a statement that our relationship had reached the point where we could share meaningful things with one another and that I wasn't just passing through her life. I was here to stay. Knowing that seemed to help Sarah hold on tight and begin to reclaim her self-respect. Standing up for herself was just around the corner.

She hugged me again and ran to the kitchen to show the house mother and some of the girls her present.

When she came back, we headed over to the living room, which had a little alcove off to one side. The Victorian lamp in the corner gave off a warm light. She sat back in a rocker. A clock ticked in the living room. The house smelled of beans and fried chicken. Dinner was an hour away.

Pouring Out the Truth

Sarah took a drag on a cigarette. She leaned back and framed herself against the light of a small living room window. She exhaled slowly with a shaky, raspy breath. Nervously, she leaned forward and fixed me in her gaze for a moment, then looked away and mumbled, "You want to hear the truth?"

I was a little taken aback. I didn't expect such a direct opening from her. Usually, we continue to hang out for a while, even joke a bit. But now I could feel the dam starting to burst. I hoped she had a lot of tissues, because I could sense a real gusher coming. I answered right back, "I'm here."

She turned toward me and looked at the floor. "Do you think you can understand?"

I sighed and let out my breath slowly. "Sarah, I hope so. But I don't know if I have to understand it all. I don't think that's necessarily the point. The point is that no matter what, I'm still here. I care."

With that, she started crying. Big, loud, messy, beautiful sobs and tears. Just knowing that it was okay to unburden some of the wounds burst her open. It's painful to see, but wonderful to experience. Her pain had been building inside her for years. Now she was going to lance the source of her infection, allowing all the pus of abuse, neglect, and violation she had endured to ooze out through her sobs and tears. In its place would be a new gauze of clean emptiness with which to build real self-dignity for herself. It hurts.

She shut her eyes tight, but the tears streamed out down her cheeks anyway. "I can't do it."

I told her, "Hey, it's okay. But I don't think you want to carry it by yourself anymore. From the look of how you're feeling right now, it's too heavy."

With that reassurance, she launched right into her story. "A year ago when my mom got remarried, it got really bad. The guy she married hated me. I think he hated me 'cause I wouldn't put out for him. He's a fat, greasy pig. Always trying to touch me. Asking me to sit on the bed with him while he'd be lying there stinking up the place with his beer and dirty underwear. I told my mom but she told me to shut up. She slapped me a lot. My mom turned against me. They were always screaming at me. Now I know they were sickos, but then . . . God! It was terrible. I kept trying to go to school and take care of myself. I tried to stay out of their way. But where can you go in a two-bedroom apartment? I've got no cousins and my grandparents are too old. Besides, they live in Florida."

She went on. "Anyway, it got worse and worse. The creep kept trying to touch me. I'd come home from school and he'd be sitting there and asking me to massage him. I hated him. He made me sick. I didn't know what to do. He was always putting his hands on me. I didn't know what he'd try next. I was so scared.

"Then one day when I came home after school, the lock to the apartment was changed. My stuff was lying out in a box in the hallway with a note that said they'd gone to California for a while. That I'm old enough to go out on my own. That I shouldn't ever come back. Could you believe it? My own mother didn't want me anymore. God, I felt so awful. I felt like I'd somehow screwed everything up."

I cut her off. I wanted to step in a bit and affirm her. "Sarah, you're not destined to have a rotten life. You're not the freak here. What they did to you was wrong. I don't care what their problems were, they were low-down and dirty."

A lot of these kids think *they're* the freaks. They blame themselves for all the bad things that happened to them. It's not hard to understand. After all, what happened to them was so bizarre that they begin to think that weird things only happen to weird people. If they were "normal," all this stuff wouldn't have happened. If they were "normal," they'd have a "normal" family. People who are abused often see themselves as victims with no way out. As they become more desperate and defenseless, they get swept deeper into the maelstrom of violence and abuse. Ironically, they seek safety on the street.

"When you found me that night, I was scared out of my mind," Sarah said. "I had nowhere to go. I was too embarrassed to ask my friends for help. I just took off on the train to the city. I had no idea what I was doing. You know what I mean?"

I smiled at her and said, "I think I have a pretty good idea. After all, I did find you."

"God, I was so glad you walked up to me. I don't know what might have happened otherwise. I probably looked kind of dumb that night. It was like I was numb. I didn't know what was happening."

"But you made a decision in spite of being so out of it," I replied. "Don't you see what happened? There you were out on the street being hit on, and you stood up for yourself. You could have stayed out in the street, but you said no way and came with me. Part of you, even in the most desperate hour, was strong. You made a decision to save yourself. Even confused, you took a stand. Kid, you stood up for who you are. Very gutsy."

She laughed a bit. "Yeah, you sound like our social worker. Or something we learn in group. Somehow, I believe it's true."

Her expression quickly darkened. "But I don't get it—how could my mom do this to me? She's my *mom!* I hate her. I hate her!" she screamed.

There's no way you can feel okay about a mother abandoning her daughter. The world is surely fractured by this. Sarah's screams still echo in the depths of my heart.

Sarah had a lot more to tell me that afternoon. It was her

bloodletting, her psychic cleansing. Her anger unleashed a litany of what could only be described as a mother's complete failure to protect her daughter.

"My mother hardly did anything with me after she got remarried. And when she did, most of the time my stepfather would get angry. It got to the point where I felt like she didn't care about me anymore. Once when she was talking to me, he went crazy—screaming things like he might as well leave because she didn't care about him and stuff like that. He was a selfish, creepy greaseball. My mom just listened to him scream and didn't do anything about it."

Sarah was facing reality, seeing things for what they were, not what she wanted them to be. She wasn't making any excuses about her family life in order to protect herself. She saw it. She saw the abuse and the ill will. She wasn't going to own it.

She was beginning to heal, to reclaim her birthright—herself. All this suffering was slowly being replaced with a newfound faith. It had begun to carry her forward to faith in herself.

She said, "Yehudah, I'm gonna make damn certain none of this ever happens to me again, and I'm not gonna end up like my mom, period."

Standing Up for Yourself

It was late Sunday afternoon. I'd caught a Yankee game up in the Bronx with my kids and slipped out at the seventh inning stretch, but not before finishing "Take Me Out to the Ball Game." There are certain rituals that are inviolate for the fan. Singing that song is one of them.

After dropping my kids off at home, I headed down Ocean Parkway and caught the Belt to Staten Island. Sarah and I had some work to do. I had a full plate heading into next week, so sometimes I start my workweek on Sunday night. I operate on the ancient principle expounded by Rabbi Tarfon, who said, "The day is short, and the work is great, and the Master of the house is pushing."[1]

Sarah was in the kitchen when I arrived. She handed me a

cup of coffee. I looked out the window and spied an old redwood picnic table in the backyard. "Let's sit and talk out in the back." Her eyes rolled a bit. I added, "Remember, I'm from the West Coast. Out on the West Coast you can have meaningful conversations outside. Indulge me. It's a nice day."

She shook her head and said, "Okay, let me get the letter."

The letter was the reason for my visit. It was part of her preparation for the upcoming family court date.

Sarah didn't want to go to court, but she had no choice in the matter. Everything had to be processed through the bureaucracy. The social worker and I had told her to use the court date as an opportunity to take charge of her life. It was a great place for her to literally stand up for herself.

The letter had to do with taking action to break from the dark pain of her abusive past. Her first task was coming to grips with her mother's ineptitude. Unfortunately, Sarah hadn't seen or spoken to her mother since she was tossed out on the street. At family court, Sarah would have to confront her—a tough and scary task. So, I had suggested that she write something to her mom beforehand. "You can send it or use it as a springboard for gathering your strength, letting go of your hurt, and moving past being a victim," I told her.

With her social worker's help, Sarah wrote the letter. She had also decided to send it, but wanted to share it with me first.

I walked out the back door, put my coffee down on the redwood table, and sat facing a pretty silver maple tree. There was a slight breeze blowing in from the west. A couple of houses away, a family was barbecuing some hamburgers or steaks. The smoke wafted on the breeze that also carried the faint odor of Elizabeth, New Jersey's chemical plants. It made my nose crinkle.

Sarah popped out the back, paper in hand, and took a seat across the table. We chatted for a while about nothing. Given all the heavy conversations I get into, my favorite topic is nothing. It creates normalcy. I cherish it.

She shifted gears and pulled out the paper. "Well, I finished it. I think I'm going to mail it. Want to hear it?"

"That's why I'm here."

She rushed on. "The letter is real short. I mean, just a paragraph or so. It wasn't easy to do. I spent days thinking about it, figuring out what I needed to say, what I needed to take care of. I'm kind of satisfied with it. It's been helpful . . ."

I put up a hand that said, *time-out.* "Sarah, it's okay. Slow down. Sorting it all out takes time. The letter isn't a magic bullet, but it's a strong step to you becoming the best you. Once, in a book by Dr. David Viscott I found an incredible insight into all of this. I think he said something like, 'If you don't really risk anything, you haven't grown or discovered a self that you feel worthy of defending.' So let's hear how you are defending yourself."

She unfolded the letter and set it in front of her on the table. "Okay, here goes."

> *Dear Mom,*
> *I decided to write you. Since you haven't called or visited I wanted to tell you exactly how I feel about what happened. I am hurt and angry at you. I don't know what your problems are, but I am taking responsibility for my life. I don't know why you didn't defend me, your own daughter, but I know now that I am worth defending. So is every kid. I also know that when I become a mom, no matter how tough my life might be, I will defend and protect my children.*
>
> *I don't know what you can do to straighten things out with me. I do know that now is not the time. As bad as things were, things are better for me away from you. I don't look forward to seeing you in court, but I'm not afraid to face you. Maybe someday you'll figure out what went wrong. I do know that as badly as I have been hurt, I've learned I can and must go on with my life. It's a big world and I have a place in it.*
> *Sarah*

She sat quietly for a few moments. The breeze made the leaves on the silver maple shimmer in the waning afternoon sunlight. She looked up with an expression that matched the resolve of her letter.

I gave her a big smile and said, "Good job, kid. I'm proud

of you. That's quite a letter. Not something easy to write. You're making peace with yourself, owning up to your hurts and letting them go. How does it feel to exercise some strength of character?"

Without hesitation she came right back, "Scary is what it feels like. Shaky, but it's what I've got to do. You know, it's strange, this standing up for yourself stuff looks like a recipe in a cookbook, but when you do it, wow, so much happens inside you."

"You're right. The secret in the recipe is the desire to unlock the ingredients." Pointing to the maples, I added, "Our sages taught, 'A tree whose branches are few but whose roots are numerous, even if all the winds in the world came and blew against that tree, it wouldn't move it from its place.' Kind of like you, now."

Sarah beamed, "Wow, I like that. You've got to show me sometime the book that came from. I do kind of feel real anchored."

Public Confession

Sarah's court date arrived. The proceedings were to determine Sarah's permanent placement until she turned eighteen. It was set for 11:00 A.M. on a Wednesday in downtown Brooklyn. I called her house mother as well as her social worker and offered to drive everybody to court. My reasoning was quite simple: Sarah needed all the backup she could get. Kids—anyone for that matter—who have been victimized, need support. As simple as that sounds, too often it's not there. I knew I wasn't going to be part of the hearing, but I planned to tag along and cool my heels outside the courtroom.

Wednesday morning arrived. I picked everyone up on Staten Island and headed to Brooklyn. We didn't talk much. That was okay. This was a time when we all had a lot to think about. It was a time to strengthen ourselves. The quiet didn't feel awkward.

We parked in a municipal lot around the corner from the courthouse and walked the few blocks. Downtown Brooklyn is a study in contrasts: moms, babies, hustlers, suits from government offices, shopkeepers, and defendants. From upscale hipsters to low-down gangsta's, the sidewalks are jammed with folks spilling over from Carrol Gardens, Fort Greene, and Atlantic Avenue.

When we got inside the courthouse, we walked up the marble stairs to the second floor. Sarah's social worker briefed her on procedures for the umpteenth time. I spied a bench down the hall near the door to her courtroom and parked myself there. Sarah came over, her eyes alternately blinking *I'm scared* and *I'm prepared.* I took her hand, gave it a squeeze, and said, "Sarah, stay within the honesty of yourself. We're all here for you no matter what. This is your day. Tell it precisely how it is. You can do it."

She took a deep breath, gave my hand a strong squeeze, and turned and walked through the door.

The wait seemed endless and it took a lot of concentration to keep my anxiety down to a manageable level. After about forty-five minutes, Sarah came out the door. From thirty feet away I could see she'd been crying. With house mother and social worker in tow, she made a beeline for me. I looked back at the door to see if her mother was around, but saw no one.

She pulled up two feet in front of me. Her eyes were puffy, her mascara smudged. I instinctively breathed in, figuring from her look that the hearing must not have worked out well. I opened both hands and said, "Well, what happened? Don't keep me in suspense."

She blurted out, "God, it was awful, and I feel great. The judge heard me and blasted my mom. I'm officially in placement. I chose not to go with her. She didn't want me anyway. I said it all. I can't believe it."

Sarah's house mother stepped in and put her arms around her. She's a tall lady. She leaned down and buried Sarah in her warm embrace, kissed her on the cheek, and said, "Honey, you'll tell the rabbi everything in the car. Let's get out of this place and go home."

Right there I saw why she was the house mom and why she

dedicated her life to giving these kids a home. She had the right stuff. She was, as the kids say, "plugged into the juice."

We got the car out of the lot. Sarah sat in the front. I was fishing around in the glove compartment for a tape, but Sarah laughed and said, "Today's my day. No sixties stuff. Let's put on Z-100 and get some real rock."

Sarah's taking a stand for herself had been more than a catharsis. She turned a corner and around the bend she was discovering that she could take responsibility for caring for, guarding, and shaping the direction of her life. Sarah knew now that she had the right to live her own life. She knew she was supported. She had friends. She had trust. She was loved. That's not too shabby of a discovery to make in forty-five minutes of family court.

One Puzzle Piece

Over the next few years, Sarah became a regular at our home. Her psychological struggles had moved from recovery to philosophy to exploring her spirituality—a natural progression.

Last year, Sarah graduated college. Her mother remained missing in action somewhere in her own private hell. Nevertheless, Sarah's graduation was a special day. I got up before dawn and took a long shower. The night before I had loaded the spray starch onto a white shirt, enjoying the sound of an iron hissing over the fabric, smoothing out the wrinkles. If only life's wrinkles came out so easily. I pulled out my best tie and put on my best summer-weight suit—actually, the only one I own.

I got the camera ready, jumped in the car, and left Brooklyn before 11:00 A.M.

I met Sarah at her dorm. She looked impossibly good, smiling and laughing with her friends. This was her day. She'd climbed another rung on her life ladder.

Later that summer Sarah left to study in Israel. At the airport she smiled and said, "Yehudah, this is another piece in the puzzle of my life. I've got to find out where I come from. If

I can know that, I can discover more about myself. But, I'll be back."

And that's the beauty of it all. Sarah's past, which caused her so much sadness and misery, was now something she could learn from. By standing up for herself as someone who was worthy of all that life had to offer, she acquired compassion for herself. She was no longer hiding her wounds in the recesses of her heart. Sarah's ability to stand up and walk completely away from what hurt her is a wonder. To this day, her strength gives me hope for every new kid I meet.

STEP FOUR

Moving Forward with Life

ALLISON'S STORY

Everything has its season,
and there is a time for everything
under the heaven:

A time to embrace and a time to keep your distance
Koheles; Chapter 3

STEP FOUR: ***Moving Forward with Life***

"Remember your Creator in the days of your youth" (Ecc. 12:1). [Because your life has changed, you no longer have desire in your former life.] Who attains complete Teshuvah? An individual who is challenged, who faces and confronts the same situation in which he or she stumbled and has at hand the possibility to commit that misdeed again, and who refrains and doesn't do it because of his or her individual Teshuvah. And this refraining is not out of fear nor lack of strength.

(MAIMONIDES, *Hilchos Teshuvah*, Chapter Two, Section One)

After standing up to the challenge, we feel renewed. This feeling is a signal that it is time to get our lives back on track. We have moved ourselves so far away from our former difficulties that we stop looking back. Instead we look ahead, and what we see is a wide-open world ready for our new sense of vitality.

We now realize that our failings taught us valuable lessons, lessons that we are only beginning to comprehend. While we will never forget what happened to us, we know that the time has come to move forward, and so we do so tentatively. It's humbling. It's as if the trauma, difficulty, and pain that we've experienced are allowing us to begin our lives again.

The journey to reclaim our lives is unique. We may feel very much alone as we work our way out of our life crisis, but we can take comfort in knowing that many others through the ages have tread similar paths of self-renewal.

On this walk, we may stumble from time to time. That possibility, that fear, doesn't hold us back anymore—by now we are committed to our walk. The point is that we are moving forward. Trying is precious. As the Talmud states, "If someone tells you *I tried but I did not achieve,* do not believe them." Trying *is* a major achievement. The goal is simply to move forward. As Rabbi Tarfon used to say, "You are not required to complete the work. Yet you are not free to desist from it."[1]

Bussing Tables

Most of the time, I have to work real hard to establish a connection with a kid. But other times, I'll just be standing around on the street or walking through a shelter and, bingo, a kid will walk up and engage me. While this type of behavior doesn't ensure a better outcome, it sure does make my work easier. Scuffling and hustling up conversations with complete strangers takes a lot out of you, especially when the strangers are kids and distrust is their guiding force.

This was one of those nights when a kid initiated contact. That kid's name was Allison.

When I arrived at the runaway shelter that night, I decided to help out in the dining room. I spotted two girls I knew, Nancy and Tanya, sitting in the far corner chatting furiously while working on their nails. Nancy worked her emery board like a master sculptor sanding the final touches on a piece of art. She'd hold her hand at arm's length, examine the nail from all angles, then sand. After six or seven fast back-and-forth movements with the board, she'd turn and blow the nail dust into the air, carefully keeping it away from the Jell-O, roll, and casserole that was her dinner. After each nail, she'd admire her handiwork and move on to the next.

Tanya was in another artistic phase of the project. Having completed *Sanding 101,* she had moved on to *Painting 101.* Her goal seemed to be getting the maximum number of color bands on all ten nails. She had her equipment lined up in a row next to her dinner tray. She worked one hand at a time, filling each nail in with the colors of the rainbow. She covered each nail like a canvas using slow, dexterous strokes. Nancy and Tanya executed this artistry while analyzing various boys and punctuating their work and talk with quick bites off their dinner trays.

I had a ringside view of this event. I was hard at work clearing dishes, wiping off tables, and giving refills of fruit punch. Most other nights, I was a counselor. Tonight, I was trying my hand at waiting and bussing.

The philosophy behind my career choice for the night was really quite simple. When kids grow up in a home where they are never safe, they lose their sense of security. They don't know what it means to be taken care of or to be nurtured.

They haven't had too many home-cooked meals or been tucked into bed with a good-night kiss. In fact, the folks who should have brought them love and trust put fear and terror into their hearts instead. That left many of these kids feeling anxious and bewildered. By cleaning up the mess they left on the dining room tables, I was hopefully getting a message to them: There *are* people who care and who feel that they are worth fussing over.

Kids have to know they are loved, and I try to nurture that love any way I can. What it often comes down to is action. Words, after all, go only so far. While kids can't get true home-cooked meals at a runaway shelter, they can get some of the nourishments that come out of Mama's kitchen. Even a little taste of caring can go a long way toward quieting and healing the soul and touching a wounded spirit. Leo Buscaglia, in his wonderful book *Loving Each Other,* underscored this very point when he wrote:

> *We talk to each other with smiles, with handshakes, with hugs, with laughter, with eye contact, with touching, holding, enfolding, and a myriad of gestures. These, too, are languages. Some of which may speak louder than words. You can tell a great deal about a person when he or she shakes your hand. A hug can send off so many messages. A glance can suggest a thousand words. Still, not too many of us respect the power of wordless messages. We do not even think about what they are telling others about us.*[2]

Some of my own best memories are of having dinner at the kitchen table as a boy. Mom would hover over the meal, telling me, "Have some more chicken." When I finished, she would swoop down and clear the table. She liked things neat, tidy, and orderly. She was aware of every piece of broccoli on the table and took great pleasure in serving. It was an expression of her love. So, it wasn't hard for me to be a waiter. After all, I'd had a good, loving teacher to show me the ropes.

As I leaned over the table to fill up the girls' glasses, Nancy gave me the once-over and laughed, "Yehudah, you sure do look good tonight. If you work at it, maybe you can get a real job in one of those fancy restaurants."

Tanya added, "Yes, sir. I can see you in a little jacket with a starched white shirt. Maybe a string tie with those nice black pants with the big pleats. Just like in the movies."

I smiled and said, "In that case, I suppose you two would be there with your dates. And because I'd be so polite, you'd give me big tips."

They both giggled. A good meal ought to have silly talk and sweet laughter. It nourishes the soul.

I moved on. I put the pitcher on a nearby tray and started clearing dishes off another table. For a moment I almost forgot where I was. After all, Tanya and Nancy seemed like regular teenagers, until you noticed the sadness lurking in the corner of their eyes. You don't have to be a rocket scientist to guess why they sought shelter. No one leaves home to vacation in a shelter for runaway and homeless youth.

Tanya and Nancy had a lot in common. They were related—not in the usual sense like sisters or cousins, but nevertheless, related. They were both survivors of physical and sexual abuse. On that note, their experience with the dark side connected them to a lot of kids I know, including most of the kids in the dining room.

Tanya and Nancy were trying to climb out, to start over. They had recently found jobs and had begun saving for their first apartment of their own. Even down in Times Square, kids pursue the American dream.

I hoped these two girls might end up being some of the lucky ones, the ones who can actually build new lives. For now, at least they had safety and shelter. To get it, they'd had to run away from their previous lives. They ran because they instinctively knew they needed help. Someone or something had to step in to make the pain stop. If you have a safe place to rest your head, a bit of counseling, some rules, and a glimmer of hope for the future, it's possible to get back into life. There's no guarantee, but it's still possible.

As the dinner hour came to a close, I took a break. I begged a cup of coffee off the cook and returned to the dining room, which was now deserted. Leaning back in a folding chair, I put my feet up on the chair next to me, took a sip of coffee, and let my mind drift. It's one of the ways I recharge my batteries. I just stare and mindlessly drift while bleeding off the tension that accumulates in a place like this.

I didn't get more than five minutes into my meditation when Vinnie and Mark showed up. They made quite a pair. If they'd had a title for their relationship it would have been *Hustler Meets Homeboy.*

Vinnie stood all of five feet six inches and wore tight pants, loafers, and a polyester shirt. He hailed from the Bensonhurst neighborhood in Brooklyn and talked a machine-gun Brooklynese. To his right, from Bed-Sty, Brooklyn, weighing in at about 220 and standing over six feet with a short set of dreds, was Mark. With his muscle and Vinnie's fast talk, they made an imposing impression. That image worked for them on the street, but the truth was that both were as naive as the day I'd met them six months earlier. At that time, they were hustling designer ties on a street corner near Wall Street. They were both homeless. Fortunately, I prevailed upon them and convinced them to come in and seek shelter.

Vinnie and Mark worked as messengers. It's a good way for these kids to enter the job market. The Manhattan business community has an overabundance of messages that need hourly delivery, so a kid can work for a messenger service part-time and still have time to go to school. These kids meet the job requirement perfectly—a thorough knowledge of Manhattan city streets and the ability to get around fast. The messengers are easy to spot in Manhattan. They're the kids riding the bikes, Rollerblading, or running down the street with packages in their arms or backpacks.

Mark and Vinnie interrupted my reverie with high fives and proceeded to sit down on either side of me. They gave each other a couple of smirks and *in the know* glances. I raised my coffee cup and gave a slow nod. Since we seemed to be playing parts, I'd be Yul Brynner in *The Magnificent Seven.* Finishing my controlled *in the know* nod and making strong eye contact, I pursed my lips and said, "Gentlemen."

It was too much for them. They looked at each other and burst out laughing. Vinnie blurted out, "Fawget about it, Yehudah. I'm not gettin' inta it. You capisce?"

I replied, "Would I have done better as Al Pacino in *The Godfather*? What do you think? We could roll that. It'd be like back in the neighborhood."

Playing with each other came naturally to all of us. Being playful is an antidote to pain. It levels out the ups and downs of life. Most of these kids missed out on happy, playful times in childhood, and while you can't recover a lost childhood, simply having fun with an adult makes it a bit easier to realize that, perhaps, not everyone wants something from you.

Mark stepped in. "Naw, listen man, don't get my little brother here started. I've bin runnin' wit' him all day. Listening to his schemes. His plans. I probably fall asleep tonight and dream about him tellin' me his next plan."

Vinnie took a deep breath. He was getting ready to go on a roll. "Gotta do what you gotta do. Hey, can I help it if I'm full of ideas? I got plans."

"So what's up, guys? Vinnie, how's work going?" I asked.

"It doesn't pay enough and I see myself more as—you know—a suit doing business," he responded.

Turning to Mark, I said, "You see it the same way? Does that mean you guys are going back to school? Gettin' the education you need to pull off your dreams?"

Mark's brow furrowed. "Been thinking about it."

Vinnie fired off. He had a bit of a temper. He was always thinking someone was pushing him around.

I just smiled and said, "You know me, guys. I can't keep good ideas to myself. I want the best for you. I want you to succeed. I'm guilty. I can't keep my mouth shut."

We schmoozed for another ten minutes about important things like John Starks's erratic three-point shooting for the Knicks as well as whether Shaq would be considered a great center. We stayed away from the Magic, Larry, and Michael arguments. We'd covered them last time. We also avoided talk about darker things. I'd spoken with them about their childhoods before. Mark had said something to the effect that his memories of childhood looked kind of like scenes out of some dark movie. He wasn't kidding. Vinnie had just nodded in agreement. He'd obviously visited that same nightmare when he was growing up.

Months later, I heard through the grapevine that Mark was going to night school. I have no idea where Vinnie has gone. I still hope that in six or seven years I'll open the business section of the paper and read about him: "Young Entrepreneur Launches Successful New Company." I know, though, that reality and opportunity for those who have resided in *The Way Beyond* is much harsher. It's a long, difficult road out of a world of violence and abuse. It takes time to build dreams when you've come from a world that shatters them. But I still live by hopes and dreams. And until I find out otherwise, my dreams keep the tears from falling like rain.

After finishing my coffee break, I moved on to make my rounds. It was still early evening, so I decided to wander into the main lounge and hang out. On the way, I said hello to all I passed, asking what's up. My strategy is simply to be available. You can't do that sitting in a corner or behind a desk. The street and environs are my congregation. Anyone I talk to is a member of that congregation. And there aren't any dues. My members have already paid enough dues.

Making a Connection

As I walked by the pay phones at the entrance to the lounge, Allison spotted me. She crossed the room and approached me.

"Are you the rabbi I heard was around here?"

I said, "Yes, how ya doing?"

She said, "I'm kinda okay. I need to talk to you."

"Sounds good, but let's go find somewhere to sit and make formal introductions. Then you can tell me why I have the honor of your company," I replied.

We walked out the doorway to the lounge next door, took a

left, and found some chairs off in a corner. It was relatively quiet. I flopped down on the chair that looked as if it had the least number of protruding springs.

We sat in awkward silence for a bit while I waited for her to offer some information. Like a detective, I use every bit of evidence and information to form a picture. I need to know as much as I can about a kid if I'm going to be of any real help. I try to put myself in the kid's place. I open my emotions so I can touch up against his or her feelings and experiences. Then, where possible, I communicate that I know what went down. That it hurt or was terrifying. That I know what it means to cry out and to know nobody is going to come and make it stop.

Although I often portray a casual demeanor, I take my role in these kids' lives very seriously. After all, this might be the last stop on the train. I can't afford not to be meticulous, to give my best effort.

I remember when I received my final evaluation at the end of my training to become a family therapist. My mentor commented that I had a problem of working *too close* to the clients. It made my work more subjective rather than objective. I often wish I could be more objective and clinical. It certainly would make it a lot easier on my emotions. But I've yet to find a way on the street to *clinically care*. The truth is, I've never met a clinician out in *The Way Beyond*. It just doesn't fit the job description.

As we sat in silence, I took a quick inventory of this young lady. She was tall with shoulder-length black hair. Rail thin. Her shoes were a pair of fraying brown penny loafers. The jeans were definitely not from the Gap. She wore a grayish sweater over a nondescript shirt, clean but stained. The yarn in her sweater was coming unraveled here and there. Her eyes were slightly bloodshot. Although I sat about three feet away, I could tell she had showered recently, had put on a bit of lipstick. She used deodorant.

She hadn't told me anything about herself yet, but I had some of the basics. She had definitely come in off the street.

She was broke and was having trouble taking care of herself, but was trying to at least be clean. She wasn't using at the moment because she was coherent in her sentence structure. I also surmised that something had scared her enough to bring her in.

She finally cut the small talk. "I heard kids like to talk to you."

"Some do," I answered.

"Can I talk to you about anything? I mean, you'll keep it to yourself?"

I chuckled to myself. Therapists have intense codes of ethics surrounding confidentiality, and religions have laws and admonitions about keeping far away from gossip and slander. But it's the kids on the street who have been victimized by poison-sweet lies. They know the consequences of a stray tongue. Most of them have been betrayed their whole lives by people they thought could be trusted.

With all the seriousness and sincerity I could muster, I said, "You can absolutely talk to me. There's only one way that I'll rat on you, and that's if you tell me something that makes you a threat to yourself or others. Otherwise, we're cool. I'm also here to get you whatever help you need. If you need help working stuff out with one of the social workers or whatever, I'll lend a hand. But you haven't even introduced yourself. Do I call you mystery girl or do I get to know your name?"

"Oh yeah, sorry, it's Allison."

"Okay, Allison. My name's Yehudah. You said you need to talk to me. I'm all ears."

She put her head back against the chair, shut her eyes, and said, "Do people ever straighten out their lives after they've really screwed up? Do things work out? Can you ever fix things and go on?"

My instincts said to be personal and direct rather than fence around the issue. "I guess what you're telling me is that it's pretty scary realizing you messed up and hurt yourself. It's probably been real tough, but if you hadn't come in, things would only have gotten worse. You're not going to just walk away from a drug habit. Problems don't go away that easily. They don't like to let go."

She looked at me incredulously. "How did you know I was doing drugs? I didn't tell you."

"Allison, it's not hard to figure out. I've spent a lot of time with kids who have put all kinds of things up their noses. But what's important is where you go from here. Have you got a plan?"

"Well, I've got an appointment with a social worker here tomorrow," she said. "I feel like crap. Things have just gotten out of control in my head. It's like I'm really lost. I don't know what I'm doing."

"How many vials were you doing?" I asked, hoping to quickly assess her drug problem. She was at a turning point and I didn't want her walking out the door and getting stoned.

"It's not like I was blowing up that much. A few months ago, when I had some money left, I just did occasional lines. Then that somehow became an everyday thing. But the worst thing happened a couple days ago—I woke up in a strange place, with a strange guy. I couldn't remember anything. I had no idea how I'd gotten there. I was all strung out. I went into the bathroom and tried to clean up, but then I looked in the mirror and felt so bad I just flipped out. I didn't know what to do, so I came here."

She shivered and put her face in her hands. Then she started to cry.

The only way you can change your life is to take some responsibility for where you are and then take steps to gain more control. But first Allison needed someone to simply help her hang on until she could get herself together enough to take some action to help herself.

I leaned forward in my chair and quietly said, "I know it's been rough. I can't tell you it's going to be all right, but I can tell you that you *can* begin to straighten things out in your life. Whatever has happened, you can find ways to understand it. But first you're going to need help to get yourself cleaned up. If you stay put in this place, you can get that help."

Her despair surfaced and she gave me a look that could melt the walls of your heart. "I'm so messed up," she said. "I don't know what's going on. I don't know what's happening to me. I feel so awful. It's like there's nowhere to go from here."

I tried my best to comfort her. "Allison, I know you feel empty now. But you're safe here and folks will take care of you so you can begin to take care of yourself. Your job is to hang on. And when I say hang on, I mean hang on to your hope."

"I don't think I can shake this. I feel so crazy. I don't think I've got enough hope to stay away from it."

"You're stronger than you think. You're going to have to use your will to pull it off. And I'm telling you, you can do it."

She sighed, "I don't have any will."

"Yes you do," I said. "You wouldn't be here talking to me and fighting to get on top of this if you weren't using your will. It's not going to be easy, but you can turn away from all of it. Just don't succumb to the despair."

She said, "I hope you're right."

I said, *"It's forbidden to despair. It's forbidden to give up hope.* A great rabbi once said that. His students took his words quite literally. In fact, when the Nazis were wiping out all the Jews in the Warsaw Ghetto in Poland during the Second World War—and they wiped out nearly everyone—that rabbi's followers came out of the bunkers and sewers with death lying in the street. They hung up banners that said, 'It is forbidden to give up hope.' Allison, you have deep reservoirs of strength inside of you. Now it's time for you to exercise your strength, your hope."

I looked at my watch and realized it was time for bed check. I had wanted to steer the conversation into specifics, but I can only bite off so much in one sitting.

"Look, Allison, you want me to come back in the morning?"

She looked a little more hopeful. "You could come?"

"I just tried to invite myself."

She gave a half smile. "If you don't mind, it would help. I wouldn't be so lonely. Maybe by then I'll know what I need to do."

I added, "You're not required to know it all right now. And you're right, it would help for me to come. You just stay strong and don't leave this place. I expect to see you in the morning."

I left the building and headed across the street to the parking lot. Thankfully, nobody approached me. I didn't have any more strength for conversation. I was thinking about how I would have to bring up the AIDS *thing* and the *sleeping around thing* tomorrow. I was too tired to think about it tonight.

As I drove home, I turned the radio on to 660 AM WFAN sports radio. I would have preferred listening to Mike Francesa and *Mad Dog Chris Russo* reviewing movies and talking Giants football with Joe from Saddle River, New Jersey, but I was happy to get Steve Sommers schmoozing sports into the night.

What's Next?

Early the next morning, I got in my car and drove to the city. I turned right off the West Side Highway at 38th and came up the back side of the Port Authority. The morning was cool and clear. It was still a bit early for the hookers to start the day shift on the side streets off the West Side. I parked across the street from the shelter and walked up the street. As I passed the corner of the lot, I spotted a couple of rats scurrying about their business. I flashed my ID to the security guard and went inside.

Allison was sitting in the lounge. She looked awful. It was obvious that she hadn't showered and probably hadn't gotten more than a couple hours of sleep. She clearly was there because she needed to be. I said a silent prayer thanking God for keeping her safe. There are no bars on the windows of the shelter. If Allison had wanted to leave, she could have simply split. It happens to a lot of kids. The street just pulls them back.

Allison, while having recently been a fairly serious user, had only fallen to what I call level one in the pit. Each level in this pit has a different bottom, a different hell. The lowest level has the real bottom—death.

I sat down next to her. She looked up and smiled. "Thanks for coming."

I said, "You look like you've had a lousy night."

She said, "Tell me about it. My mind's been in overdrive. I ache inside."

"I'm happy you're still here. You've got guts. It's not easy surfing with your fear."

She twisted her head at a slight angle. She wasn't feeling particularly heroic—more like walking depression. She let out a long breath. "Well, at least something good's happened. I've got my first session with the social worker today."

That was a wonderful piece of news. So many times I've watched kids hit bottom and then fail to get the counseling they need to climb out because of a lack of resources. Then the street just comes back and reclaims them.

I said, "You couldn't have asked for a better shot. You stayed the night and now you get to find some help. Good news." Then, to begin our next conversation, I asked her an obvious question: "Where are you from?"

She replied, "I grew up in Iowa—Des Moines."

"Probably a nice place to grow up," I said.

She sighed. "It was nice, but things just fell apart. When my father died, I got myself into so much trouble. My dad would feel so bad if he were alive."

I raised an eyebrow. It seemed we were going to get personal. "You loved your dad a lot?" I asked.

"He was so great," she said, "but he'd been sick for a long time. I was in the middle of my second year of community college when he died. I was never close to my mom at all, and after the funeral, I just had to get out of there, so I decided to travel. I took all the money my dad left me and split to Europe, and just got way in over my head."

"Have you called your mom since you got in here?"

She closed her eyes, and tears leaked out. "I'm too ashamed. We were fighting so bad when I left. She didn't want me to leave, but at the same time she said, 'You're on your own.' I'm just so scared. I've got to clean up, then I'll get in touch. I can't let her see me like this."

She started crying harder. "My dad worked so hard his

whole life and left me all that money. And look what I did. *Look what I did.* I just threw it all away. I spent almost every cent of it and on what? On getting screwed up."

I let her cry. It was lousy. But at the same time she was experiencing a deep awareness of her actions. She saw the consequences, and they were leaving great pain and shame in her heart. That wasn't necessarily a bad thing. Pain can be a great teacher sometimes. While it's true that we can't rewrite our past, we can, through Teshuvah, repair the spiritual damage done.

I didn't cushion her reality. "Realizing how much you messed up hurts a lot. But what counts is what you do next."

"That's what I'm trying to do—what's right. I wish I had seen all this coming when I was in Europe. I just traveled, partied, moved from guy to guy, and got stoned. I just blew my inheritance without thinking. It could have been such a good experience, but look how I blew it."

I said, "What it's gotten you is a wake-up call to fight for your life, to reclaim your dignity. You may not know it now, but you can discover a lot of powerful things about yourself if you really clean up. You can learn to move forward with your life. Let me tell you something deep: *Sometimes you have to search through the ashes to find a single spark.* A great rabbi, Rabbi Dov Baer of Mizritch, said that. Allison, you may not see it, but I do—you've found that spark. Don't let it go out. As humbling as all this is, you can begin again."

I knew I was getting into my spiritual rap, but I wanted her to open her eyes. Ironically, when people fall into darkness they become able to hear and see things of spiritual importance. Ask any Twelve Step follower—it all begins with finding a Power greater than yourself.

The spark story struck a chord in Allison. "Somebody else told me something like that two weeks ago at a Grateful Dead concert," she said.

I simply responded, "Wharf Rats."

The Grateful Dead scene has a number of loosely organized heads who have fought their own battles with drugs and other trouble. They've even organized themselves into a self-help group and have stationed themselves at the band's concert venues. True to their path, they call themselves *Wharf Rats.* Now, that may seem like an odd name for a group of folks working on their recovery, but if you're familiar with the band's 1971 album *Grateful Dead*, you know that it includes a song called "Wharf Rat." And yes, it's about people struggling *to get back on their feet someday.* In that world, it was a natural fit.

"You know them?" she asked.

"Well, I'm acquainted with the scene and know of their work. So what did this Wharf Rat say?

With reticence she said, "It's kind of embarrassing to talk about."

"I didn't think you spent the last several months running the straight and narrow," I said.

"Well," she paused and collected herself. "Well, I was running out of rope by the time I hit that Dead show. I was nearly broke. I'd spent months traveling around Europe, like I told you. I came back to the States thinking I would just clean up my act. But before I knew it, I was doing cocaine and downers. I kept saying to myself, *I've got to straighten up. I've got to stop sleeping with these guys.* It was like I was selling myself. But I'd just end up doing more coke and going to bed with anyone. Using up my money. Staying wherever.

"So I was staying with this guy out on the Island and he decides we're going to go see the Dead. I was there and was so wasted doing ludes and I don't know what else. I don't think I want to tell you everything." She stopped talking and stared out into space.

I let her just tune out. This was not an easy admission to blithely talk about. Each experience must have taken away more of her dignity. Each time she'd try to regroup, she'd start at more of a deficit and she'd feel overwhelming shame over what she'd done. Without her realizing it, a process had begun where she was giving up more and more of herself trying to avoid the pain, slipping deeper into the cycle of trouble and shame. And at every step of the way there were people waiting to fulfill their own nameless and sordid desires. She became numb to herself—a precious soul on the way down, afraid to latch on to hope.

She shook her head and looked at me. "I was so stoned and out of it at that Dead concert, I just started crying. I was so down, so empty, just walking and crying. It was like there was a hole in my chest, and the hole sucked in everything. It made me feel like I was sinking. I was so sad, and it wouldn't go away. Then this guy came up to me and sat me down. And, like, he knew where I was at. He wasn't coming on to me or anything. He just wanted to share and help me straighten out."

"I guess you could say you had hit bottom."

She took a deep breath and let it out slowly. "It's like that guy said, something like I have to live with what I did. I have to accept my life and see that I'm not powerless. He said that if I surrender to a higher power, I can find hope and meaning. It was something like that. Kinda like being able to find the spark in the ashes. Like you said.

"Well, I'll tell you one thing. It sounds to me like you're ready for a change."

She nodded, "That's why I'm here, I guess. I want to be finished with it."

I smiled but said nothing. She'd know soon enough that you're never really finished with it.

We chatted quietly until midafternoon, when it was time for Allison's appointment. "Will you be in touch with me?" she asked.

I got out a piece of paper and wrote down my home number and handed it to her. I've never carried business cards. What would I put on them? "This is my unlisted number, Allison. It's only for you. You call when you want a visit. You'll find me around here, but you call just the same."

She took the paper and gave me a big hug. There's nothing like being appreciated.

"Thanks, I'll call soon." She looked scared.

I said, "Trust in your heart, kid, and God will give you

strength. I believe in you. It's okay to be scared. When you're ready, we can talk some more."

She hugged me again. Leo Buscaglia would have been proud.

"You'll be there when I call?" she asked.

I said, "You've got the number."

She said, "I want my life back."

The look she gave me reminded me of the look my daughter gave me when she headed off to camp for the first time. Unfortunately, this wasn't camp.

I fought the traffic all the way home to Brooklyn. They'd closed one lane of the Battery Tunnel during rush hour. When I finally got home, I hung out on the stoop talking sports with my next-door neighbor Billy, then helped my kids with their homework. Later that night I caught an episode of *Taxi* and then switched to *Letterman.* Dave had on some dog doing *stupid pet tricks.* This dog madly chased its tail every time the audience applauded. It just ran round and round. Kind of like me on a bad day.

In the old days, I would have had a scotch, but I'd stopped drinking. I fell asleep before *Letterman* was over.

First Call

Two days later my wife, Elliesheva, and I were sitting in her office, editing my institute's self-help inspirational newsletter, *Family Watch,* when the phone rang. I went into the kitchen to have some privacy. It was Allison. In an enthusiastic voice, she said, "Yehudah?"

I started chuckling. "Well, welcome to Brooklyn by phone."

"I guess you know who this is," she said.

"Well you don't sound like Charles Bronson, but from the sound of your voice, yesterday was a banner day. Did you win the lottery, get a medal, survive a triathlon, Rollerblade through Central Park, or what?"

"Huh?" she said. "What are you talking about?"

"Don't pay attention to my ramblings. You'll get used to it. I just picked up on the happiness in your voice."

"Well, you're right. I had a real good session this week. It was an eye-opener."

I said, "Uh oh, sounds like a new-person alert. Does this mean I don't get to talk with the depressed and stoned kid?"

Allison gave out a good, strong laugh.

I'm a firm believer in laughter. Laughter lets you take risks with yourself; it makes you brave. Joy takes the edge off the sadness, allowing you to face sorrow and bear pain. I was well aware that Allison had only begun to touch the top layers of her pain, and that she would need lots of laughter to make it.

I pressed forward. "So you realized some things that gave you pause?"

"Well . . ." I heard a faint sigh. "I see that I hide from things. It's like I've hidden parts of me to keep from getting hurt."

I bluntly said, "I guess you figured wrong."

"Tell me about it. It sure didn't work out. I guess I screwed up."

Heroically, I added, "But remember, you met foes and beasts. You had many battles. You were hurt. You were wounded. But you survived."

She laughed. "You sound like one of those epic novels."

"I do read a lot. But life's real heroes and villains come up through the ranks of everyday living. Every moment creates new opportunities to change and grow. It all depends on what you do with what God gives you."

"I still wonder how I got into all of this," she said in frustration. "I still don't know why I just didn't stop. You have no idea how many guys I've been with. When I think about everything I've done, I feel like I've taken a shot in my heart."

The masquerade party was over for Allison. The masks were taken off and the costumes were being put away. Without them, Allison realized who she saw in the mirror.

"It's true that you didn't stop, Allison, but you have now. The way you're going, you are absolutely going to find your self-respect. You've stopped hiding from the pain. That's a huge first step."

"Whoa! I didn't realize that what I told you meant all that."

I replied, "That's why people have conversations. Speaking of which, I think we have had enough heavy conversation for a first phone call. Let's turn the burner down to simmer and have you over for a visit."

"I'd like that," she said

"Okay, that was easy. You're invited."

After making the arrangements and giving directions, I hung up the phone and walked back to the office. Elliesheva looked up from the computer screen. "I finished the newsletter," she said.

"I finished the phone call and invited Allison over," I said.

"Good idea."

"It was either that or stay on the phone all day. I don't think my neck could take it."

Elliesheva gave me a look. Who knows me better than my wife? She puts up with me, my anxieties, and my weird hours. She also loves me.

"Okay, okay," I said.

From the first day of our marriage, my wife and I have understood that we were going to share our lives with others, that every loving relationship extends outward.

As my outreach to kids grew, I knew I couldn't provide the warm and caring environment they needed in an office or a classroom. My wife and I understood that the best environment to nurture the healing these kids needed was in our home. By spending time with us, they could feel what it's like to be accepted, understood, trusted, and respected for who they are. Through this, they could learn to love others.

While at times this decision has made for complications, there was no other choice. Every time my wife or I answered the phone in the middle of the night to hear someone's desperate need, we knew we had to respond. The morning I stepped out the door at 6:30 only to be greeted by a sad-eyed kid who had been standing on my stoop most of the night, afraid to knock on the door to ask for help, and too scared to go home, we knew we had made the right decision in opening our home.

Our three children have grown up in a home filled with people from all walks of life. They have been enriched by our guests and have learned about compassion in action. They respect people's struggles and differences, not because of what they've read about, but because of what they've lived with.

Nothing is more powerful than a home. Nothing is more healing than a deep discussion over a home-cooked meal, and nothing is more refreshing than a family living, loving, and squabbling together.

The Wee Hours

Over the next six weeks, Allison took some major steps in her life. She got a job as a receptionist in a doctor's office. She moved out of the shelter and found an apartment to share near New York University. She became a regular visitor at our home.

However, I continued to worry about her. It wasn't that I thought she'd fall back into her old lifestyle; what concerned me was that she kept coming up with excuses for not getting tested for HIV. I knew that until she faced her deepest fear and got tested, she wouldn't be able to heal from her inner shame. To face your inner demons, you first have to confront them in your daily life. Before Allison could put away her anger and tears, she was going to have to let them out of the recesses of her heart.

I took the approach of relentlessness. I became a broken record, and in every conversation I'd return to that theme: "Kid, you're going to learn something from all your mistakes. While you can't forget the past, you're going to make new discoveries by moving forward with your life."

I got up one morning when it was still dark. I went downstairs and put on a Stevie Ray Vaughan tape. He was singing about having a real bad feeling. I sat in the living room drinking coffee and looking across the street at an old brick apartment building. The streetlights gave off a misty yellowish glow, shimmering off the windows of the building. It's at times like these, when the city sleeps in the wee hours before dawn, that I attempt to take stock of my life. It's also a good time to review my worries, which are at times immense, and try to make sense out of them.

I began rummaging through the bookshelf that contains my spiritual books. I picked up the *Kedushas Levi* by Rabbi Levi Yitzchak of Berditchev. He lived in the late 1700s, but what he said then is still relevant today. His all-embracing love for people and his titanic spiritual advocacy for the fallen inspire me. I picked it up, thinking that perhaps I could find, within the pages of his book, a tidbit of spiritual light to help me find solace and direction in the shadow world of *The Way Beyond*. As I opened the book, the binding made a familiar cracking sound and the Hebrew letters danced before my eyes. As I snuggled into an overstuffed chair and prepared to lose myself in the book's pages, the phone rang. I jumped out of the chair and quickly caught it on the second ring. I didn't want it to wake the house. It was Allison.

"You're in trouble," I said.

"Sort of," she said.

I said, "Is the trouble 3:30-in-the-morning trouble or is it 10:00-in-the-morning trouble because you thought you'd be leaving a message at this hour?"

"It's more like 10:00. I'm kind of embarrassed that you picked up. I figured you'd get my message first thing in the morning. I've got the day off and I wanted to come over and talk. I didn't expect to find you up."

I let out a long sigh of relief and said, "Well, I didn't expect to be up, either, but I think I'm becoming an insomniac. So yes, I was up thinking and trying to sort out the universe. How about you? I hope you're not going to tell me you've been partying on a Wednesday night."

"No, I couldn't sleep. I've been reading a book and thinking a lot."

"Happy thoughts?" I asked.

She said, "Come on. Happy thoughts? With how I'm feeling, I can't even find a happy thought."

I said, "I know. You didn't call in the middle of the night to get an early start on your day. So later's fine. How about ten?"

"Ten would be great. Thanks, Yehudah. I really mean it."

I hung up the phone. The tension coupled with tiredness hung all over me. I did some stretches and deep breathing. I felt better. I went back to Rabbi Levi Yitzchak. I wanted to see if he had any advice for me.

I started reading but was a bit distracted by Allison's call. I told myself that at least she had called and that this might be the phone call I'd been waiting for. It was better than the knocks I sometimes get on my door at three or four in the morning. It was better than that snowy morning when I walked out the door to find the kid who'd been huddled on the stoop most of the night waiting to talk with me. It was better than a lot of things.

I knew the coming talk with Allison was going to be a gut-wrencher. Calls at three in the morning are not courtesy phone calls. I fell asleep with my feet propped up on the desk and the book in my lap. I was thankful it was a very comfortable chair.

The Subway and the Yankees

By 9 A.M. I was just beginning to function. The second cup of coffee started clearing out the cobwebs. After showering, I put on a pair of Dockers, my best Yankees T-shirt, and my black knock-around sports jacket with the rolled-up sleeves. I looked in the mirror, smiled, and gave myself a wink. Elliesheva laughed at me and we went downstairs to the office to wait.

Allison arrived right on time. Elliesheva got the door, gave Allison a big hug, and we all sat down in the living room to have some tea. I chose some chamomile to balance out the caffeine. It's always a good idea to carry out ordinary behaviors, even in times of stress. It helps to keep everything from looking like a crisis.

"The D train was on time today," I said. "It stopped at Avenue M?"

"Since I was going against the commuter traffic, I even got a seat on one of these new graffiti-proof trains," she said.

Subway talk is part of the New York scene. Most people take the trains. It's convenient, even if at times a bit scary.

"The D's my train," I responded. "I always cast my ballot for it when they have this contest on the marquee at Yankee Stadium. There's the D, the C, and the 4 train, and they have this race to see which train makes it to the stadium first. Everybody screams for their train. It's a very cool cartoon with this true New Yorker calling the race."

Elliesheva looked at Allison. "Don't pay too much attention to my husband. He's just trying to get the conversation over to the Yankees. Since the boys are at school and his friend Billy is in the city, he feels deprived."

I shrugged my shoulders and looked as innocent as possible. I put down my cup, turned to Allison, and said, "We can talk in my office or take a walk over to a neighborhood park. This time of day the park will be pretty empty and there are some benches and some trees."

She said, "The park sounds good. I could use the fresh air."

Moving Forward with Life

We walked out the door and down the brick steps of the stoop and turned left down East 14th. The day was cool and crisp. I patted the trunk of the silver maple tree I planted in front of the house. Allison looked at me. She was getting used to my idiosyncrasies.

We crossed Avenue P and Kings Highway. The neighborhood is filled with small ethnic shops. On the street you hear Yiddish, Hebrew, Russian, Polish, Spanish, Korean, Chinese, and Arabic. New York is still the place where so many new Americans set out to find the American dream. If you don't think that dream is alive, go ask any Korean shopkeeper.

I said, "I bet this isn't at all like Des Moines."

"It's incredible," Allison said.

As we crossed Kings Highway, the subway train rumbled by on our left. We were on our way to my favorite park up toward Avenue T. It doesn't have any grass, but does have nice basketball and hardball courts. It's got benches under the trees. Most of all, it has a good feeling to it. I've never run into any gangbangers there. I attribute it to the fact that a Tai Chi master and his students work out there every morning. This part of the neighborhood is decidedly Asian.

We grabbed a bench under a majestic maple tree. As I predicted, the park was empty, except for a young mother with a baby stroller sitting on the other side of the park.

I opened. "Well, I guess it's time for our talk. I know it must be important because of what time you called."

Allison winced. "I hardly know where to begin. Part of me thinks that you can't possibly understand what I've been through. But then I remember what we talked about in terms of my moving forward with life. That we have to learn from our failures. That you get changed by all the pain and that pain can motivate a person to live their life again."

I just nodded and said, "True."

"I've been real down on myself. I've been crying a lot. Sometimes I feel like an apple that looks all nice, red, and normal. Then someone takes a bite out of me and it turns out I'm all rotten inside."

She gulped in a big breath and went on. "Sometimes I'll have a few hours where I'll see I'm really involved in good stuff. I feel like I'm really moving along. I even forget the things I did, the person I was. Then, out of nowhere, I remember something awful; I see myself doing something disgusting. My heart sinks right into my stomach and, I know this sounds weird, but I start to smell sewage and I feel dirty. I know I'm imagining it, but God, when that happens I feel so messed up from just throwing my body around with all those guys. All the things I let them do to me—it makes me feel so bad.

"I got my HIV test back and it was negative. I thought that would make me feel better but it didn't really. I still feel rotten. It's like I'm haunted by the thought that the real me is the *stoned slut,* and the good person I'm trying to be isn't real. She's only someone I'll always hope I can be."

She started crying quietly. It wasn't easy sitting with her and all her heartache and anguish, but there was no way she could avoid the pain and no way I could make it go away. If any of her new shoots of growth were going to emerge, she had to go though the humbling sacrifice that is served on the heart's altar of suffering. Once through it, she might find herself able to accept her imperfections and failings. In their wake, she might discover the deeper values of compassion and caring for herself and others.

My job here was more than simply to empathize. It was to take enough edge off the pain to let her deep inner perspective begin to assert itself. Inside, we all embody something that's trying to make sense out of what's happening, and I needed to help Allison let that something—that spirit—out.

She looked up at me, wiped her eyes, and smeared her mascara. "I feel like I just completely messed up my life, like it's over."

"Allison, you're right," I said. "It is over. All that stuff that happened is over. Do you understand? *That's* what is over. What is happening now is a new beginning."

It would have been nice if I could have had a magic wand to tap on her head so she would get it. Instead, she blinked at those words, blew her nose, and let out a long, protracted sigh. The words seemed to be slowly sinking in.

"You know, yesterday I was getting my hair cut," she said. "And the hairdresser and her friend were talking about this girl. They said, 'So-and-so is going to bed with everyone. She is so disgusting. She's just a whore and everyone knows it.' I mean, I was sitting there and listening to this. First, I got mad that they were being so mean and judgmental. Like, what did they know about her? Then I realized they could have been talking about me. I felt so rotten."

I stopped her and said, "Let me ask you a question. If you were those people, would you talk that way? If someone came to you loaded with problems would you say, 'Hey, you're damaged goods. You'll never be anybody. Give it up'?"

She raised her eyebrows and said, "Of course not. I'd never do that. I don't believe in being cruel. I care." Her eyes popped a bit after saying that.

"Good. I'm glad you agree with what I'm saying. We're on the same page."

"I get what you're saying, Yehudah," she said. "But you don't know how bad it was."

"Good for you. You've got to test the theory. Check it out. Leave no stone unturned. A rabbi once said that if we could hang all our sorrows on different pegs on the wall and then pick up the ones we liked best, we would invariably pick back up our own because all the other sorrows would be even more difficult to bear. So, you're right. As difficult as all our lives can be, each of us has to get a grip on our own confusion. We have to face it and accept it so we can move on. I can't take the walk in your shoes. Things don't work that way. But I can give you feedback on where you've been and where you're going. I can support you and tell you I care."

Something I said made her explode: "I just never knew where to draw the line, Yehudah! Someone would hand me a drug; I'd just take it. Or a guy would start coming on to me, and I'd let him just keep going, even though I didn't want to. I'd let him do whatever he wanted to me. It was just pure damn luck I didn't end up with some homicidal maniac, 'cause I'd be dead now. I'd do it with two or three guys in a night, right in the club or hallway. Then I'd go home with another guy. I'd wake up some mornings in these creepy lofts filled with all kinds of S & M stuff and I didn't care. How could I have not cared then and care so much now? You tell me how that's possible."

"It's a flat-out miracle," I said. "That's how it's possible. Sure, I can give you a formal family systems rap and talk about issues, but you've got a therapist for that. So I'll say it again from a spiritual perspective. When you hit the wall, you can discover God's grace—the turning point to spiritual awareness. The soul wakes up and says, *Enough of this.* Now that is a pure gift. The universe cares about you. While we can't minimize our sufferings and struggles, we can use them to move toward the light. We can move on."

"That's a special way of seeing things," she said.

"It's a close approximation to the truth," I said. "Someone is the tender of souls on this planet and that someone, so to speak, is God."

"But what I did is so unforgivable. If you're an alcoholic, you can go through the Twelve Steps and get it together, and it's okay. If you do drugs, you can clean that up. So many famous people have done that, and it's okay. And if a guy screws around, it's somehow okay 'cause he's a guy and guys are guys. But what I did as a girl, that's never okay. People think, she's the lowest of the lows. She threw away her virginity and then the worst of the worst."

I had to admit she was bringing up some interesting cultural issues, but she was still missing the point. She couldn't be worrying about other people's perceptions; she had to get herself straight. She had to salvage the good, redeem the bad, and move forward.

"You have a point," I said. "But no matter what has happened, you have to be the best you. You can't worry about what others think. That's what you used to do and it got you into a lot of trouble. You've got to ride the new inspiration that's freeing you to get to a better place. And that's for the sake of all the people you are going to love and all the people who are going to love you."

"But . . ."

"There's no but on that," I replied. "Stuff happened. You'll never forget about any of it. But what can you make better? What do you need to do?"

Trying again, she said, "But . . ."

I decided I had time for one more *but.* So I let her go on.

"But like I've ruined my chance to even marry a good guy. What will happen when I find someone I like? He'll find out. He'll know I kept secrets from him and why."

I came right back. "You're thinking sideways. You know you're not going to be with a guy who doesn't understand. Period. That's it. Your world is changing and honesty and compassion have to be a part of it. The old you was afraid to let the real you out, and that's where the trouble started. So don't try to find a way to be dishonest.

"The guy who's going to fall in love with you—and a guy is going to fall in love with you—isn't going to care about where you've been because he'll be falling in love with who you will have become. Little by little you'll continue to build more of the new you, which will outshine all that old stuff. The strength of your resolve and commitment to all the good things you now do with your life is all he will see. There will be no doubt in his mind—as there is no doubt in yours—that you would never *never* go back to doing any of those things again."

Tears began to stream as she nodded her head and said, "You're right." Then she really started to cry. She'd try to stop and say something, but the sobbing would just start all over again—two handkerchiefs' full. I waited it out until she finally stopped.

She blew her nose again, and it honked, which made her laugh. I joined in and we laughed together.

"I feel a whole lot better," she said. "You're right. Thanks."

I said, "I feel better too."

We walked back to the house. On the way home I introduced Allison to Mr. Kim, my favorite neighborhood Korean grocer, and to a warm Hassidic couple who own another grocery store farther down the block. After all that intensity, it felt good to end our talk on a normal, positive note.

No Other Way to Be

Over the next several months, Allison made significant strides. She went back to Iowa to visit her mother. Although it was far from a miraculous reconciliation, new seeds for future growth were planted. As time moved on she continued to move forward with her life. She even began dating. After just a few months of dating, much to her surprise, but not mine, she began a serious relationship with a young law student. Besides loving her, he encouraged her to go back to school.

In the middle of her senior year in college, she called me

and said, "I want you to be one of the first to know. I'm applying to social work school. After all I've been through, I want to be there to help other kids who get in trouble."

I said, "I can't say I'm surprised, but I can say I'm proud of you. And anyone who has the privilege of having you reach out to lend them a hand will only be better because of it."

She said, "Thanks. And thanks for believing in me when I had trouble believing in myself."

I said, "You're welcome, but there isn't any other way to be. It's the requirement of the job. You'll do the same."

"I hope so," she said.

"You know I'm big on hope."

STEP FiVE

Straightening Out Personal Business

TRACEY'S STORY

Everything has its season,
and there is a time for everything
under the heaven:

A time to mourn and a time to dance
Koheles; Chapter 3

Transgressions between an individual and another are never forgiven until you reconcile your debt and appease your friend. Even if you return said individual's money that you owe, you need to reconcile and ask to be forgiven. Even if you upset someone by saying certain [hurtful] things, you must appease this person until you are forgiven. If the individual doesn't forgive, go back to that person two or three times. [But] if the individual doesn't want [to forgive you], you may leave the matter and go. The person who refuses to be forgiving is considered a sinner.

(MAIMONIDES, *Hilchos Teshuvah*, Chapter Two, Section Nine)

Before our lives can move ahead smoothly, before we can be ready for the wide-open world, we have to ask for forgiveness from the people we hurt. We are now emotionally strong enough to endure the discomfort of repairing the damage.

It's not enough to say we're sorry. We have to do everything possible to find satisfactory resolutions. There are two parts involved: paying back and seeking forgiveness. Both are necessary. When doing them it's important to go the extra mile.

How can we get straight with ourselves and God unless we're willing to get straight with the people we cheated, hurt, or worse?

It's scary to return what we took, pay up a debt, or admit we lied. But never attempting to take care of these problems means never being free to live an authentic life. Pay up your debts. Do it diplomatically, but face the music. According to circumstance, write a letter, make a call, or, if possible, visit those you hurt and ask for forgiveness. Don't expect miracles. The people you've hurt have their own pain to deal with. Trust that your sincerity will go a long way.

After the Game

Spring is always a welcome sight in New York. The crocuses and daffodils break ground early, although the spring warmth doesn't really arrive until May. The chill of early April provides a magical opportunity to bring your kids to a ball game. I've always tried to make it to Yankee Stadium for the first Thursday night game of the season.

I try to give my kids life markers that underscore the beauty and poignancy of this world. In the world of play, I've given them baseball because I think it gives them a vision that reflects an inner spiritual value. My father gave it to me—the love of the game. It's a gallant metaphor of triumph and struggle that reflects so much of life—of living in the moment and giving your all.

The late Bart Giamatti captured baseball's essence and spirit when he wrote: "It is designed to break your heart. The game begins in the spring, when everything begins again, and blossoms in the summer—filling the afternoons and evenings. And then as soon as the chill rains come, it stops, and leaves you to face the fall alone."[1]

On this particular Thursday night, the Yankees were playing the Texas Rangers. The gates opened at 6:00 P.M. and we went in and headed to the field seats in left field. The Rangers were taking batting practice. My son Benny, all of eight years old, had on a Yankee hat that didn't quite fit. While I sat down, he pushed his little frame right up to the edge of the barrier, stuck out his glove, and prayed a kid's prayer—to get a ball. Getting a major league baseball is a mythical quest for little fans. It's a priceless treasure and memory. I still have two baseballs from my childhood. To this day, all I have to do is look at them and I remember the warm summer nights at the ballpark with my dad.

This was Benny's night. Monty Fariss, one of the Texas Rangers, picked up a ball and put it into Benny's baseball glove. For Benny, it was a moment of pure happiness and joy. Later, as we sat in the fog-shrouded upper deck, Benny turned and said to me, "It'll never be better than this. Too bad I can't stay a kid forever."

Because Friday was a school day, we left the game during the seventh-inning stretch. By 11:30, the kids were sound asleep. I was feeling particularly satisfied and at peace. Then the phone rang.

I shook my head, knowing that a call at this time of night could only mean someone was in trouble. I caught it on the third ring. A young lady's voice sadly said, "Yehudah . . ."

Recognizing the voice, I replied, "Beth?" I could hear in the way she said my name that something terrible had happened. Most of us, at one time or another, have heard that voice. I took a very deep breath and said, "What happened?

She said quietly, "Can you come over?"

I suddenly felt drained. After all, I was just about ready to call it a night and didn't particularly feel like rushing out the door. Beth was a club girl and a regular at my Sunday night classes. Sunday Night Class was an open spiritual gathering that I ran out of my home in Brooklyn for many years. It was a nexus point for all kinds of people who were searching for ways to make their ideals manifest in their lives. Beth always paid close attention to what I taught and would often stay after class to go over a certain point. I'd never heard her sound like this, and her voice was working its way into my heart.

I said, "Kid, it's almost midnight. It will take me over an hour to drive to Hoboken. So why don't you clue me in on why I've got to come?"

The silence on the phone line was eerie. After what seemed like a minute, Beth spoke. "Yehudah, I know you didn't know Tracey very well, but . . ." I could hear her fighting to choke back the tears. "Well, a few days ago she was at a party, and she didn't drink that much—she never drinks much—but after, on her way home, she lost control of her car. Yehudah, she died."

I let Beth cry. During that time my adrenaline kicked in, and I shifted gears. I was wide awake and focused. I've never met a crisis that didn't bring me right back up to speed. When you're needed, you've got to leave all your personal baggage at the door.

Beth was right. I really didn't know Tracey that well. We

had spoken after class a couple of times, but the conversation was always casual. However, I knew the statistics and I read the newspapers. By drinking and driving, she might as well have used a gun. We lose a lot of kids that way. The message is plastered everywhere: "Don't drink and drive." Yet ignorance prevails, and children lay down and die.

"I've invited a bunch of her friends to come over to my apartment and talk," Beth continued. "We just need to be together. I really need you to come over and talk with us. I think it will help us sort through what we're feeling. When everyone gets here there will be about fifteen of us. Monica's here. And so are Sara, Anne, and Susan. Bill, David, and Leticia are coming later. I don't think you know anyone else."

I knew six of the seven kids she mentioned. They generally hung out together and had all gone through hard times. They were all in their late teens and early twenties. Sara, Anne, and Susan I knew from the clubs. Sara and Anne held down jobs as secretaries and Susan was a waitress. Monica I couldn't place. Leticia was in college, and Beth was a receptionist in an office on Wall Street—standard fare for a club girl. Bill and David had at one time been hanging out in billiard parlors, hustling games and committing petty theft. I had helped both of them land jobs through the good graces of some of my friends.

All of these kids were still partying hard, but they were straightening out. Some of them had battled drugs, and during their high school years most of them had been kicked out of an endless array of schools. But somehow they all survived their high school days, graduated, and had put a semblance of order into their lives. Leticia and Beth were even regulars at Sunday Night Class.

Beth was still waiting on the phone for my reply. I told her, "Beth, I want to come. But do you have anything you specifically want me to do? Otherwise, you know I have no problem just hanging and talking."

She quietly said, "Maybe we could just talk and you could bring something along that we could talk or think about to help us understand what's happening. We're all kind of shaky."

I answered, "It's pretty tough to get perspective right now. But I'll try to help out in any way I can."

After giving me directions, Beth hesitated and then said, "Yehudah, Tracey's death is getting to me more than I can tell you over the phone. There's a lot you don't know about me. I don't know how to deal with what I'm feeling. Maybe we can talk about it later."

I assured her that we would, and that I'd be there in around an hour. I hung up the phone and stood in the silence of the living room. I let my breath center me before walking upstairs. I quietly told my wife what was up, got a change of clothes out of the closet, and turned on the shower. I ran it hot, soaped up, let the hot water sting my skin, then turned it to lukewarm. After toweling down hard and putting on some comfortable clothes, I felt much calmer and more focused.

Downstairs, I stopped by my library that stretched from the living room to the dining room to choose the books I would bring. I have accumulated several hundred books that I've arranged systematically. The Talmudic books and commentaries are to the far left. Next come the Biblical commentaries, followed by the Hassidic and Kabbalistic texts. On the far right sit the ethical and self-help works known in the trade as *Mussar* works, along with a small section devoted to works of Judaica in English.

I picked out two books. One was devoted to understanding the impact of good and bad tidings. It included a lengthy spiritual discussion of how to bless the good along with the bad things that happen in life. The other is my constant companion. It's a little book called *Aish Kodesh,* which means Holy Fire, and it was written by a Hassidic rabbi in Poland during the Second World War. It is a compendium of his teachings to his disciples in the Warsaw Ghetto. Written at one of the darkest times in modern history, it is filled with the power of hope when facing the heart of darkness. I naturally relate quite well to it. Sadly, the rabbi perished in Auschwitz, but his books miraculously survived.

I knew that opening up either one of these books tonight

would slip everyone into a timeless journey where the voices of sages speak to us as if they were still with us today. The teaching is a powerful medicine. As I went past my desk, I rummaged through the papers piled in one corner. I was looking for one of the eight steps—Straightening Out Personal Business. I knew one thing for sure. Tracey's death would be a strong wake-up call for these kids to straighten out their own lives. I figured I owed it to the group to discuss it.

Opening the Door

I turned on the alarm system in the house and went out the door. I figured the traffic would be light. I headed through the Battery Tunnel up the West Side Highway and under the Hudson via the Lincoln Tunnel. Hoboken became a pretty popular place for singles and yuppies during the eighties. It's a stone's throw from Manhattan and a whole lot cheaper.

As I drove, I thought about how when I was a kid, drunk driving and auto wrecks were big items in a teenager's life. Now, we've added more dangers to that list. We've got OD's, drivebys, and gangbangers also taking kids down.

The drive took a little more than an hour. I found a parking space a block from Beth's building. The neighborhood revealed a unique charm with clapboard row houses, walk-up apartments, cafes, and specialty shops.

I got out of the car and walked to her apartment, a three-story walk-up in an old rambling corner house. From the street, the lights from the third floor spilled out into the night. The front yard was filled with English ivy wrapped around a couple of yew trees in need of pruning. I rang the bell and was buzzed in. As I made my way up, the stairway creaked under old, frayed carpet. At the second- and third-floor landings, there were two single light fixtures. I felt right at home heading up the stairs. It reminded me of walk-ups in Brooklyn.

The door to Beth's apartment was open. I walked in. The living room was spacious with a sloping ceiling. It was framed by what looked like an elegant Victorian couch with a matching velvet love seat. In one corner next to the window was a rolltop desk with a Victorian lamp sitting to one side. The curtains were rich and full, and they matched the decor. On the other side of the room, near the hallway to the kitchen, sat her stereo system—some kind of surround-sound machine. No doubt a high-end model with very sophisticated electronics.

An ornamental fireplace filled another corner of the room. Another ornate Victorian lamp graced one corner of the mantle. From the look of her place, Beth's tastes went well beyond her receptionist's salary. I guessed that she was either getting a lot of help from her folks or she was dealing in trouble. I shrugged off my suspicions. They come from what seems like a lifetime of dealing with hustlers from *The Way Beyond.*

Everyone was sitting and talking quietly. The room was thick with sadness. I took a breath and stepped in. My tongue felt sticky; it tasted of sorrow. A few of the kids who knew me came over and gave me a hug. Nobody spoke, as if speaking would break a sacred ring of silence. After all, what had happened was beyond words. Looking at the kids, I saw a mixture of awkwardness, sadness, confusion, and reverence.

I found a spot near the fireplace, on a plush Oriental rug. Seeing that it would be impossible to get everyone's chair in a circle, I sat down on the floor and motioned for everyone to sit with me. When the kids had all gathered around, I moved to get everyone focused. I asked them to sit quietly and meditate on Tracey's memory. We sat there quietly breathing in and out Tracey's remembrance.

I wanted the kids to open their hearts to touch the upswell of emotions they felt surrounding Tracey's death. Quiet contemplation is a good tool to open the door to the heart. When death crawls into our lives, we are confronted with mysteries that can't be answered intellectually.

To find a beginning measure of peace, you first have to surf the waves of pain, sadness, fear, loss, sorrow, and emptiness. That's where the healing begins. Underneath all those emotions is a great expanse of love. To get to that love, you first have to fight through the fear and pain of loss. And if in that struggle you can open your heart, you can receive the most precious gift anyone can leave in this world—the gift of their love. It's important to concentrate on these emotions first. Philosophical discussions could come later. They'd certainly be of no help now.

We sat. I taught them the blessing one says when bad tidings are given. We spoke. They cried. The room filled with angry tears and sad tears. Tears of missing memories. Tears of shock. Tears of love. I let them roll out across the room. Everybody felt bad, but it's always best not to hide from reality.

After the first round of tears, we let silence come and rest its healing presence on our hearts. We spent a little more time studying. I read them a passage from the *Aish Kodesh.* The rabbi said that when grief and destruction are overwhelming the world, God cries with us, so to speak, over our pain.

I pulled out the sheet of paper that I had folded into one of my books. I said, "I brought this piece of paper along because I think we're ready to learn something from it. This is a sad time. Everything feels empty. It's like we all have big holes in our hearts. You've lost your dear friend Tracey, and I can't help thinking that somehow losing her is also making you question your own lives. I mean, any one of you could have been in that car and gone to that party. And when you think about it, you've probably told yourself that Tracey's death somehow has to mean something. I think the message you're looking for goes beyond not drinking and driving.

"Doesn't losing someone precious throw open the question, 'How do I straighten out my own life?' I mean, if I knew I'd be gone tomorrow, could I honestly say that I wouldn't have any loose ends with anyone? To those I've hurt, I've asked forgiveness? To those I owe, I've paid my debts? Imagine that I could tell you that tomorrow you could get up and know what you needed to do to get that straight. Given what's happened, who wouldn't want to do that? The sad irony is that Tracey's passing has upset you enough to get a glimpse of who you are, what you've done, and what you've got to do to correct it. I'll tell you this, though. I don't think any of us wants to face death knowing that there are things we did that we never straightened out, came clean on, and asked forgiveness for.

"That's why I brought along this passage written about seven centuries ago by Rabbi Moshe Ben Maimon, better known as Maimonides. One of the things he wrote about was just that—straightening out our personal business. Here's what he said:

> *Transgressions between an individual and another are never forgiven until you reconcile your debt and appease your friend. Even if you return said individual's money that you owe, you need to reconcile and ask to be forgiven. Even if you upset someone by saying certain [hurtful] things, you must appease the person until you are forgiven. If the individual doesn't forgive, go back to that person two or three times. [But] if the individual doesn't want [to forgive you], you may leave the matter and go. The person who refuses to be forgiving is considered a sinner.*

I put the paper down and looked around. "The principle of what's written here is very simple and direct. It's about how we can straighten out our personal business when we have outstanding debts. We can't get straight with ourselves and God unless we're willing to get straight with the people we cheated, hurt, or, God forbid, worse. After all, God can't pay back your debts, only you can do that."

You could have heard a pin drop in the room. Maimonides' words had gotten everyone's attention. Most of the time we're more comfortable with ignoring the mystery of life, of not thinking about what we're doing. But now, with Tracey gone, it was impossible for these kids to feel okay. Everyone felt the pain of her unfulfilled dreams. Her life would always be an unfinished story. Her memory would cling to them and haunt them in the quiet of the night.

I continued: "You see, Tracey's passing calls our life into question. It forces us to ask, 'What am I doing here? How can I become the best me? If I don't clean up my debts—if I know they're out there, and I don't do anything about them—how will I ever be free to live an authentic life?'

"If you're looking to make a new beginning, we can talk about what you might do to straighten up. If Tracey had a chance to do it all over again, she wouldn't have gotten into the car. It didn't work out that way, but if she had made it, she would tell us. And we have a chance to honor that now. I think we all know that if we don't straighten out our debts, we just go on living a lie. And it never goes away."

I've lost my share of friends and loved ones. Each loss has always been a sharp message for me to reexamine my own life. I've learned that if I don't pay attention to my own personal business, it keeps me literally away from living with honesty and integrity. It holds me back from giving my all. I know from my own battles that I have to keep a watchful eye on myself in order to keep straight.

My talk was effective. I saw it in their faces. Beth put her head down and cried. Leticia just sat there with tears streaming down her face. Bill and David got up and stood silently in a corner of the room staring out the window. I ended my speech: "There. I've said it. Tracey's memory and the message of her life are in your hands. The rest is up to you."

We had sat long enough. I got up, stretched my legs, and went into the kitchen to get a cup of coffee. I knew I was hitting overload. I also knew that the death of a friend opens you up like a can opener. From the looks on everyone's faces, it was going to be a long night. The fire of sorrow that had started dancing in their hearts was beginning to burn. It burned like pitch-covered wood, with heavy smoke and lots of sparks.

Homegrown Teshuvah

Beth's kitchen had a little alcove off to one side. In another era it would have been called a breakfast nook. The ledge was lined with African violets. The windows were old four-paned jobs whose edges were filled with cracked putty. I decided that would be my office for the night. I sat down and waited.

Leticia came into the kitchen and saw me staring out the window. She took the first appointment. The chair cattycorner to mine looked inviting. She plopped herself down with a considerable sigh. Normally, when I'd bump into Leticia at a club, she would be a walking fashion show, but tonight, given the circumstances, she wasn't about to pose. She had her hair pulled back in a tight ponytail and was wearing a cotton running suit. Her shoes were an old worn-out pair of Reeboks. She had remembered to put her three earrings into her ears.

She didn't waste any time. "Yehudah, what do I do now?" She gave me a forlorn look. Her eyes were brimming with tears.

I said, "What do you think you need to do? What does your heart say to you?"

She took another long breath. "Tracey and I had such good times together. She was like a sister. I can't stand it that she's gone. It scares me. Then, you gave that talk about being honorable to yourself and to your friend's memory. I've got a big trail of screwups and lies that I've got to do something about. I don't want to go around with it anymore."

I felt as if I was suddenly sitting in the catbird seat watching people's lives unfold. I blinked hard to get back on the field. I said, "It's never easy to carry a basket full of screwups and lies and it's even harder to confess to them."

"It's just that I lie sometimes to my friends," she said. "Tell them stuff that isn't true. I've gotten jealous and lied to get them to hate a guy or another person. I do it. Now I feel like a creep. Tracey's death just made me feel . . . you know . . . life can be so short . . . why do I get so petty? See, but I don't know what to do about it. Other than stop, but it doesn't feel like enough. My lies are out there, and I'm responsible for them. Do you know what I mean?"

I spread out my hands and nodded, "Letish, you're talking about reclaiming your dignity. Your dignity is very important. You've let yourself see the real you when you look in the mirror. Some of it you don't like. So how do you think you ought to straighten up this lying streak? Do you think you can just clamp down on it and stop it cold?"

She shook her head. "No. I got to do something else." She started to cry. I waited. The tears stopped after about thirty seconds. She took out some more Kleenex and blew her nose. She looked at me. "God, I must look awful."

"No, you look wonderful, because you're being yourself. You're being honest. It may not feel good, but it's truthful."

She whispered, "Tracey knew I lied."

"What did she tell you to do?"

"She didn't, except she told me to cut it out."

I said, "So you're at least clear on that part. Now you've got to figure out the rest."

We live in a world of easy answers. The trouble is, easy answers don't heal the soul. Healing's hard work. The ability to keep an open heart goes a long way toward giving chase to the demons. More than that, it melts the fear of ourselves and allows us to accept our broken hearts. Then we can experience a glimpse of the divine in this world.

Leticia went on. "Yeah. I've got to get up the guts to tell some of my friends what I did to them. I feel I've got to do it even if they hate me for what I've done.

"It's really weird, but since Tracey died, I never know when it's going to happen, but I'll be somewhere and I'm sure I hear her say something to me. Whatever's going on, I get this eerie feeling like she's there with me, right then, and that I'd better be able to give her a good report. Like I'd better have been straightening up my life. And when this happens, I always think of something I haven't done or someone I haven't been straight with. It's like I think Tracey's going to be with me my whole life, keeping me straight."

I thought to myself, this is true penance. This is homegrown Teshuvah—the spiritual power for someone to turn her life around and begin to grow straight from the garden of her soul. In an instant I understood why Teshuvah was part of God's plan in the creation of the world. I had read that, but now I was seeing it.

Leticia fixed me in a stare from across the table. "Why are you smiling?" she asked.

I said, "There's not much to say, is there? You're on track. Seeing you dig in makes me feel warm and confident. Your decision confirms the good things in life. It affirms my faith. It tells me Tracey must have been really special because she had a friend like you."

Leticia and I chatted some more. After a while she got up. She said, "I still feel I need to do something else for Tracey."

I replied, "Take care of this first and talk with your friends. Then call me. See what you come up with. You need to straighten out your own house before you climb the hill and look around at the world. Then you'll see what else you need to do from there."

Over the next hour, several other kids sat down to talk. They spoke of new resolutions, of forswearing old habits, and of asking friends for forgiveness, of making amends. They spoke of thoughtless words, of anger, of hurts, of abuse, of pain, and, most of all, of newfound attempts to straighten up their past actions.

It was as if the instant karma of Tracey's death awakened within them a sense of urgency to get sober with life. They weren't looking for bottom-line results to heal their lives; instead, they were searching for lives that didn't ignore the consequences. They were attempting to become more sensitive and more responsible in each moment for their actions. Not a bad place to be.

Friends and Family

A couple of hours had passed. Most of the kids had gone home. I expected a lot of phone calls in the next few weeks. I was getting pretty tired. I'd switched from coffee to club soda with ice. If I had any more coffee, my thoughts would turn sideways and my brain would melt into a puddle of exhausted babble. But I was still waiting for Beth.

She had organized the evening, going to great lengths to call Tracey's friends. She had also opened her apartment and prepared some refreshments. I figured that she was carrying a big load. It wasn't that I was cynical about her goodwill; on the contrary, I admired it. But I also knew there was something off base about the life she led. From the look of her apartment and her clothes, she lived beyond her means. While I didn't know what was going on in her life, I assumed I'd soon find out. I didn't have to wait long. She came into the alcove and sat down.

Beth's stunning good looks usually mixed well with her designer wardrobe. Tonight, she wore sweatpants with an extra-large T-shirt. With her tall, thin frame, short brown hair, and green eyes, she normally looked like someone in a photo shoot for *Mademoiselle*. Tonight, she looked a mess.

"You've been busy tonight," she said.

I answered, "I expected no less, given the circumstances." Her eyes darted around the room anxiously. I waited for her to unravel knots of trouble that had come undone with Tracey's passing.

She began. "This seems so unreal. Tracey and I were out partying just last week." She turned and looked out the window. "Now she's gone. It's all so confusing. So sad."

"I know." I waited for her to go on.

She turned back and looked me in the eye. Her forlorn look reminded me of a Keene painting, as if all there was left of Beth were her big sad eyes. But she was no waif. "Will the pain ever go away? I just ache and ache. I'm hardly able to sleep. I wish somehow I could have been there and stopped it all, had her over that night, gone with her to a movie. Something."

Beth pushed away a tear. I said, "You're always going to miss her. You can't change what happened. But you can mourn for her, and that's precious. Where would you be if you didn't hurt? If you didn't feel the pain? If you slept like a baby? There's a relationship between your love for your friend and your pain. We are given emotion because we have the capacity to care. If we could transcend those feelings, we'd lose our humanity. If we couldn't cry, we couldn't love."

A tear slowly ran down her cheek. She didn't wipe it off. She carefully said, "I miss her so much. It hurts. It makes me question so many things in my life." Beth then leaned in close, looked around the room, and said, "Tracey told me something in a dream."

Voices floated in from hushed conversations in the living room. I asked, "What did she tell you?"

"I had this eerie dream. It scared me. After I invited everyone to come here tonight, I had some time before they'd arrive, so I took a nap on the couch. I really didn't think I was dreaming, but Tracey showed up at the door. She came in and I told her, 'It's really weird, but I thought you were dead.' She laughed and started walking around my apartment and pointing to everything I own and telling me that I have to give, like, my TV back to my parents and my stereo back to this old boyfriend of mine, and other things to other people. In the dream, I didn't get it, but then some friends really did show up at the door and woke me up. I realized it was a dream and I got scared. It's like I knew I was going to have to make things right in my life, like Tracey was literally knocking on my door."

A chill prickled its way up my back as I realized that both Beth and Leticia had experienced some kind of communication from Tracey. I'd felt that chill before. Almost everyone I've spoken with who's experienced a loss has reported similar visitations. I've even had a few of them myself. Tracey's spirit had reached out and touched them.

She blew her nose. It was beet red. Her eyes were bloodshot. She looked up at me and took a sip of her cold coffee. Her nose wrinkled.

"Pretty bitter isn't it?" I said.

She asked, "The coffee or my life?"

"At this moment I'd say probably both."

Looking straight at me with eyes that revealed the depth of her sorrow, Beth said, "That dream was Tracey telling me to stop this thing I do, but I've always done it. And to stop would mean having to admit it to everyone."

"It sounds like whatever it is you do isn't exactly commendable."

Beth took a deep breath, put her hands on her lap with a thump, and said, "Well, ever since I was fifteen, whenever I needed extra money, I've tricked people into giving it to me.

My friends, my boyfriends, my folks. I practically stole. I'd borrow things, like my old boyfriend's stereo, knowing I'd never give it back. I figured I'd just break up with him and keep it. I never let myself think about what I was really doing, but now I feel sick. Like I'm going to vomit."

It all clicked into place. Her lifestyle had always been a mystery to me, but this explained the expensive clothes and the niceties in her apartment. I said, "Tell me, how much did Tracey know?"

"She caught right on to me one day when I tried to get money from her. I had spent a lot of money partying the night before, and she knew how much. The next morning we were having coffee and I started to come on to her about how I was going to be short on the rent and maybe she could help me. She just looked at me and said, 'Beth, I saw the cash last night, remember? What are you pulling on me?' She wasn't mad. She just said, 'You've got a real problem. Straighten it out now or you'll lose everything, even your friends.' "

She was crying again. I didn't like to see it, but I know that she couldn't heal if she didn't fully experience and work through her feelings of immense regret. If we've hurt someone, it's not enough to simply ask God to forgive us. Teshuvah doesn't work that way.

After a couple more minutes, she started calming her breath. She let out a long sigh and then launched into a machine-gun confession. "It started with me taking money from my folks, straight out of their wallets. Then I did the same thing at my best friend's house with her parents. It was so easy, and I didn't get caught. Then I'd lie to get money. I'd tell my folks that lunch at school cost twice what it did, and I'd make a tuna sandwich and pocket the money. Later, when I left home, I kept going. I told my folks the damage deposit for my apartment was way more than it actually was. When the money would run out I'd come up with another lie, like I had a high dental bill. Then I started borrowing money from friends and boyfriends by telling them some crazy lie. I said I'd pay them back, but never did. If they made a thing of it, I'd just disappear, stop getting together with them. If they didn't say anything, I'd just keep on making like nothing happened.

"It makes me sick to think about it, but I'd even hustle dates for cash, like some cheap low-life hustler in a movie. And all the time I'm buying expensive stuff and going out to dinner and partying hard and renting limos everywhere. God, it's pathetic, and what's worse is that I've gotten used to it. My conscience would tell me to cut it out, but I'd just block it out. Then I stopped even caring. Then Tracey found out, and she went and died."

I said, "The real question is, how are you going to straighten this out?"

With a quiet voice she said, "I've got to do what I've always dreaded the most. I've got to go back and tell everybody what I did. I've got to figure out how to pay them back. I know. I've thought about it. That's what Tracey was telling me in the dream. I've always known I'd have to do it someday. I just pushed those thoughts away. It's really scary."

I gently added, "What's even scarier is not dealing with it. Living a lie eats slowly into your soul. If you lie to yourself, you never can be straight with others. It affects everything. That's why you had the dream. Deep down, you've got to change and Tracey is the messenger straight from your conscience."

"I know. It's like when I'm with someone. Even if they like me a lot, or I like them, I'd always think, *If they only knew what I really was about, they'd hate me.* Then, when I got close with Tracey and she found out, little by little I realized that she still loved me as a friend. All I had to do was to cut it out. Now that she's dead, I know I have to finish it. I can't hold back. But God, some people are going to really hate me."

"Yeah, that probably will happen. But some folks will forgive you, and you'll forgive yourself, and you'll pay everyone back. There's no way you can avoid the pain or the shame, but there's no way you can go on and live the lie."

Beth went on, "I don't think you know how bad it's really been."

I said, "I won't know if you don't tell me."

She shivered and swallowed hard. "I probably owe people maybe over $8,000 or $9,000. I owe my parents the most. I'm so ashamed of this, and I'm scared about how everyone's going to flip out when I tell them. And *how* am I going to pay that back? Yehudah, what am I going to do? What am I going to say?"

She leaned forward across the table, "Yehudah, I'm really scared. What would you say to someone like me if they came and told you what they did and offered to pay you back?"

I sat for a moment trying to gather my thoughts. "Beth, the truth is that this has happened to me. And there are still people running around out there who I thought were my friends. They ripped me off and disappeared. So what would I say if one of them showed up? For openers, I'd tell them that I've been pretty hurt and angry at them for a long time. I'd tell them that what they did reflects their character, that it's got some big flaws. But I'd forgive them. No doubt about that. I don't think we could become friends, but if I saw their sincerity, I'd forgive them. It's the right thing to do. Everyone makes mistakes, and it's the fortunate ones who wake up and realize what they've done and straighten up. Not forgiving would be an act of cruelty on my part. I'm not going to add to the bad vibes in the world if I can help it."

She immediately said, "But not everyone's going to do that."

"That's true, but you have to do what's right, even if you have to take a bath in someone's anger," I replied. "There's no choice, is there? I think Tracey's death has helped you see that. You can't stay where you are, and you can't move forward until you do this."

"I know," she whispered.

I added, "Look, what you did happens to a lot of people. I mean a lot. But that doesn't make it any less disreputable. Think about it. You rip off your friends. They grow to hate you. Now if you magnify that hatred to include every friendly rip-off, what do you get? I'll tell you—you get a tremendous amount of hate in the world. And what's worse is that people get used to hurting their friends and people get used to hating those who hurt them. It's a bad scene. Don't you see now why one of the Ten Commandments is 'Don't steal'? It creates ripples of bad feelings. It hits people's livelihood. It steals people's time. Clean it up, Beth, and you'll open a new door for yourself.

She wasn't crying now. Resolve was starting to work its way into her heart. "I'm going to do it. No matter how scared I might be, I'm going to do it. Besides, I feel like Tracey is somehow listening in and is going to follow me around to make sure I do it."

"I'm rooting for you, Beth. You might have to be a bit persistent in your quest to straighten all this out. Even with someone who gets angry at you and doesn't forgive you, you've got to try and go back to that person until it appears you will gain success, or until you see there's no possibility for forgiveness. Then you can let go of it. It'll be over then either way. But remember, to find forgiveness we have to seek forgiveness, we have to ask for it. You can ask God to give you the strength to ask people to forgive you, but the people you've hurt are the only ones who can grant forgiveness. It's practical and real because it's downright spiritual. Let me know what happens." With that, I said my good-byes and headed out.

By the time I got home, the sun had already lit up the eastern horizon. The neighborhood had begun to come alive. At 6:00 A.M., enough people are on their way to work that I had no trouble finding a place to park. I stood out on the stoop and watched the lights go on in the apartment building across the street. I thought about Tracey, Leticia, and Beth. Maybe this was the time for Tracey's friends to get it right. I knew I always could hope.

Straightening Out Personal Business

The problems I encounter with kids fall under a handful of categories. For a good number of kids in trouble, lying and stealing make the list. They come from family systems where, among other things, their parents discount who they are as individuals. They grow up lying in an effort to gain their parents' respect. Stealing generally comes later as they begin to devalue other people's feelings after having learned to devalue their own. Through subsequent conversations, I learned that Beth and Leticia both fit the profile. I was happy they were close friends. I hoped they would find a way to help each other straighten out their personal business.

The next several weeks brought on, as I suspected, a lot of phone calls. I felt like the duty sergeant in the police station. These kids, like so many others I'd been privileged to meet, needed somewhere to report. Some days the phone lines were filled with upbeat reports, bubbling voices, and lives filled with conviction: "I took care of it." "I feel better about myself." "I learned a lot about myself." "I feel as if a weight has been lifted from my heart."

Other times the storm winds of inner work would take hold. The phone would fill with tears and hurts. "I feel rotten." "After I told him he screamed at me. It was awful." "Why did I do this?" "I messed up real bad."

To the ecstatics, I'd remind them that behind every high there is a low and that the secret is to continue the work through both the good and bad times. To the depressives, I'd remind them that fear, hurt, and recrimination weren't a sign of failing, but of acceptance of who we are. We are all filled with imperfections. We heal and hurt at the same time.

A couple of weeks after our meeting, Leticia called me. I said, "Hey, Letish, how's business?"

"It's been some week, Yehudah."

"Well, kid, I hope that there's been at least some value to the week."

She let out what sounded like a half groan. "I don't think I can be the same me anymore. The more I've been owning up to my lies, the weirder I feel. It's like I'll tell one of my friends that I lied about all that stuff I did in high school or that I lied about what a guy did, and it's not so hard telling them, but afterward I feel so shaky about myself. Am I making any sense?"

I came right back. "Yeah, I think I understand what you're saying. After straightening out a bunch of your lies, you've discovered that you've been covering for yourself for such a long time and you can't do that anymore."

She piped in, "Right."

I went on: "So, what makes you nervous now is that you can't be the person who lies and makes up stories anymore. You were used to embellishing yourself, and now, because you're not going to do that anymore, you're just stuck with plain old you. You're not used to that and you don't know who you are underneath the stories. You don't have your lies to protect you anymore."

Her voice began to break. "Yeah, it's like, my whole life, I've lied to my folks and lied to my friends. Then it's like, bang, Tracey dies, and whoa! I've got to take care of my life. I see it so clearly it hurts, Yehudah."

"But you're doing it," I told her. "You've taken measure of yourself and found your honesty. Maybe you ought to focus on that. From where I sit, I see your integrity shining through. It takes strength not to live a lie; it takes courage to really care for yourself. Tracey's passing touched you so deeply that you've now chosen not to live underground in a world of lies. You've surfaced to become yourself. If you cherish and nurture the new you, you can only find true value in who you are. What you toss away is untruth. What's left is you."

I could hear her breathing through the phone. "You know it's funny. It's like if I look at who I was and try to hold on to that, I can't and get very shaky, 'cause it wasn't real anyway. And now, you're saying that stuff is gone. I need to look at what's me. The honest me."

I added, "You ought to write that down as a reminder. Put it on an index card: 'Leticia is an honest, courageous person. She tells the truth and keeps far from lies. She does this to keep her business clean. She does this because she cares about herself and others.'"

She laughed. "Thanks for cheering me up. I might just do that."

Beth also was having a rough time, but she did find the resolve and the courage to be honest about her past and about who she really was. One day she reported, "Yehudah, I spoke to my mom. It was awful."

I asked, "What happened?"

"She forgave me," Beth said sadly. "She hugged me. Told me she was glad I was being honest. Then she said, 'I raised you to be honest. You did a terrible thing, but I know this is not easy for you. You're trying. You're my daughter and I love you.'"

I knew full well why that had felt awful, but I said, "That was awful? Sounds pretty good to me."

Beth replied, "Her forgiving me hurt so much. It made me cry. Here I did this to my own mom and she loves me and understands anyway. God, it hurt me to see what I'd done. I felt real low, like I didn't deserve her forgiveness or that kind of love."

"But you took it in and accepted it," I said. "Now you have a taste of how strong the ripples can be from love and forgiveness."

She quietly agreed, "Yes. It's hard to believe I lived with such deceit. But don't get me wrong, my mom didn't let me off the hook. I'm paying her back too."

Not every call from Beth went so well. While many people exercised good judgment and were willing to let go of their anger as long as they were paid back, a couple of people really unloaded on her.

She called one day after a particularly harrowing experience. "I spoke with this guy I used to date," she said. "I told him I ripped him off, and that I was sorry I told such goofy stories and lies. I said I wanted to pay him back. He saw it as some kind of macho thing. He said I was dirt and a no-good bitch. He said disgusting things and then laughed and said for me to keep the money. Then he added, 'You're nothing but a whore.'"

I asked, "What did you say?"

"Well, I mean, I felt like crying," she answered. "I was really confused. Then I started to get real angry. I was going to tee off at him when I remembered what this was all about. I was taking care of *my* personal business. *I* was the one who started all of this with him. I used him. Who was I to get angry at him even if he is a creep?

"I just left, went home, and then walked to my special spot. You know, when Tracey was alive, we used to walk to this spot between two buildings where you could see Manhattan through some trees. It was so beautiful that we used to just stand there, stare, and talk. Now, when things are rough, I go there, you know, to clear my mind. Afterwards, I feel a lot better. It's like Tracey's friendship gave me the guts to take care of things in my life."

As time went on, Beth began to sort her feelings out. Her relationship with her mother continued to be positive, but her mother also was forcing her to stay honest. A good sign. Once, she called and said, "I just got off the phone with my mom. She won't let me off the hook. Every time we talk, she asks me if I'm paying everyone back on time. It just makes me feel, I don't know, bad again or useless and mad. I'm mean, I'm taking care of it. Why doesn't she just cut it out? And to top it off, she's always saying, 'Do it for Tracey.' "

I said, "She's your mom. It's her job."

"What do you mean by that?"

"She's concerned," I said. "She wants to make certain you're being responsible. Forgiveness and responsibility go hand in hand. She has a piece of this too. After all, she raised you and you ran out on this limb and almost sawed it off. Don't think for a moment she's not questioning herself and her parenting. But she's being responsible and isn't running away from what she sees is her job. A mother's love can be at times the best reminder to you. Every time you confront your past, you're not only being brave, you're being loving to yourself."

In time, the phone calls became less frequent. I felt relieved and happy.

Good Deeds

One Saturday night I was in the Village catching a struggling rock 'n roll band whose front man is a friend and a tremendous guitar player.

It was between sets. The place, although small, was packed. I glanced to the door and spotted Beth, Leticia, and two other girls whom I recognized from my night at Beth's house coming through the door. They saw me and headed right to my table. I stood up with flourish and said, "Welcome ladies. Are you here for the show or did you decide to track me down?"

They laughed and Beth said, "Nothing all that dramatic, Yehudah. We called your house, found out you were here, and, since we were heading to a club on the West Side, thought we'd see you in person. We wanted to thank you and to tell you some good news."

The girls all looked more at peace. Leticia had a less severe look on her face and Beth's wardrobe reflected what she really could afford—clearly not from some upscale designer boutique.

I smiled and said, "I appreciate the thanks, ladies. But remember, you did the work. You took the risks to get straight. It's like . . ."

They all shook their heads and Beth spoke for all of them when she said, "Yehudah, we're not in session with you."

I laughed and held up my hands in surrender and said, "Well you never know."

They were, of course, right. But I always like to err on the side of caution. Better to drop some insight into someone's lap on the spot than to turn and let the moment slip away.

"So here's the news," said Beth. They all had such eager looks on their faces that I figured I was in for a real treat. "A bunch of us have been talking about how Tracey affected our lives. So much happened to all of us after she died. We're all trying to do things differently. Anyhow, we were thinking, we've got to do something for Tracey. You know, to honor her memory. We miss her so much."

She paused, and I said, "You've got my attention. So what is the something you're going to do about it?"

With a big smile, Beth said proudly, "Well, we've picked out a couple of organizations that could really use some help and we've been taking up a collection. We're going to keep adding more money for the next couple of months and then we'll give the organizations the money in Tracey's memory."

If we hadn't been in a noisy club when Beth said that, there would have been a beautiful silence. Four pairs of eyes stared at me, waiting for my reply to their announcement.

"If I could climb a hill and shout a big *yes,* I would right now," I beamed. "Seldom have I been prouder or more impressed at the splendor of who you kids are. This is something I'll carry in my heart all my life. You are wonderful, terrific, and beautiful. There is no greater reward in life than performing acts of charity and splendid good deeds."

I saw a tear well up in Leticia's eye. It was a wonderful moment filled with life's exquisite beauty. It proved again that underneath all the hard and desperate stories are hearts of goodness and kind deeds. I thought to myself, *I'm the fortunate one.*

We schmoozed for a bit. The band members came back in and my friend came over, guitar in hand, to say hello. He was dressed in one of his outrageous hats and posing clothes. He reminded me of the late Andy Wood, whose legendary band Mother Love Bone vanished with his passing, only to rise again when two former members went on to help form Pearl Jam. The girls enjoyed being introduced. He then popped back onstage and the band got ready to play.

I said, "You girls ought to stay and catch a set."

Beth said, "I'm sure it's great, but were heading uptown."

I said, "Yeah, I know. You're stuck on dance music. You're going to miss something special."

They got up anyway. I walked them to the door. Their happiness was infectious. Out on the street, I turned to Beth and said, "No limo?"

She smiled. "No more limos or any of that stuff."

I said, "I'm impressed and I'm proud of you."

They all nodded and said thanks. And it was a sincere thanks. They started toward the street corner to flag a cab.

Halfway down the block, I shouted to them, "Girls, you be careful. You watch out. I want to keep getting phone calls from you at regular hours."

They waved and disappeared around the corner.

I walked back into the club as the band began "I Will Find You." I felt blessed to have found these kids.

STEP SiX

Confessing Your Actions in Public

RiCK'S STORY

Everything has its season,
and there is a time for everything
under the heaven:

A time to throw away and a time to gather together
Koheles; Chapter 3

STEP SIX: ***Confessing Your Actions in Public***

It is exceedingly praiseworthy for an individual to do Teshuvah by confessing in public and acknowledging and making his or her sins known to others, and revealing the transgressions that occurred between the individual and his or her friends. The individual should say to them, "I sinned against so-and-so and I did such-and-such. . . . Behold, I am this day doing Teshuvah and express my regret.

(MAIMONIDES, *Hilchos Teshuvah*, Chapter Two, Section Five)

Once we've set things from the past straight, we move forward by sharing with others what we have learned. We strengthen ourselves tremendously by talking about how far we fell, how we hurt ourselves, how we hurt others, and how we struggled to climb back to where we stand with them now.

This accomplishes two powerful things. First, there is a great lesson in humility that accompanies a public admission to another person. Second, by baring our souls to another, we help those we've wronged recognize that our regret is sincere.

Confessing to others lifts a burden. When others know what you have done, you have nowhere left to hide from your life. Baring the soul can lead you inevitably to unburdening your heart to God.

Rick's Mission

People are of the opinion that my line of work is exciting and daring, that it's gallant. They'll come up to me and say, "Gosh, I read a Robert Parker novel that read like the story you just told." Or, "Your life reminds me of *NYPD Blues*." Or, "Your work is like an episode of the *Equalizer* I saw on TV last week. Did you see it? Is it really like that out there?"

While I admit to having a curiosity about how complicated troubles can get, that's as far as I go. I've held too many crying kids in my arms to romanticize the drama of what I've seen. I'm sure any cop would tell you the same thing. Reality is an entirely different trip.

Over the years I've had so many stories poured over my

heart that my memory has blurred. There are names I've forgotten and stories I've buried. I'm afraid that if I remembered them all, the pain would cripple me. After all, out in *The Way Beyond,* most kids don't make it.

But there are some kids I'll never forget. I can close my eyes, see their faces, and be touched in my heart. Even if I can't recall their names, I can hear their voices, see their smiles, and embrace their vanished dreams. They show up from time to time in my dreams. I'm certain there is something mystical about these encounters. It is as if, in the realm of souls, they are there to heal something. But then again, I'm no seer and I'm not privy to mystical sight.

Everyone's legacy has to be carried by someone, so I let these kids' faces walk in my mind and visit my dreams. Perhaps it is because I've spent a good deal of my life in the land of the forgotten that I am privileged to carry their memory.

Rick was one of those kids who will stay with me forever. He stood out on the mean streets. I'd find him at 2:00 A.M. on the edge of a stoop trying to stay out of the rain. I'd see him walking like a ghost on the West Side Highway docks. I'd bump into him in a cafe in the Village. His rail-thin body was always on the move. His clear brown eyes shone with the light of the next world. Rick was dying of AIDS, one of the many victims of the hustler's paradise. There was, though, one difference with Rick. He was on a mission.

He came right out and told me. "I'm dying, man. I messed up a lot of things in my life. I'm out here to tell kids not to do what I did, to get out of the life. I tell them, the money's not worth it. Look where it got me. I just got sucked into all the easy money, and all the tricks I turned gave me nothing but AIDS.

"There's other young gay hustlers all around here who started out just like me, but they can't see what's on the other side of the door. I've got to try and tell them. I left home because no one could accept me, but look where it got me."

I didn't know Rick all that well, but I'd heard bits of his life story. He came from a small town. He was gay. His growing up was full of confusion, and this had led him to seek a new life in New York, ultimately on the streets and in big trouble. When he saw so many others heading for the same fate, he decided to do something.

"I'm not trying to be heroic," he told me once. "I'm just trying to set some things right. I don't have much time left to do some good in the world."

Encountering Rick was like stepping right into a buzz saw. His words chopped everything to the core. His heart heard the wing beats of the angel of death, and he knew he had to get ready to fly. He prepared himself by engaging in the deepest act he knew. He went out to save others.

Rick was fragile, yet strong. Broken, yet dignified. He kept talking. He knew his words might keep someone alive.

Early one evening I ran into him near Christopher Street in the Village. The late summer sun's rays were warm, but the air was filled with the first hint of fall. The street was alive with young people making their way across the West Side Highway to party on the docks. Even from two blocks away, you could hear the music and see the crowd. Rick was sitting at a window table in one of the many small restaurants that populate the Village. As I walked by, he tapped on the window glass. I turned, squinted, and stepped up to take a look at who was beckoning me. Seeing him, I ducked inside and made my way to the table. Rick was having a salad. To his right sat Joaquin.

Joaquin I knew from the street. He was a nineteen-year-old hustler on the way down. When I first met him, he was on top of the world, full of cash and flash. His young body rippled with muscles and was covered with fine silk. But turning too many tricks and smoking too much crack had left him HIV-positive and with a nasty drug habit. He still had puppy dog eyes, but now they connected not only to a lost innocence, but also to a cavernous sadness.

Joaquin and I had sat on a stoop in the Village one hot summer night, and he had shown me his "trophies." "Yehudah, want to see my tattoos?" he said and took off his shirt, slowly turning in the shadows of the yellow-white streetlight.

His tattoos turned out to be knife scars with stitch marks that crisscrossed his arms and torso.

"That's quite a display," I said. "Looks like you've been in and out of some major league trouble." I tried to make my words sound cool and hip, but my insides were ripping apart.

"Yeah. Johns did this to me. I'm a regular at the emergency room." He proceeded to enumerate in detail, with a good deal of pride, who did what to him and when. He rambled on like a war veteran recounting tales from the battlefront.

While I admit I've seen a lot of strange things in my day, I wasn't quite certain if Joaquin was telling the truth or was instead a victim of some bizarre sadomasochistic ritual. Maybe he came right out of the books of someone so wounded and in need of caring that he had developed a bad habit of slashing himself to reflect the voracious holes inside his soul. Then again, the street is violent. I've met so many cut-up kids, he certainly could have been telling the truth. What was clear to me was that his whole life had been a tragedy for which I had no explanations.

As I reached the table, I gave Rick and Joaquin big hugs, told them I was happy to see them, pulled up an extra chair, and ordered a seltzer with lime. Joaquin was an excellent candidate for Rick's lifesaving work.

Rick smiled and looked up from his half-eaten salad full of alfalfa sprouts and sunflower seeds. As he polished off a mouthful, a few of the sprouts clung to the side of his mouth. Pointing to the salad with his fork, he said, "Lemon oil dressing with good cold-pressed oil. It's supposed to help my immune system, which is, by the way, currently shot."

I couldn't help wincing. He matter-of-factly continued: "I was in the hospital last week. Didn't think I'd make it out alive and neither did the doctors. My T-cell count was down to zero. I couldn't hold down anything. I was in IV-land. Then, I sweated out a monstrous fever. The next day I felt better, and I checked myself out of the hospital. I'm feeling pretty good now." He checked his watch. "I gotta go. I'm going to get out tonight and talk to some more kids."

Rick finished off the rest of his salad and got up, so Joaquin and I did too. Rick gave me a hug, held me at arm's length, and took a deep breath. He looked straight into my eyes, as if he wanted to connect his spirit with mine. I wanted to hold him and tell him everything would be all right, but he'd gone too far down the road for that. He didn't have the luxury of a lifetime to work his problems out. All he had were his speeches and hugs. I reached out and squeezed both his biceps hard. Leaning close to his ear, I quietly said, "Rick, I'm with you."

With that, he laughed and said, "I know."

We both knew if we stood there any longer our eyes would begin filling with tears, so he walked over to the cashier, paid his bill, and waved as he went out the door. Joaquin tagged along after him.

No Joke

I finished my water and then headed down Christopher Street. The end of Christopher bumps into the West Side Highway. The bottom end is flanked by bars and adult S & M toy shops. The establishments stand in stark contrast to what's going on up the street at the AIDS hospice. I figured I'd put in another couple hours of work. Maybe I'd hang out with Rick and talk to some kids.

I spotted Rick across the highway, talking to a kid I knew well, Jonathan. Heading their way, I thought of Jonathan's struggles as I walked by an adult toy store. I used to laugh at how people could go home loaded down with implements of bondage like love leashes, whips, hoods, riding crops, blindfolds, and wrist shackles, then sit back, pop porno flicks into the VCR, and be set for the evening. My laughing ended when I got to know Jonathan.

He was about nineteen or twenty, tall and angular in a bony kind of way. The sides of his head were buzzed. The top was mowed down to about a quarter inch and dyed orange. He loved to take his western shirts with the imitation pearl snap buttons, cut off the sleeves, open the shirt, and show off his washboard abs, belly button, and pierced nipples.

Jonathan spoke like a Georgia Peach. He was a Southern boy who had moved north to turn tricks and get his body plundered in Manhattan's dark paradise. Underneath his good ol' boy exterior smoldered a kid who wasn't afraid to get violent. Hustlers as a general rule aren't into peace and love. One time he told me, "Yehudah, I'm a performer."

I said, "Down here?"

"Not in cars, silly," he said. "Y'all know I've got class. I perform in gentlemen's houses or condos."

I reacted like I'd been fed a hot pepper. Turning tricks in private residences is, in my book, spinning the roulette wheel with death.

I had to lay it on the line right there. There was no guarantee I'd ever see him again. This wasn't about building a relationship with this kid; it was about grabbing him before he fell off the cliff.

"Jonathan, you're playing on dangerous ground," I said. "You might get really wiped out. Vanished. Poofed. Snuffed. You've got to cut that out."

He just gave me a good ol' patronizing southern smile and said, "Now don't you worry none. I can handle it. Nothing's better than kneeling and submitting to your master. These guys love it and they pay for their love."

"Yeah, but what happens if you pass out or panic? Or if some john decides not to untie you?"

He laughed, reached into his backpack and pulled out a pair of fancy scissors and double-ended safety snaps that attached to the end of ropes. "You see, these are ambulance scissors. You know, used by rescue workers to cut through belts, hoods, or boots. And these beautiful snaps let you bypass untying the ropes. It's all safe and consensual."

I came back and said, "You might have good equipment and the right vocabulary for consensual bondage, but the fact is you don't know who you're going to hook or who's gonna hook you."

At that, Jonathan started to rummage around in his backpack again. I stopped him, adding, "I don't need to see your weapons. I don't want to know about them. All I'm telling you is that some of your johns are going to play rough. What's the guarantee they'll untie you? And don't tell me some cornpone answer, 'cause you've got none. You're pushing it and someone can snuff you just like that."

I know I snapped at him. The whole conversation was giving me a headache, but I had to try. The outcome was not in my hands, but caring was within the reach of my heart. So was creating a space for love in a loveless world.

Tonight, as I looked across the highway, I felt hopeful that Rick was talking to Jonathan. Then, he wandered off to talk with someone else. I jaywalked across the highway, one-armed a jump over the concrete abutments, and made my way over to Jonathan.

Instead of Jonathan's usual cut-off sleeves and open shirt, he wore a scarf around his neck and a billowing country western shirt with French cuffs. Noting his new wardrobe, I said, "You've changed your outfit. What's the deal?"

He had a faraway look in his eyes. Something was up. Without waiting for a reply, I added, "What happened?"

He tilted his head back and closed his eyes down to little slits. It made him look angry, dangerous, and scared. "The son of a bitch nearly strangled me. Look at this, will you?"

He pulled up the sleeves of his shirt. There were two ugly bruises etched like smeared purple tattoos around his wrists. He then carefully pulled down part of the scarf around his neck. The skin was raw and bruised, tinged purplish pink and red. The scarf was stained with antibiotic cream and pus. Clearly, he'd had a bad run-in with a john.

"You've seen a doctor?"

He didn't hear me. "You see what he did? But I got him. I beat the crap out of him. Stomped him till he begged me to stop. I had gotten a weird feeling about him so I had worked the rope so I could get free."

Then, as if his brain was on a delay, he said, "It's not infected. If I get a fever, I'll go to St. Vincent's and have someone check it out."

I put my hand out and touched his shoulder. He tensed, then shuddered and relaxed. "Jonathan." I spoke slowly and gently, "Don't you see selling yourself doesn't work? The deal's not going to go down right. Besides, I can't stand to see you hurt, and that temper of yours can get you blown away. I don't know what demons you're fighting, but without letting anyone in to care about you and give you a hand, the party's going to come down hard. Do you understand what I'm saying? I'm standing here looking at you, and I'm worried as hell."

Jonathan just stood there and stared at the water. I didn't know whether my words were sinking in or he was building up new walls of defense against his pain.

Turning, he looked me in the eye. "You can't understand this." He swept his right arm over the docks, then pointed up to the Village. "You just can't understand. Being a hustler, it's my freedom. It's like huntin' possum. It's like being out in the pines. It's my paradise out here. When I was a kid, my parents were like monsters. They were horrible, and I was this good little boy. I was afraid to go up against them. I didn't have the guts. They told me what to do and I let them do things to me. Then I got away. I just get off on it all—the danger, the sex. Out here it's a pleasure factory. I know you care, but stay out of it. This is what I do."

Most of the time, kids like Jonathan who turn to hustling come from homes filled with physical and sexual abuse. They learn to flee to their inner hideaway to escape their attackers. They put their innocence into the recesses of their souls. In some confused way, they think they've found a place where nobody can touch them. In the process, they lose touch with themselves and get propelled into deeper cycles of abuse. They get abused, and if they survive, they grow up to become abusers.

I winced at Jonathan's words, but what was I going to say to him? The weight words carry out here sometimes pushes people away. The street isn't the place to operate a debating society. I simply said to him, "It's possible for someone to care about you. It's possible to make other choices. It's even possible to be loved."

He frowned at me and said, "Yeah, right podna. No thanks, but thanks anyway. I gotta go."

He turned and walked off down the docks. I just stood staring after him. About twenty yards across the vast expanse of concrete, he turned and looked back at me. He gave me a smile. I gave him a salute back.

With his looks and his attitude, Jonathan was a premium product for those who wanted what he had to offer. He was something prized to prey upon. I watched as Jonathan vanished into the crowd. I wondered if he'd ever find his way out.

Street Epidemiology

I spotted Rick again later that night. As I walked toward him, my feet dragged on the concrete, scuffing my soles. After my talk with Jonathan, I felt defeated. I stopped and looked up at the stars, letting myself be refreshed by the sky. It's not easy finding a bit of heaven on the highway to hell, but I felt better. I caught up to Rick.

The crowd at the south end of the docks had grown to maybe a couple hundred people. Someone had brought the inevitable boom box and the thump from the speakers carried up the docks. Rick was leaning out over the abutments that line the Hudson. From ten feet away, I could see that he was engaged in a serious conversation. I quietly approached, leaned my back up against the concrete and waited. A tug pulled up the river. The bottles, trash, and sheen of spilled oil on the water reminded me of the street.

Rick turned, smiled, and said, "Yehudah, this is Tom. He's filling me in on various treatment options. He volunteers with an AIDS awareness group in the Village."

I shook his hand. Rick went on. "Tom, Yehudah's a rabbi who does a lot of work out on the street."

"Gentlemen, I don't mean to interrupt," I said.

"We're almost finished," Rick said. "Besides, you could learn something."

Tom smiled and said, "Rabbi, it's a pleasure to see anyone out here lending a hand. I was just going over some basics with Rick, just to make sure he knows what's happening to him. You're welcome to listen in. So as I was saying, any time your T-cell count goes below 600, you're wide open for OI's."

Looking at me, he added. "OI's are opportunistic infections. With you, Rick, since your T cells are so low, you've got to consider yourself at serious risk."

Rick just nodded. I was up to speed at this phase of the conversation. T cells are a main part of the body's immune system. They're a type of white blood cell that allows the body to fight off various diseases and infections. HIV attacks and kills T cells and is especially damaging to CD4 cells, a type of T cell. The count, which refers to the number of CD4 cells in a microliter of blood, is a good barometer to use in determining what's going on in a patient's body.

Rick added, "You know, I just got out of the hospital. I had a bad run-in with pneumonia. I could hardly breathe. They treated it with high doses of pentamidine. I was delirious and figured I'd come down with toxoplasmosis, pure brain rot, but I hadn't."

Tom looked very serious. I kept my mouth shut. It was clear that this was street epidemiology at its best. Tom took Rick's hand and tenderly said, "I gather they took a biopsy."

Rick nodded.

"Look, the pneumonia you had is called Pneumocystis carinii pneumonia. It can easily kill you. Are you taking Bactrim every day?"

Rick nodded again and asked, "But what about my bone marrow? You know I take AZT. I heard that Bactrim can affect my blood cell production."

Tom replied, "Both AZT and Bactrim do affect bone marrow, but if your bone marrow is just a bit shut down with AZT, a little Bactrim every day won't mess you up. Your T cells are below 200. You're high risk. You need to get your blood work done regularly. If you get allergic to Bactrim, there's other stuff to take. If you get a yeast infection, take acidophilus milk or yogurt."

Rick stood there, absorbing as much as he could. It's got to be hard enough fighting for your life, keeping up a good attitude, and struggling daily with the illness and the gnawing worry of having to get your life in order right now. But added to the soup is a full-blown course in pharmacology, epidemiology, and nutritional management as well as a network that keeps you up on the latest research. There was Rick, a street hustler with an active case of AIDS, having to learn a whole new language to gather information about his health. Still he had energy to do what he thought was most important: warning other hustlers to watch out for the virus that had taken down so many. The more I thought about it, the more it took my breath away.

The conversation ended a few minutes later. I shook hands again with Tom. Rick turned to me and said, "Let's walk."

A Spiritual Favor

The first thing Rick said to me as we walked along was, "I saw you speaking with Jonathan."

I said with a little sigh, "Yes."

"He's a walking dead man," Rick told me. I winced. "We can hope for miracles, but he's running hard down a bad road," he said.

I thought of Robert Johnson, King of the Delta Blues Singers, who sang about having a hellhound on his trail. "It does look that way," I said. "We can hope."

Rick switched topics and said, "I need to ask you a favor because you know a lot of spiritual stories and stuff. I need a list."

I asked, "What kind of list?"

"For when I'm walking around or sitting, if I'm sick in the hospital," he said. "I'm alone a lot. I think about how all this happened to me, about how I'm probably going to die. I want to make better use of my time. I want to get stronger spiritually, especially when I'm really scared. So I thought you could type me a list of a few things. You know, just one page on, say, the power of forgiveness. It would help me out a lot. I could read it and let it sink in. It would help me organize my thoughts and feelings. Maybe make me see a little clearer now that I'm not hustling anymore. You think you could do that?"

I looked at him. His face seemed suffused in a warm, faint light. Every time I saw that light around him I was touched by its glowing warmth. It was as if his face was turning away from this world.

"For you to ask me is an honor," I said. "It would be my pleasure."

Over the few months that we'd known each other, Rick and I had had very intense conversations, different from those I'd had with other kids. Rick had his own inner agenda and was wedded to it. My job was to provide him with information. From time to time I'd ask him, "How do you do it? How do you keep so focused? This can't be easy. How do you manage to pull yourself out here?"

With Zenlike precision he'd say things like, "All there is, is today." Another time he said, "My past is only filled with bad memories. My future is gone. What else do I really have but today, to do what I can right now?"

I'd share in all this and be transformed by it.

That night, as we walked toward the main expanse of what used to be a parking lot, he paused, turned, and stared out across the Hudson toward New Jersey. "I've been thinking. This is what makes sense to me right now: I can't control what happened to me. Things just happened. I can't forget it, but you know what gives me strength?"

Turning, he looked right into my face, smiled, and said, "I can forgive." He went on: "When I realize that, I get new energy to come out here and talk to kids. Most of the time I'm not afraid of dying anymore. I just know somehow deep down that I've got to try and tell kids not to follow what I did. Look where it got me. I thought I had it all."

I said back, "True heroism is knowing you're not a hero but doing the right thing anyway."

I heard his breath catch in his throat.

I added, "It's all like good compost."

"What?"

"Well, you gather up all the garbage," I explained, "but first you've got to know what the garbage is. Then you take it out of your house because you can't compost in your house. You put it all in one big container and add to it every day. You stir the pile, and it heats up. When it's finished composting, you take it out and like magic, the garbage has turned into fertilizer for your garden. I mean, you know it was garbage, you can't forget what it was, but now it's been transformed. It now has a use, and it's nutritious."

He started laughing. "You have a way of taking a heavy conversation and rolling it around."

I said, "Well, the metaphor works. It says that life works even without the 'expected outcome.' That's what you're telling me, isn't it? That your life's on the compost heap and you're using it now to nourish a new garden."

He shook his head and laughed. "Enough with the garbage. I get the point."

"What do you expect from me?" I asked. "I majored in botany in college."

Working Out with the List

I got home around 11:30 P.M. The house was quiet. Everyone was asleep, but I was wound up tight. I went upstairs, put on my running shorts and shoes, and headed down to the basement to run a couple of miles on the treadmill. I figured a good workout would help get rid of some of the tension.

I turned on the lamp next to the couch. The light made the room feel warm and cozy. I did leg stretches against the drainage pipe that stood next to the treadmill, then got on the floor and did some back stretches. I then sat quietly, just following my breath. I felt more relaxed, but still had a substantial knot of anxiety in the middle of my chest. I trusted the treadmill would wash enough endorphins through me to settle me down. Sure enough, after thirty minutes of good, hard running,

I felt better. I was ready to clean up and go to work on the list.

While I'd prepared for countless classes, given lectures, worked up translations, and quoted many spiritual sources, including Hasidic tales and Talmudic aphorisms, I had never written a list of spiritual insights for someone who was dying. I searched my heart, asking, *how do I prepare myself for something like this?* I prayed, and in the end simply accepted the fact that this was what Rick wanted. He'd picked me because I was available and in his life. Somehow that made me worthy enough to be up to the task.

I knew where to look. I chose a simple format. I would give him a source translation from the Hebrew and then add some of my understandings of the text based on classic commentaries. It was important to transmit the material as authentically as possible. Rick deserved the best I could provide.

I started out in the Talmud, with Yoma 86:

> *Confession*:
> It is written, *Happy is the person whose transgressions are covered* (Psalm 32:1). But it's also written, *Somebody who covers up their transgression will not succeed* (Proverbs 28).
>
> There seems to be a contradiction between the two scriptures, but in truth there is no contradiction. . . . Rav Zostra Bar Tuvia says in the name of Rav Nachman, *Behold the first scripture is talking about transgression from one person against another person.* (Those are covered with a public confession.) *The other scripture refers to those transgressions between an individual and God.*
>
> The point here is that when you do things against others, you ought to make it known to them. This brings about forgiveness. But the things you need to get straight with God need to be confessed in the privacy of your heart.
>
> *Effort:*
> *Return to Me, and I will return to you* (Malachi 3:7). The point here is that when you do your Teshuvah, God will be there to give you divine help in your task.

Open for Me like the little eye of a needle, and I will open wide for you the gates of heaven (Zohar 3:20A). Our efforts may seem small. We may have power to open ourselves no more than the needle's eye, but even that opening can open the gates of heaven.

Love and mercy are at the root of forgiveness:
As I live, says the Lord God, I have no pleasure in the death of the wicked, but that they turn from their ways and live (Ezekial 33:11). God is always ready to forgive us. But to find that forgiveness, we have to discover that turning away from our past gives us a new way to live.

Patience is part of forgiveness:
For the sake of my name, I will be patient. And for My praise, I will restrain [anger] from you, that I not cut you off (Isaiah 48:9). Even though it took a long time to get ready to seek forgiveness, even though so much happened, we are not cut off.

I looked at the list, felt satisfied with my progress, and called it a night. It was 1:45 A.M. I got up from my desk and climbed the stairs. As my head touched the pillow, I fell right to sleep. My last thought was of Rick's glowing face.

The Search

The following Thursday night I headed out, list in hand, to find Rick. I drove up the West Side, making a pass by the West Side Highway. It was still pretty early, but a couple of young kids were already working the traffic. Driving into the Village, I parked in a lot off Houston and headed out on foot. I roamed the side streets, window-shopped the restaurants, and cut by the Bitter End on Bleecker. After an hour it was getting dark. I checked into Tower Records on Broadway. Still no luck. Finally, I made my way over to Christopher Street which was packed with overage hipsters and young boys out strutting the evening stroll. By the train station I sidestepped a homeless man urinating in a corner alcove off the edge of the sidewalk.

After an hour and a half of exercise, I hoofed it back to the parking lot and drove up to Times Square, leaving my car at the Park 'N Lock on 42nd Street. I cruised the video parlors, the Port Authority Bus Terminal, and a good number of shops that line 42nd Street and 8th Avenue. I ran into a couple of girls who I thought knew Rick, but had no luck. Disappointed, I gave up for the night. I wasn't worried though. Rick had made it very clear he was a loner.

I once invited him to come over to the house, figuring that a home-cooked meal and some relaxation wouldn't be such a bad idea. He said, "Thanks, but I'll pass on the invitation. I really don't have the time."

"Okay," I said, "the invite's an open one. What do you mean you don't have time?"

"Look, when I'm feeling well, this is where I'll be. I don't know how much time I have. If I'm feeling good, we can meet each other here. But going to Brooklyn will blow an evening that's better spent here. For me, socializing is over."

I didn't push it. I simply took him at his word. But I was also aware that opening a door in his heart to a family at this stage in his life would be difficult. A family, playful children, a mother, a father—all of these represented worlds and experiences that had brought him a lot of misery. Coming to my house could churn up too many memories.

Another time, when I asked him about his family, he matter-of-factly said, "Yehudah, I come from a very traditional family in a very small town. Everybody knows everybody else. Everybody found out I was gay, and I mean everybody. It was clear I no longer belonged there. My mom tried to accept me, but my dad . . . well, he couldn't handle it. My brother somehow thought I was a threat to his manhood. So I left. I wish it was different. When I called and told them I had AIDS, it didn't move them. They told me not to call again."

A legacy of rejection, abuse, and scorn delivers up so much pain that it's no surprise to see so many kids hustling to survive. Even with all the violence out on the street, they feel safe there. After all, they are away from their abusers and they are no longer rejected. We might not be able to understand their choice of fate, but none of us should be so proud to think we couldn't be broken just as easily. We ought never to forget that trouble could just as easily have worked its way through the basement window and up the back stairway in our own houses.

I didn't know how to respond to what Rick had told me about his family, so I just hugged him. Inside I twisted. Instinctively he said, "It does hurt. It hurts a lot, but I've done my share of trouble too. I'm not going to get to fix it all up, but at least I'm not running from myself anymore. I've accepted things for what they are. It's easier that way."

So when Rick disappeared, I too, accepted things for what they were. I couldn't visit him in the hospital. I'd never know when he'd be going in. I wanted him to come over, but I knew he wasn't going to visit. I wanted to find him, but I knew I had to leave our meetings to fate. It was a hell of a way to do business, but the toughest part was learning to accept it.

I went back to my car. It had started to rain, and the oil and water misted up off the street and smeared my windshield with a rainbow sheen. As I drove home, I remembered something I learned long ago: *The biggest obstacle to changing ourselves is our own discouragement.*[1] At least Rick wasn't discouraged. His motivation was like a pure arrow guiding his life. Good things ought to come out of childhood: love, hugs, cuddles, laughter, understanding, and some fun thrown in. Kids like Rick never got that. What they got were heavy doses of fear. Somehow, Rick was putting his share to good use.

Confessing Your Actions in Public

I finally found Rick a month later. He was working the street, talking to young hustlers, plying his trade, doing his own private Teshuvah. The air signaled the onset of fall. In another month, the pretzel vendors with their briquettes would be out in full force in the city.

Rick was halfway up the block from the Port Authority. He had sandwiched two kids into a doorway that stood between an all-night nude dance theater and a peep-show and porn-video parlor. The street was filled with lost kids hanging out, dealers, assorted hookers, commuters, homeless people, occasional psychotics, street-corner preachers, vendors handing out leaflets, and patrons of the theater district on their way to gourmet restaurants and five-star Broadway shows. This was, after all, Manhattan.

I slipped up right beside Rick and joined the meeting in the doorway. I recognized one of the kids. His name was Eric. I had spoken with him a couple of times uptown. I received nods of recognition.

Rick continued talking: "No, you guys listen to me. You don't see me for a while, and you think it's a joke. You assume I was in Rikers, in prison. You just figure I did some time or was living with some john, right?"

They both gave him a look that said, *Yeah, so what else is new?*

Rick went on. "So how do you think I'm looking?" He did a quarter pirouette and sashayed his hips. "Think I can still pull down some good tricks? Do I still got the looks?"

They both looked a bit bewildered.

"Come on. Am I good or not? You're a couple of evil girls. You tell me who's hot. Am I hot?" He puckered up and blew them a kiss.

They laughed until they saw me staring hard at Rick. Then they picked up that something wasn't right with the picture.

Eric took the lead. "Okay, Rick. What's up? What you trying to prove here? You're pushing something."

But Rick had his attention and wasn't about to give in easily. "So you tell me. I mean, you know me. How do I look?"

Eric shook his head and said, "You smoking something? Is that it?"

Rick eased up a bit. He smiled and said, "No more smoking for me. I just want to know what you think."

"Okay, you still got it," Eric finally admitted.

Rick sighed, "That's what's so weird about it. I look good." He paused, took a breath and quietly said, "I've got it. I've got AIDS. I'm not just HIV-positive. I'm real sick. I'm probably dying."

It's moments like this you don't easily forget. I looked again at this scene, feeling as if I were hovering outside my body. Rick's words made the air feel sticky and thick. I felt his heroic effort, his attempt to attach his fear and hope to his words and stick them on the walls of Eric's and his sidekick's hearts. I shuddered. What does it feel like to say things and know someone's life could depend on it? A chill wrapped around my heart like a cold vapor. I thought, *Will his sacrifice now find favor in God's sight? Would the cracks in his soul and heart find a measure of healing and peace?*

Before he got AIDS, Rick had his foot down on the accelerator of life. Before he danced with the angel of death, he thought life was death and death was life. Now he embraced his pain and gave great dignity to each passing day. He was gearing up for that big day that comes to all of us, but sooner for Rick than for most. His work now was at the scene of the crime, in the same territory where he was brought down. He brought his confession back to where he saw the beginning of his fall. When I was a little kid I learned, *Know from where you came, where you are headed, and before whom you must give an account for your life.*[2] From where I sat, he had those three bases covered. Maybe with God's mercy and grace, he would steal home.

"We all get unlucky," Eric said.

"I'm not talking about luck, guys," Rick countered. "I'm talking about getting off the streets. Don't you understand turning tricks gave me AIDS? I've been in and out of the hospital. I'm sick. I used to think the same as you: *It ain't going to happen to me. I'm cool. I'll watch myself.* Look here, I'm standing with one foot in the grave. The next time I go in the hospital, there's a good chance I'm not coming out."

Eric just looked at him and shook his head. "I'm sorry you're sick. I know it's bad, but I know the score. I'm careful." He pulled out a couple of condoms from his front pocket. "See, I know."

Eric's sidekick, a kid who looked no more than seventeen, just stood there with his hands awkwardly jammed into his front pockets. Rick took in all of Eric's resistance and remained unmoved. After all, a year ago, in what seemed like another lifetime, he was an Eric. On top of the world. Turning $100 tricks as if there was no tomorrow. Only now he knew that tomorrow *does* come, and so does the end.

"Eric, at least go in and get tested. It's completely private. Do that. Find out."

"I don't need no doctor," Eric replied.

"I know," Rick replied. "I was afraid too. I didn't get checked until I was real sick. If I had gone in earlier, I probably could have responded better to the medicine. Don't be afraid to find out. One way or the other you're going to find out. And the sooner you face it the better."

Eric shrugged and said, "Maybe." His sidekick just looked uncomfortable.

Rick said, "*Maybe* means you'll think about it. Good. But think fast, girls, 'cause it's no fun finding out you've been positive for a long time and could have helped yourself but didn't."

Eric pulled back and took a step out toward the street. "Gotta go. Take care of yourself, Rick." The sidekick moved with him.

Rick said, "I hope I see you again. I hope you'll try."

Eric came back and gave Rick a hug, then faded with his sidekick into the flow of street traffic on 8th Avenue.

Rick turned to me and flashed a big smile.

I said, "So this is what you do for a living."

He just nodded. I handed him the list and said, "You want to get something to drink and we can talk?"

He was slowly scanning the paper. He looked up and said, "This is great. I've got to read this tonight." Looking at me he added, "I'm real tired."

I said, "I understand. So, tonight's off. But I've been on the lookout for you. You're not easy to find."

He lifted his eyebrows and said, "I know. How about we get together next week at that natural food place in the Village. Say next Thursday night. By then I'll have some questions."

"Okay, let's say around 8:30. That way you can get back to work if you want."

He laughed and said, "You're on."

I gave him a hug. "You might not have gotten too far with Eric, but you moved me."

He said, "With the Erics, it takes time. I'll see him again. This wasn't the end of it. Besides, he hung around to listen. Other kids see me coming and they split. Okay, *ciao*, Yehudah."

"Adios, amigo. Vaya con Dios."

"You too."

Ten minutes later I was back in my car. I felt beat. The guilty voice inside me started up and said, "Yehudah, if Rick can stay out here, you can give it a few more hours. What's wrong with you?" Then the voice that tries to look out for my own good said, "You're tired and you have to process all this. You're not going to be of any use if you're not on deck. It's been a long day. Get some rest. Go home. Tuck your kids in bed." I headed home.

On the drive back, I thought of a friend of mine who's been HIV-positive for about twelve years, but completely symptom-free. A few years ago, he told me he spent a good portion of his time taking his sick friends on special trips. He tended to them. He nursed them and gave them the best care he could provide. We were talking on the phone last summer, and I asked him, "Who are you taking on a trip next? Where's the next destination?"

"I don't do that anymore," he replied.

"Why not?" I asked.

"All my friends who needed that died. There's nobody left."

I held that conversation in my head until I got home. It started to rain lightly. I stood for a moment underneath the silver maple tree in front of my house, listening to the raindrops fall on the leaves. I thought the sky was crying.

Anybody Seen Rick?

The following week I was filled with anticipation. I'll admit I was pretty attached to Rick. The prospect of our spending time deep in talk was spiritually uplifting, and I felt I had to prepare myself mentally for such an encounter. I do try to give my all to everyone I meet, but the quality of this conversation required extra effort. I had to reach inside and pull out my best understandings.

In preparation for our meeting, I added a couple of miles to my jogging route, extending the run all the way down to Avenue Z, giving me more time to think. I put in extra hours studying traditional texts on Teshuvah in the backyard at the old redwood picnic table.

I thought a lot about my father, a physician, who had passed away the previous year. I drew strength from remembering the endless conversations he had on the telephone with patients who were struggling with their lives. I called my mom, talked with my sister, played with my kids, and took long walks with my wife. Finally, Thursday night arrived.

At about 8:25, I popped into the restaurant Rick had suggested, ordered a Dr. Browns Creme Soda, and settled in at a table that sat cattycorner to the street. I relaxed and listened to the soothing meditational music that floated through the place. By 9:00 P.M., Rick still hadn't showed. Okay, he was late. It can happen.

By 9:30 I was working on my third Dr. Browns. I knew he wasn't coming. I paid my bill and hung out on the street for another twenty minutes. Rick did not appear. I went home, disappointed. But then again, I knew this was par for the course. Kids failed to show all the time. I refused to let the creeping dread leak into my chest. I just let it go, figuring I'd check things out the coming week.

The following Sunday, and then again on Wednesday, I drove around and checked out Rick's usual haunts. There was no sign of him. Another week went by and I started asking questions. "Anybody seen Rick? Anybody know what he's up to? Where he's hanging out?"

No response. He'd vanished. I thought, *Okay, maybe he's back in the hospital. I'll check that out.* The only problem was, I didn't know Rick's last name. I wasn't even certain I had his first name correct. I used to be amazed at how protective people were of their names out on the street. First names got changed to street names. Life stories, when given, got routinely switched around to avoid identification. I learned that these lies were thrown up to create a smokescreen of protection. Deception became another tool to divert someone's attention away from where you were going, although most of the kids I met had no idea where they were going.

Rick, however, knew. He had faced the twisted turns of fate that led him to the doorstep of AIDS. While he might not have worked out all his issues, he had done enough housecleaning to find some measure of peace.

My calls to hospitals didn't pan out. I hadn't really expected them to. Six weeks went by, and every time I thought of Rick my insides were awash with the kind of burdens that stalk my dreams at night. I didn't like it.

After three months I realized I probably wasn't going to see Rick again. I didn't want to think the best and I didn't want to think the worst. I just tried to see the situation for what it was. He was gone. I had no idea where or why. I never found out, either. Maybe he reconciled with his family. Maybe he took off to take his confession and healing home. Maybe he died alone. Maybe he'd had enough of the street and just got up and got off it. Maybe . . . The maybes were endless and he didn't owe me any explanation. If Rick hadn't been successful in turning kids away from the hustler's paradise, he was certainly majestic in his effort.

Holy Men and Old Cowboys

Fall was passing into winter. The sidewalks were etched with the dark stains of fallen leaves. The gray cement was tinged with browns and blacks, and the storm sewer drains were piled high with leaves and trash. With every strong rain, puddles quickly grew into ponds on the street corners, making it difficult for the elderly and children to get around. In Brooklyn, you walk everywhere.

I needed to get closure on Rick's disappearance, so I decided to take a day off and work on that. I wanted to seal our time together in a warm and secure place in my heart. In

Judaism, actions or deeds play a large part in an individual's service to God. A thought is best when attached to an action. It means taking that which is unmanifest and making it manifest. It's a fundamental principle of the process of Teshuvah. Rick implicitly understood this in his unabashed street confessions.

I needed to get away to sort out my feelings, so I drove out to the wharf on Sheepshead Bay on the eastern end of Brooklyn. It's a little marina filled with charter boats that will take you fishing on the Atlantic. Seafood restaurants line the street. The parking is easy, and walking around the docks makes you forget you're in Brooklyn.

I wanted to visit a special man who plays old-time country music with his pick-up amp every Sunday down at the bay. His music is a rough combination of Hank Williams, lonesome blues, and the mournful train tunes of Jimmie Rodgers. When I first heard him, I thought, *My gosh, here's a modern-day incarnation of Hobo Bill's Last Ride*. While I've never spoken with him, other than to find out he came here years ago from the Oklahoma Panhandle, his music soothed my nerves and stretched my soul outward.

I grabbed a park bench, bundled up against a stiff breeze coming in off the Atlantic, and took in the music. I went inside myself and worked on my heart. In a few minutes I was lost in a memory twenty years old.

I remembered taking a bus on a Friday afternoon from Tsefat in the north of Israel back to Jerusalem for the Sabbath. I was spending a year in Israel as a first step on my way to becoming a rabbi. I was about the only person on the bus who wasn't a soldier; the others had pulled duty all week and were on furlough for the Sabbath. The bus was old or at least in need of a tune-up. Every acceleration and shift produced a cloud of diesel smoke as we wended our way across the Israeli countryside. Some of the soldiers were singing and others were lost in animated conversation. We were a military camp on wheels.

The route flowed along olive and almond orchards. We passed by legendary kibbutzim and new settlements. Every ten or fifteen miles, the bus would stop. Groups of soldiers would jump off the bus to make their way down dusty roads, through biblical fields to their homes on kibbutzim or moshavim. Halfway to Jerusalem, we stopped for a solitary man, a beggar of sorts. He stood out in the road in a long dirty black coat. He wore a wide-brimmed black hat and carried an old bag with a broken zipper. He mumbled inaudible phrases to himself as he shuffled down the bus aisle. Before he sat down two seats in front of me, I saw that he wore under his coat several loose cardigan sweaters. What I noticed most were the pockets. He had sewn pockets everywhere so that the inside of his jacket looked like a makeshift utility closet. Every pocket had a bottle, all different shapes, sizes, and colors.

He sat down. The cadence of his mumbling picked up, and he began to draw the attention of other passengers. Reaching into his coat pocket, he pulled out an old sour mash bottle. It was filled with a bright red liquid. He held it high over his head. He laughed, took the bottle to his mouth, popped the cork with his teeth, mumbled a blessing in Hebrew that sounded more like a mystical incantation, and drank. He smacked his lips and pulled out another bottle from the inner recesses of his wardrobe. This one had a bright blue liquid in it and reminded me of the old milk of magnesia bottles that sat in our bathroom when I was a kid. He sipped from a third bottle filled with a green liquid. Time and again he would pull out a bottle, wave it around the bus, laugh, and mumble his incantation.

The noise level in the bus continued to rise with each bottle the old man pulled from his coat. What started out as laughter soon turned to derision, as if this old man became the focus of everyone's anger. The tension inside the bus became incredible. The old man kept pulling out bottles, laughing, and drinking. The catcalls rose higher and higher. Even the bus driver started yelling. Suddenly, the old man reached into his bag and brought out a whistle. He began blowing it, and the bus erupted. Some of the soldiers started to poke the old man, who only grabbed more whistles. I felt as if I was floating outside my body witnessing a surreal event or as if I had been rocketed into the middle of a Fellini film.

Somebody grabbed the old man's jacket and pulled his arm out of the sleeve. He continued mumbling while bending down and reaching for something between his feet. With what seemed like great gusto and satisfaction, he pulled out a poorly crafted bamboo flute. He brandished it like a broadsword in the face of his newfound tormentors. Suddenly, he put his mouth to the flute and began to play. The tune started off-scale, the sound as harsh as the energy that bristled throughout the bus. Three bars in, the melody shifted. The old man's eyes twinkled. The melody took on a poignant, ethnic sound, its keening rising higher and higher. The tune pressed its way into my chest and I wanted to cry. Looking around the bus, I saw that everyone was being touched by the song. Stillness reigned where thirty seconds before cacophony ruled.

In my astonishment, I turned to one of the soldiers and asked him, "*Mah karah?* What's happening? *Mi hu?* Who is he?"

The soldier simply said, "*Ata lo yodeah?* You don't know? *Ish kodesh hu.* He is a holy man."

I made a mental and spiritual note. I knew, at that moment, that all the stories about the holy beggars were true and that the world is full of disguises. If you're willing to look and listen, and not run away, sometimes, just sometimes, the layers get pulled away. The inner light then shines through. I promised myself then that I'd never look away, even if what I saw was something too difficult for my heart to bear.

With that thought, I snapped out of the memory. The old singing cowboy had lit a cigarette. He took a couple of drags and then wedged the cigarette down into the strings at the base of his guitar. He started singing Waylon Jennings's "Luckenbach, Texas." Most people just passed him by. They missed his song.

But I heard it, and I realized again that each of us has a song to play deep in our hearts. Like Rick and the mysterious holy man on the bus, we can create a melody that will bring us to the gates of anger and confusion, or take us to the threshold of acceptance and understanding. I also knew that most of the time we just pass each other by and miss the magic of our songs.

I thought to myself, it really is too easy to label the Ricks of the world. It's so easy to say someone's damaged, to write him or her off. It's too simple to run from a beggar's song because we think he'll make us dirty or tainted. In truth, we are afraid. We are afraid of other people's failures. We are afraid to look into the abyss, lest we fall in. But what if we knew that it isn't an abyss at all and that even in failure, there is hope.

Maybe if I wasn't raised the way I was, I'd be running from the Ricks and the holy beggars of the world. But I was taught that you have to be there for others when you know there's no one coming for them. I grew up knowing that caring for people isn't a choice. While I admit it's gotten me into some tough scrapes, I've also gotten to hear and carry forever the magical song in another person's heart. I've gotten to glimpse inside and sense the preciousness of another's heart, beneath the veils and illusions. I've been touched by the beauty of someone's song.

I got up off the bench, walked over to the cowboy, and dropped a five into his guitar case. He nodded his head. I said, "Thanks, podna," and then headed to my car. The sky was turning blue-black. A young couple walked arm in arm alongside the docks. A gust of wind kicked dust in my face. I got in my car and made a U-turn. The old cowboy stood alone singing his song.

Winter's Song

Winter came to New York. The streets were piled high with snow and ice. I got up one night and sat by the window overlooking the street. I thought about Rick. The snow was blowing hard. The flakes danced in the wind.

From that third-floor window, I watched the snowflakes fall, remembering that no two snowflakes are alike. Each has its own pattern. Some land on the street and some in the gutter. Some touch the rooftops and others nestle in the trees. I thought about life. Each of us falls into this world. We each have a unique pattern, shape, and size. But it's also true that where we fall is by God's grace, even if we fall into the gutter. Perhaps that's the most difficult lesson of all to learn: that in spite of our fear and pain, there is grace to be found in our suffering. Rick knew that. In spite of what anybody thought, he got beyond it all and made peace with his pain.

I went downstairs, put on my winter coat and boots, and walked out the front door. I stood listening to the snowflakes that were quietly dropping on my shoulders. I told myself that if I'd learned anything from Rick, it was that we seldom know each other unless we're willing to risk everything to tell the truth of our lives to another. Turning our eyes away from what is in front of us only hardens our hearts, and in the end, we only touch the cold steel of this world. We miss the early morning rain, the owl up on the ridge, our children's laughter, and love's gentle eternal caress and song.

STEP SEVEN

Living Your Forgiveness

DARREN'S STORY

Everything has its season,
and there is a time for everything
under the heaven:

A time to guard and a time to let go
Koheles; Chapter 3

An individual should not wonder and say, "How is it possible for us to do what we want and thus be responsible for all our actions?" The Creator desires that individuals have free choice and be responsible for their actions without being forced or pulled. It's forbidden for a person to be cruel and not be appeased. Rather, a person ought to be easily appeased and difficult to anger. When someone who sinned against you asks you for forgiveness, you should forgive with a complete heart and a willing spirit. Even if that person caused you pain and wronged you many times, don't seek revenge and don't bear a grudge.
(MAIMONIDES, *Hilchos Teshuvah,* Chapter Two, Section Ten, and Chapter Five, Section Four)

After speaking to others about our struggle, we continue onward through life, conscious of our great responsibility to make wise decisions. We must look around in the world and find ways to make positive choices for our lives.

We are now keenly aware of how we are responsible for every move we make. No one is forcing us to choose one way or the other, but we no longer consider choices that could take us in the wrong direction.

Being unforgiving in any way keeps us from making positive decisions. When we forgive someone, particularly someone who caused us pain, we pave new paths upon which others will travel the road of forgiveness.

We previously sought forgiveness from those we hurt, but memories of how others hurt *us* tend to linger. Our willingness to forgive is a sign that we have truly been transformed. Without holdouts and grudges, we are free to touch the sky.

The secret to gaining inner strength is to be strong enough to forgive. To forgive requires true strength of character, and the greatest source of our forgiveness is love. When people approach you for forgiveness, your ability to sense their sincerity reflects on your own ability to be sincere and forgiving to yourself. Choosing to hold on to our anger and pain keeps us away from the life we all crave—one filled with heart, spirit, and love. Holding on to anger only leads to scoring points with our ego and being cruel to others. After all, people who ask forgiveness from you are doing so because of their regret over the anger and pain they dumped on you. By forgiving them, you can forgive yourself and put an end to the pain that has damaged your own life.

Forgiveness is a great marker in life. It is a statement of our change and transformation.

Video Parlor

The entrance to Penn Station is next to Madison Square Garden and across the street from the General Post Office off West 33rd. At night, Penn Station is home to the homeless, and the video parlor within is a meeting ground for the lost. The station spreads out for what seems like blocks underground. It was 11:30 P.M. on a cool, crisp night. I parked on the back side of the Garden, east of the post office, and headed toward the station. I was out making my rounds, looking for kids in need.

I stopped to gaze up at the buildings, to catch a bit of sky. It was somehow reassuring to spot a star or two over the Manhattan skyline, especially before going underground.

I quickly cruised the main waiting area, which I call the hotel lobby. It has rows of attached plastic chairs with metal bottoms that are welded together and placed back-to-back. In the daytime they provide travelers a brief respite while waiting for a train. At night they become beds for dozens of homeless people who sleep sitting up in those chairs. The transit police rouse them every hour or two, and they shuffle from one chair to another all night long. I guess it's safer than sleeping in the subway tunnels and a lot warmer than a metal grate on the street.

I walked quietly by each sleeping body, checking for runaways. They weren't difficult to spot. After all, how many sixteen-year-olds are spending the night sleeping in Penn Station? From there I wandered over to the tunnels and spent about five minutes talking with the transit police on foot patrol.

It's always a good idea to check in and remind them that I'm looking for lost kids.

I moved on toward the subway platforms, which smelled of stagnant water and stale cigarette smoke. It had rained the night before, and I spotted a rat drinking from a pool of water next to the third rail. The subway station lights reflected off the oily sheen of the water.

As I walked, I tried to read the faded old painted signs that silhouetted the tunnel walls. They were advertisements for long-gone local barbers, tailors, and neighborhood clothing stores. Those signs represented better times, when life was less complicated—when being in the neighborhood meant friends and family, not gangbangers and drive-bys.

The tunnels were quiet. My footsteps echoed off the concrete. When you're alone at night in those tunnels, you tend to get jumpy. It's not just the rats that send rushes up my spine. Down in the netherworld I've run into some pretty off-balance people who like to be left alone. Some of the looks I've seen in people's eyes would put Jack Nicholson in *The Shining* to shame.

When I first started visiting *The Way Beyond,* I thought I had stumbled into hell. How else could I explain what I was seeing? Later on I didn't hide behind my mind's attempt to protect me. I took it straight on. This was reality—there was good and evil. I was there to resist the evil, champion the good, and above all, to try to be helpful.

I headed back toward the hotel lobby. I planned to look into the video parlor, but first I needed a cup of coffee. I popped into a doughnut shop forty feet away from the video game room, and even at that distance, I could hear the action. It sounded like the Fourth of July melting into Green Day.

Inside were a couple dozen kids working the machines. I've never found a runaway hanging out in the video parlor, but I've talked to dozens of kids who might as well be added to the statistics of abandoned youth. They might have an apartment to sleep in during the day, but they've got no one in their lives loving them. Daddy's long gone, Momma's beamed out, and little Junior's been working the streets since he started walking.

The irony of it all is that they are still trying to make it by mastering a skill. The tragedy is that making it means being the best player of Mortal Kombat, NBA Jam, or Primal Rage.

I got my coffee and wandered into the game room. Humped over a machine in a corner was Darren. He was locked into Primal Rage with another skinny kid whose name I can no longer remember.

The muscles on Darren's neck and forearms hung like thick ropes tied in knots. A mesh shirt stretched across his chest, pulled so tight against his muscular frame that I thought it might split if he made a sudden move. In spite of his build and intensity, he didn't look mean. As he worked the game, he was cracking jokes, laughing hard, and smiling broadly.

As I drew closer, I saw his hands flashing over the controls in a blur of motion. The real good players meld their bodies as close to the machine as possible. As one kid said to me, "You try to line up your body so you feel like your nervous system's jumping to the circuits in the machine."

I said to him, "I can't wait to see what happens to you when we jump to virtual reality."

He nodded his head and said, "That's when we disappear, man."

All of Darren's six-foot frame was focused into the Rage. The game revolves around a cataclysmic event that awakens monstrous gods and sorcerers and, as the game says, they are angry.

I peeked over Darren's shoulder and saw that he had picked the god Blizzard. He was in the final battleground, battling the likes of Savran, Chaos, and Armadon. The action was furious and Blizzard was ripping his opponents to pieces. I thought, *Maybe this kid isn't too angry. After all, he did pick Blizzard.* As the game instructions tell you, Blizzard is a noble god. His animal power and age-old wisdom make him almost unstoppable. He didn't pick any of the others, whose descriptions include "foul beast wallowing in filth for eons" and "cannibalistic god that eats humans in order to remain immortal."

During a sudden break in the action, I stepped in and took out a card that listed the services provided by the local shelter I often work with.

Darren shook his head and said, "No thanks, I know you guys."

I smiled and said, "Well, that's cool; now that we're finished with the formalities, let me introduce myself. I'm Yehudah."

Darren wrinkled his brow. His head moved back a couple of inches. "So, you out here tonight to try and save me?"

I laughed and said, "Are you drowning? I don't see any water. If you want, yeah, I can give you lifesaving lessons. But before I rush in and save you, I think I want to challenge you to a little game of Primal Rage."

I learned long ago that without some kind of connection and thread of relationship, you can't reach out and touch another person's heart. If it worked any other way, I could just stand around on street corners and give speeches to the hustlers.

He closed one eye and focused on me with a stare that said, *You got to be kidding.* "You? Play me?" he said.

I said, "What, you afraid to take me on? Afraid I'll embarrass you? Think I don't know this game? I'm too old to be quick? Is that it?"

That got him laughing. "Well, why not? This is a first. A rescue worker challenging me." On the street there are always sudden changes, so I've learned to do the unexpected. Humor and curiosity have the power to break through walls of pain and suspicion.

"Who you gonna pick?" he asked.

"Well, let's see, since you've got the only cool noble god in this game, I'd better pick evil incarnate to prove that the badder you are, the badder things get for the good guys."

He chewed on my little bit of moralizing for a couple of seconds. "It's just a game, man."

I laughed and said, "My kids say the same thing to me all the time. Okay, I pick Diablo. So let's see if you can save the planet before I burn it and you along with it."

I popped in the quarters and the game started. I got wiped out in less than a minute.

Darren turned to me with a look of satisfaction. "I thought you were good at this. I annihilated you."

"Of course you did. I'm lousy at this. I am too old. I've got slow hands and bad hand-eye coordination, but I couldn't pass up the opportunity. So again, I'm Yehudah."

He gave a snort and laughed. "You're crazy." He shot out his hand and said, "I'm Darren."

"So, champ, this is where you hang out. This is where you spend your life?"

Seriously, he replied, "I hang out mostly here and some other places."

I surveyed the scene. "Are you the best player here?"

"Some nights yes, not always."

I gently probed a little further. "How late do you stay here?"

"I usually go home around four."

"What's your mom say about all this? I mean, hanging out till four in the morning."

He gave a look that told me to back off. "She doesn't like it, but it don't matter."

I quickly switched subjects. "How long does it take to get good at a new game?"

The conversation wandered on for another ten minutes. I convinced him to give me a rematch. He called over a couple of his friends to have a good laugh at how bad I was. After another bad loss, our conversation continued, interspersed with bits of information about myself. I wanted him to know who I was, what I was doing out there, and what I had to offer. But other than that, I didn't push. I let Darren know who I was and that I could help if he wanted, and then I took my cue and left.

In *The Way Beyond,* kids are always suspicious. Many of

them have so many defenses up that it takes weeks to convince them you care. And the rules on the street are different. Imagine what it would be like if you were lied to most of your life. Imagine if the people you're closest to betray and abuse you. That would lead you to set up a minefield of defenses to protect what little bit of innocence and purity you have left. After a while, kids naturally close themselves off; they don't let anyone know them or see who they are. It's how they stay safe. The trouble is that they get so caught in the lying and the running from the abuse that they lose themselves. It's hard enough helping someone heal a broken heart, but what do you say to kids who have lost their own hearts?

Street counseling is always a tough balancing act. I like to compare it to something Tommy Lasorda, Hall of Fame manager of the Los Angeles Dodgers, once said during a TV interview: "I believe managing is like holding a dove in your hand. If you hold it too tight, you kill it. If you hold it too loose, you lose it."[1]

It's a learning experience. I've had to discover new instincts. For instance, by nature I'm a hugger, but out on the street you don't give a hug to a kid you've just met. Doing so means you're at best a john, or someone more sinister—a potentially dangerous person. Walking up behind someone you know and saying hello by tapping them on the shoulder can invite a violent confrontation.

What holds true with your actions also holds true with your words. Words contain great power. Out in *The Way Beyond,* a wrong word can push a kid further over the edge. At the same time, not responding can give an equally negative message—that you don't care.

Family Tradition

Over the next several weeks Darren and I continued to meet at Penn Station. In the beginning, I think he got a kick out of me. As time went on, a tentative bond formed between us. I hadn't been able to piece together much of his story, but I knew he hadn't graduated high school and was probably a small-time hustler. He didn't do drugs, he was fierce in defense of his mother, and his eyes burned hot whenever the conversation turned to talk of his father.

"Listen up, Yehudah. My mom has worked herself hard for me and my sister. She's raised us to be good people."

"I've no doubt about that. You're not hanging out in the neighborhood. But what's this?" I swept my arms around in a big circle covering every game in the joint. "This is what your momma raised you for? Where are you going, Darren?"

He smiled at me emptily. "Don't worry so much about me. I won't be here forever. I got plans."

"Okay, I've said my piece for today."

To my surprise, he had a comeback. "You? Finished for today? You're never finished. You've always got more to say."

I grinned and nodded. I wasn't going to lie.

He continued. "It's me, my momma, and my sister. My dad . . ." His eyes narrowed. "He knows better than to ever show up again. I'm not a little kid anymore." His muscles flexed.

Darren's words jumped at me like a live wire snaking on the ground. Our society cuts a lot of slack for adults who hurt children. And Darren was obviously one of the kids who was hurt because of that. He was carrying a lot of misery and pain. It was not something he would ever forget. But left to itself, that pain could turn into an incubus that would eat holes in his heart.

I reached out and put my hand on his shoulder. He shuddered and then instantly relaxed. I told him, "I know that whatever he did was beyond bad, but you can't let the darkness win."

He gave me a puzzled look. "What do you mean, win? I'm not like him."

"Listen, Darren, this is the real tricky part." I took a deep breath and went on. "The stuff your dad did to you has got you spending your life out here in Donkey Kong–land. Your anger is keeping you from going after dreams for your own life. When your dad hurt you, you labeled yourself 'loser' and 'damaged goods.' It put you out of your game plan. You're going to have to forgive yourself for your choices and accept what happened. Maybe it's time to see yourself as you really are rather than playing video games while you wait to get revenge. You'll just end up a victim. Your dad was probably someone else's victim. Maybe you can put an end to the family tradition. Maybe you can gather all your good points rather than just holding on to all that anger and pain. Look, it's up to you. You can let it burn in your stomach or take an antacid, treat yourself to a milkshake, and go after your dreams."

Darren's glare softened. "Maybe you're right."

I might have set off my self-indulgent rocket ship with that speech, but I couldn't help myself. I used to rationalize giving speeches like that by saying noble things like, *Somebody has got to do it.* Now I know that's not the reason at all. You see, I had a father too. He raised me to be the way I am by his own example. Family traditions run deep.

I sighed and said, "We have to learn to be strong. The secret to gaining strength is to be strong enough to forgive. Somewhere along the line, you're going to have to find a measure of forgiveness for your dad and a load of forgiveness for yourself."

He shook his head. "Sometimes you sound like a book."

I laughed. "Well, as a matter of fact, I did write those last sentences. It's something I'm working on."

"They're good," Darren said with an approving nod.

"One more thing," I added.

Darren recoiled a bit and said, "What?"

I smiled and said, "Nothing too heavy. Just that it was good talking with you. I know it wasn't easy talking about all that stuff."

Mr. Trouble

I learned long ago that there is no timetable to the healing of the spirit. Perhaps I can best explain how I grew to understand this through the words of Rabbi Uri of Strelsik.

He taught, "A person is like a tree. If you stand next to the tree, constantly watch it, and don't move your eyes from it in order to see how much it has grown, you will see nothing at all. But if you look after it, prune it a little, and take care of its dead branches, over time the tree will sprout new growth and grow. So too with each of us. All we need is to remove the obstacles that keep us from the path of good, and in time we will grow. But it's not possible to constantly examine how far we are growing on the path of good."[2]

In my book, a good helper is a good gardener, someone who keeps out the weeds and lets the garden grow. That's what I try to do. The trouble with that formula is that out in *The Way Beyond,* you're rarely given enough time to weed anything in the garden. Sometimes, though, the grace of God shines on you.

It was 2:15 A.M. I had just lost another game of NBA Jam. I had run with Ewing and Starks, but never stood a chance against Barkley and Johnson. I'd been blown out. The video clips in the game thundered *Boomshakalakah* and *He's on Fire.*

After the game, Darren and I moved away and stood off in a corner. He was sipping some Sprite and I was blowing on a cup of bitter coffee topped off with chemical sweeteners and milk. I'd been pushing on him to get enrolled in a GED program.

"Listen, Darren, you've got to finish high school and move on past this scene. You're bright, and I want you to know that."

I handed him a list of places that offer GED programs. "Take a look at this list. I can call ahead for you and let them know you'll be making an appointment. What do you say?"

He glanced up and down the list. "So all I have to do is go a few days a week and study? Then take a test and I'm out of high school?"

We seemed to be getting somewhere. "This is the deal. You study. The people who run these programs will teach you what you don't know. It's going to take time and hard work, but you'll feel good about yourself if you do it. You can even go to community college after you get your diploma. Who knows, maybe you'll become a computer engineer and design games for Sega."

Shuffling a bit, he carefully folded the paper and put it in his pocket. "I don't know, Yehudah. I've got to think about it."

I moved to affirm him. "Right. You've got to think about it because it's important. I've got faith in you, kid. I know you're smart and talented. Look at it this way: You haven't beamed out on drugs, you communicate well, and you've got skill. You know the score and you haven't gotten messed up with the police. But now I want to see something happen in your life. Somebody's got to lean on you. Somebody's got to tell you, in spite of whatever's happened to you, that you can go for your dreams. Down here, dreams die. I don't want that to happen to you. You hear me?"

Darren did what he always did when I got his attention. He gave me a quick stare and nodded.

I pushed on. Out on the street, you have to load up conversation, counseling, spiritual support, and education all in one package. You never know how long you have with a kid.

"If you get up enough courage, you can get past all the stuff that hurt you when you were growing up—all the pain. Remember, the secret of finding your way in life is to accept what's happened to you, fix it as best you can, and be tough enough to forgive yourself for what happened."

I was always amazed that he let me give these lectures. He never would share much of his private life, but I'd seen enough kids to understand what he'd been up against.

"Well, should I stop?"

He chortled, "You're on a roll. Why stop now?"

"Just checking."

Darren suddenly turned and looked over to the entryway. An armadillo of a man had walked into the room. He looked about five-ten, weighed maybe 220 pounds, and had a shaved, bullet-shaped head nailed to his shoulders. From across the room, I could see the sweat bead up on his forehead. I looked at his feet. He wasn't wearing regular shoes—strictly army/navy surplus boots, black with steel toes. This looked like one tough, angry young man. If the video machines could have responded to his amperage, the whole place would have short-circuited.

I turned back to Darren and realized in a flash that Mr.

Trouble was coming our way. The muscles on Darren's neck corded up. Darren quietly hissed, "Be cool. I'll handle this. Nothing's going to happen to you."

I looked back. Mr. Trouble was getting closer. From ten feet away, I could smell the beer fumes billowing off his breath. When I looked into his eyes, I couldn't tell if he was drunk, beamed out on PCP, or both. But when he approached us, the hair started to ping on the back of my neck, my stomach knotted up, and my palms began to sweat. I shifted my weight back and froze. I'd been around enough in my life to recognize danger. Bullet-head immediately got aggressive. "I've been looking for you, Darren. I told you to stay away from Michelle," he growled.

"Tony, you don't know what you're talking about. Cool it, man. Don't tell me stuff you'll regret later. You're bent. See me tomorrow."

Darren's words just bounced off Bullet-head. Tony was obviously in a violent mood.

Instead of keeping quiet as I'd been advised to do, I stuck my foot in my mouth. Stepping in as the adult, I restated Darren's words: "Tony, whatever you've got planned, forget about it. It's not happening here. You can talk with Darren tomorrow."

Suddenly Tony was in my face. "Who you? You telling *me* stuff?" he roared. It didn't go over very well.

The whole scene escalated. A crowd even began to gather. The smell of violence always attracts the bottom feeders.

Darren's voice changed. It was menacing. "Tony, don't even think about touching him. I don't want trouble. You know me. This here is my friend. Move on him, you move on me. Either you leave, or we leave."

I was seeing another side of Darren. Outside he was cool and noble, but inside angry and violent. That naturally made him dangerous.

Tony turned and poked a finger into my chest. He shoved me, and then his right hand moved toward his coat pocket. A bad sign.

Darren snapped five words to me. "Get out of here NOW!" I couldn't move. Where would I go anyway? Darren immediately whirled and slammed his fist into Tony's gut. His fist made a crunching sound and Tony dropped to the floor gasping for air.

We left Tony lying next to the Terminator 2: Judgement Day game. It had all lasted less than a minute.

We walked out of Penn Station. I've been in deep trouble like this a few times in my life. I've been shot at and have endured a couple of assaults. The world never looked the same after that. The uneasiness is always there.

Walking out into the night air, I felt the familiar sweat tickling the sides of my chest, and then, an odd sort of calm. It's always that way with me. After a moment of violent confrontation, the rush of adrenaline somehow pushes me into a place of calm and clarity. It's only later when I think about what happened that fear leaks in. A few days from now it would get worse, then it would begin to fade, but the fear would always be there, just beneath the surface. Tony's imprint would always remain in the shadow world of my mind.

Saving the World

As Darren and I headed down the street, I said, "Nice friends you've got."

"Tony used to be all right," Darren said. "Now he's all messed up. I don't know what's gone down with him. He's gotten bent. I mean, Michelle's my cousin. He was making no sense, but he would have hurt you. No doubt about that. But it's over. He's not hurt bad. Tomorrow he won't even remember what he was so pissed off about."

I got serious. "Darren, you protected me back there. I'm deeply grateful."

"I did what was right," he replied.

I smiled and inwardly thanked God. There is nobility and good to be found in the darkness.

We walked out on 33rd Street, turned right, and walked around the plaza on the west side of Madison Square Garden opposite the post office. We chose a spot to sit by one of the locked back doors of the Garden. I was still trying to shake off the adrenaline. It felt like a pair of cold hands had ahold of my heart.

As if he could read my mind, Darren said, "Tony's a scary guy. Especially the first time you see him worked up. But I've known him for a long time."

"No doubt. There's a lot of scary people out here."

The sky was gray and overcast. Dawn was around the corner. The building lights cast dark shadows on the street. It had been drizzling earlier. You could still smell the faint odor of urine that drifted out from the corner doorways of the Garden. An occasional cab or truck worked its way down 8th Avenue. Solitary businessmen's footsteps echoed across the street as they made their way to the General Post Office to get a jump on the business day. They looked very lonely. It's true the city never sleeps.

I looked at my watch. It was hard to believe it was almost five.

I looked up and Darren was staring at me. "You okay, Yehudah?"

"Yeah, I'm okay, just trying to cool out from what happened. I'm not a big fan of that type of scene. I've been in too many scary spots not to get scared. It's gonna take a while till the fear gets out of my chest. Do you know what I mean?"

"I do. I mean, with so many people carrying something or packing heat, I either got to strike fast or run. I usually run. I've seen too many lying in the chalk."

I pursed my lips and got Darren to look me straight in the eyes. I was feeling immense gratitude. "Darren, you saved my life. Years ago, another person saved my life. When I asked him what prompted him to step in and rescue me, you know what he said? The same words you said: *It was the right thing to do.*"

"So what happened to that guy?"

I asked, "You want to hear his story? You've got some more time?"

He laughed. "You know you've got me curious. You know I've got the time, and you know you want to tell it to me."

For a moment I couldn't believe I was going to hang with him till after the morning sun, but I wanted to let him know the depth of my gratitude. "Okay, here's the story. It took place years ago, before I was married. I was working in northern California. . . ."

California's Golden Sun

I vividly remember how the late afternoon summer heat baked my arm as it hung out the window of my Volkswagen bus. It was the mid-1970s, and I was working near the Sacramento Delta in northern California, teaching and running a school program for the kids of migrant farmworkers. I was driving down a two-lane blacktop road in the delta. Levees and an occasional walnut tree were all that broke the horizon. This was a tomato canner's paradise.

The canning factories were running twenty-four hours a day. Downwind from one of the companies, the air smelled like a giant kitchen with smokestacks belching steaming tomato sauce. At night the harvest machines with their eerie lights crisscrossed the endless miles of tomato fields. They were like giant dinosaurs in a grade-B Japanese horror movie, consuming everything in their path. Rows of migrant farmworkers lined the metal walkways of those machines. They worked day and night, endlessly sorting tomatoes after the machines had ripped them from the ground and onto the conveyer belt.

The work was sweaty, dirty, and at times dangerous. Workers had to be careful to keep their hands out of the belts. The machines also harvested rats, a most undesirable commodity.

I pulled into housing camp 422, a cluster of small Quonset huts with metal roofs out in a dusty field. The license plates on the cars parked there read California, Arizona, New Mexico, Texas, Colorado, and northern Mexico.

There were sprinklers on the roofs of the huts, providing cheap air conditioning. If it was 110 degrees in the shade, it was 135 degrees or hotter on the sheet-metal roofs. The houses never got much over 100 degrees inside, midday.

It was early evening, around 6:30. I got out of my car and took a deep breath. The dust made my nose crinkle and twitch. The hot, dry wind made dust devils dance around in the fields. They jumped the irrigation ditches and then meandered off to the west. The grass rustled with a mantra that echoed like some lost ghostly melody.

It was Thursday, my night out to the camps. The program I ran at a local junior high school was in session from spring through fall—the tomato season. It had become part of my routine to visit the parents of my students.

The first day I arrived at the junior high, I met the migrant kids. They were a group of down-and-out students shunted to the side. In the social studies class I visited, the teacher had seated the migrant kids in the back of the room, where they cut and pasted pictures out of magazines. They might as well have been with the first graders. You couldn't blame the teacher, though; he didn't speak Spanish. The fact of the matter was, nobody except the Spanish teacher could speak with these kids. So there they sat.

Later that day I pulled them out of every class and started up a bilingual program. I hoped to eventually build an intensive English as a Second Language program to help move these kids into the mainstream. In the meantime, I taught all their courses in Spanish. It was no surprise to discover that these kids were bright and talented in spite of their nomadic life.

The Case for Another Reality

My family visits were extremely important. The families' emphasis on work was strong. Everyone pooled their wages to survive. Children worked full-time as soon as they turned fourteen, sometimes younger. They followed and worked the crops. There was no way out.

My job was to build the case for another reality—education. The parents had a simple formula: If your kids worked the fields, there was more money. Education simply wasn't relevant. Survival was relevant. Food was relevant.

If only I could pull a few of these kids through high school, I thought, *others would follow*. In my classes, these kids were being opened to a world full of possibilities. They had begun to dream of new jobs and better ways of life. Learning gave them hope, but the tomatoes gave them food. Life in the camps swallowed down ambition. Still, I was determined.

I was on my way to visit the parents of one of my students, Angel Rivera. Angel loved school and wanted desperately to go to high school. My visit to his parents was helping to build my case for Angel's schooling one brick at a time. I was making progress. He was coming back to school the following year.

The meeting lasted half an hour. After I said good-bye, I walked over to play soccer with some of the camp boys, another Thursday night ritual. I immediately ran into Armando, Genaro, and Miguel hanging out by the laundry.

"*Eh vatos, que pasa?* What's happening? Are we going to play or what?"

They replied, *"Si, mon."*

They sounded a little gloomy, so I asked, "Armando, what's up with you guys? You don't look like you're going to a party. What is it?"

The looks on their faces gave me that sinking feeling. Armando sighed, "*Muy malo news, Maestro*. Bad news, teach."

I took a deep breath. "Okay, guys, you all look afraid. What's happening? We'll deal with it."

Miguel turned his head toward the road outside the camp and said, "Esteban Morales is coming next week."

I opened my arms, shrugged my shoulders, and asked, "So who is Esteban Morales?"

Genaro scowled and spit. "He's real bad. A real bad cholo. The vatos are afraid of him. He comes here and he's the man. He'll change everything."

Shaking my head, I said, "Let me get this straight. There's thirty of you guys in this camp. He shows up, and he's the boss. Come on! How old is he?"

Genaro turned to me and opened his eyes wide. "He's fourteen. He's muy malo. You'll see."

I didn't get much more of a picture except that Esteban traveled with his mother and two sisters. No father. That made him an anomaly.

I decided to return to the camp and meet this Esteban Morales before he came to school. I made a mental note to visit him on Friday afternoon the following week on my way to San Francisco.

Low Riders and Murphy's Law

Friday arrived. When I pulled into camp, I ran into Julio. He was Miguel's little brother, seven years old and full of energy.

"Julio, *que pasa*? Where you going in such a hurry?"

Panting, he blurted out, "Hey, Maestro, I was going to get Pablo. There's going to be a fight. *Una lucha*."

Stopping him for a moment I asked, "Who's getting into a fight?"

He took off running, calling over his shoulder, "Esteban and Luis, but it's probably over. Estebán fights quick. He's good with his feet."

I followed him to the fight, but it was already over. Esteban had gone after Luis, kicking him once in the stomach. Luis immediately went down with the wind knocked out of him. That, thank God, was his only injury.

I scanned the area. Esteban was easy to spot. He was hanging out in the parking lot laughing with the Lopez brothers, a couple of low riders from Brownsville, Texas. These guys were mean drunks. You wouldn't want to run into them late at night, alone.

Their car doors were open and music was blaring. Estebán was sitting in the front seat of Pablito Lopez's ride. He was smoking, laughing, and generally acting important. After all, he was hanging with the vatos. He was cool.

I walked across the narrow dirt driveway toward their car. I could see Esteban looking at me out of the corners of his eyes. He wasn't going to lower himself and look me straight on. Under his Corona beer T-shirt, he was rippling his muscles, sending me a message.

I walked off the driveway to buy a Coke from the vending machine that stood outside the washroom. When I saw Esteban step out of the car, I walked over to him. Five feet away, I paused and smiled. "Esteban , you know who I am, right?"

He turned and took a step toward me, tough. "Yeah, you're the teacher."

I stayed in charge. "Good, I'm looking forward to seeing you in school."

He smirked and said under his breath, "Yeah, sure."

I wanted to let him know that with me, there was going to be no nonsense. "Just wanted to tell you that school's different with me. We study hard and we play hard. We'll spend some time talking Monday. *Nos vemos lunes*. Okay?"

He turned toward Pablito and blew a smoke ring. It floated lazily in the air. After watching it for a while, he said, "Okay."

Pablito and his brother didn't even look my way. It was their scene and their turf. They were macho.

I walked across the parking lot, got in my car, and headed out. As I moved out, I glanced back toward Esteban. His eyes never registered my glance.

Looking back, I realize I was young, idealistic, and too sure of myself. I could have used a quick refresher course in Murphy's law: *Anything that can go wrong will go wrong.* Things weren't going to work out for Esteban and me.

Verguenza

When Esteban came to school that Monday, he immediately stepped onto my turf. This was school, period. My way and my rules. Esteban, on the other hand, made it clear that he was the gang leader. He intimidated the other kids, so I rode him. I kept telling him to cut the crap. Yet being near him also gave me an unsettled feeling. The hair on my neck moved up and down like a crawling stream of small ants.

I soon discovered that Esteban was smart, very smart. But inside, he was smoldering. Getting close to him was like hugging a block of ice. Sometimes I'd think I had a good grip on him and could feel him melt a little, but underneath was only more cold. Then he'd simply slip away.

I kept trying to get the message through to Esteban that there was another way to go. Unfortunately, he didn't see it that way. Too much had happened in his life. He was fourteen and already invested in a life of violence. Little did I know that my efforts were hurting his *orgullo*, his pride, his machismo. And I was going to have to pay. I didn't see any of it. Nor did I see what was coming.

Summer school was in full session. It was a Thursday evening out at the camps and I was ready to play my weekly soccer game with the guys. Earlier that day Angel and Luis had told me that Esteban had been coming on real strong to Josephina and Amelia at lunch. I planned to talk with him before the game. When I got out to the camps, he wasn't around. I went out to the kids who were waiting for me at the soccer field.

I remember how the heat of the early evening breeze caressed my cheeks. In another hour and a half it would be dark. Over by the irrigation levee the crickets were starting to chirp. The dust was kicking up on the soccer field. It was time to play.

Soccer is the most exhausting game I've ever played. Even though I jogged three days a week, an hour of nonstop sprinting up and down a dusty tomato field always wore me out. We'd been playing about twenty-five minutes. I had just run down the field and kicked an alley-oop pass to Ramon. He sprinted ahead, took flight, and head-slammed a shot-on goal. It was an act of pure grace and fluidity. After I made that pass, I was doubled over, gulping for air, trying to catch my breath. I didn't see him coming.

Esteban's hands were like Vicegrips. He locked them down on my neck, and I went down. I couldn't breathe. My cells were already oxygen starved, and I felt the exquisite pain of blackout and strangulation take over. I remember thinking, *This is where I'm going to die.* Esteban was going to kill me. There were no words for the desperation I felt.

Suddenly, Esteban's hands let go. I lay there on the ground, curled up and gasping. My ears kept popping. Lights flashed inside my head.

After about forty-five seconds, I opened my eyes and slowly stretched out. When I got to my knees, I saw Angel by my side. His nose was bleeding, but clearly not broken.

He helped me up and looked at me hard. "Don't worry about me, it's nothing. You okay, Maestro?"

I gasped. "Okay isn't the word, Angel. No, I'm not okay. What happened?"

With great seriousness, he said, "Esteban tried to do you in, Maestro. He jumped you when you were out of breath. It was his *verguenza*—his vendetta on you. But it wasn't fair. So, I pulled him off you. His fist slammed at me a little, that's all."

I realized what Angel had done and said, "Angel, you saved my life."

He shook his head and gave me the bad news. "It's not over yet. You've got to fight him. A fair fight. Genaro, Luis, Armando, and Cesar are holding him for you. You've got to fight him now."

I snapped into focus and looked around. About twenty-five young men stood silently in a circle. Esteban was standing in the middle, glancing my way.

I remember thinking, *This isn't how it happens in the books. What's the teacher doing fighting with a student?* But I never thought about *not* fighting him. Somehow I knew that would be even more dangerous. This had to be settled now. At the same time I knew I couldn't hurt him. I was his teacher. I was being forced to teach Esteban his idea of a lesson.

I quickly calculated that I had a few things going for me—no weapons, for starters. Also, I knew that Esteban was a street fighter. He was quick with his feet and brutal with his fists. He liked to wade in kicking and then knock you down. After that, he started stomping with his boots. He wore big boots.

I looked over at him. He wasn't glancing at me anymore. He looked me straight in the eyes. He wore a bright feral smile. I realized he was really enjoying this.

I thought fast. In high school, I had been a pretty good wrestler. Esteban didn't know that. I hoped it was true that a disciplined fighter will always take out a street fighter. All I had to do was absorb a kick or a punch, then I'd take him down.

I moved in quickly. He threw a punch, which I sidestepped. It was followed by a roundhouse kick that snapped by my knee. He pulled back. His smile was gone. He spit at my feet and moved in. He whispered loud enough for me to hear, *"Nos vemos en infierno, Maestro."* See you in hell, Maestro.

His next punch slammed into my shoulder. His knee jumped up like a jack hammer into my stomach. It felt like it went clear through and bounced off my spine, but it was my opening. I wrapped my arms around him and lifted him up, did a quick leg sweep, and body-slammed him down to the ground with a thud. I was on him in a moment, pinning him in a full cradle. I tucked my head in tight against his chest, keeping my face away from his fingers. I didn't want him to scratch out my eyes. He was mine. Completely pinned.

Esteban had never met a wrestler before. He had never been pinned. He struggled and wiggled for two or three minutes, but I held on tight, every so often loosening my grip. I'd give him the feeling that he might get out, then completely pin him down again. I knew it was over. He'd lost, yet he wasn't hurt.

The guys standing around us started taunting Esteban You couldn't blame them. He wasn't so tough anymore. But I yelled at them to shut up. I wasn't going to have Esteban any more humiliated than he already was.

I held Esteban there in that dusty tomato field for what seemed like an eternity. I whispered in his ear the whole time I held him down. Reminding him how I was now in charge. He'd lost to me. He wasn't going to make any more trouble. He was going to work hard in school. He was to show me respect at all times. He had to acknowledge the new rules. If he didn't, I'd hold him down all night. I told him I had plenty of time.

He gave in and finally stopped struggling. He got up and

walked away alone across the field back toward the camp. His shoulders drooped.

I stood up and looked for Angel—my angel in this world. He was standing with Armando, talking. I walked over and grabbed him.

He backed away from me laughing. "Hey, Maestro, don't fight with me. You know I'm tough."

I gave him my warmest *abrazo*, hug. "Angel, I owe you my life. You truly are an angel. Your friends and I have a special privilege now. We know a real angel. What made you do it? Step in? Pull him off me?"

He smiled and quietly said, "It was the right thing to do, Maestro. It was the correct thing to do."

Angel and I walked back to visit his parents. I wanted to express my gratitude to them for raising such an esteemed son.

After this, it seemed that Angel had somehow been transformed. He continued to do the right thing in his life. It was as if by saving my life, he stepped into a new world for himself. His parents granted him permission to go to high school. He went on to graduate.

When you completely give of yourself, you transform the world. The Talmud teaches that whoever saves a life saves a world. Angel saved my world and transformed his own. He was willing to step in and help. By helping others, you help yourself too. Today he owns his own fast-food franchise outside of Bakersfield, California. He was the first one in his family to graduate high school and get out of the camps.

That could have been a day of great transformation for Esteban too. In his defeat, he could have also turned his life around. Unfortunately, he didn't. Esteban never came back to school. A few weeks later his family left to pick apples in the Okanogan in Washington State. When the camps opened the following spring, Genaro and Miguel told me that during the winter in Brownsville, Esteban had gotten in a fight. He'd pushed a kid down on a sidewalk and then kicked him in the head. The kid's head split open and he died two days later.

Esteban was sent up to do three to five years on manslaughter.

I remember how a sadness shuddered up my spine when I heard the news. For a moment I felt very cold. We never spoke about Esteban again. But to this day, I'll never forget Angel.

After finishing the story, I turned to Darren. He looked at me and smiled. He then interlaced the fingers of both hands, stretched out his arms until his elbows straightened, and popped his fingers. It sounded like popcorn banging in the microwave.

I got up and stretched. It was late. In another hour, the city would be in full swing. Traffic was picking up as some of the early work shifts clicked into gear to turn the Big Apple. Up over on 10th Avenue, the hookers were finishing up another night's work.

"That was some story," Darren said.

I nodded, "Angel was a stand-up guy. Good, honest, and determined to do something with his life. I see that same courage in you, Darren. I see your strength and your caring. Remember, the greatest source of our strength is our love. And the key to opening the door to our love is forgiveness. Now, if you can take a big chance and care about yourself, forgive the past, and seek a better future like Angel did, the door to your life will be opened for you."

Imagining the Best

Several weeks went by. I walked through Penn Station every Thursday night, but I didn't run into Darren. A month went by and he still hadn't surfaced. I asked around. "What's up? You seen Darren? Is he okay?" The replies were all basically the same: "He don't hang here no more." Or, "I think I saw him about a week ago and he seemed okay." Or, "I think he's hanging somewhere else."

Whenever kids disappear, I get nervous. There are too many bad things going down on the street to assume that they're okay. They never just go home to momma and papa and everything's fine. I had no way of tracking down Darren, and since the word was that he was okay, my only choice was to exercise patience and wait for him to show up. Besides, while Darren and I were close out on the street, I was not in his personal life. If anyone owed him something in this relationship, it was me. After all, he got me out of the jam with Tony.

So with Darren, I had to trust that things were working out for him. It wasn't easy. I worried. I got anxious. I worked hard to cultivate acceptance. In time, I let go of the notion that I would see Darren again. I didn't let the dark thoughts creep into my heart. I made myself imagine only the best for him.

Living Your Forgiveness

A few weeks later, I was making my way by the Port Authority. The late afternoon sun bounced off the windshields of the endless stream of cabs that snaked their way through Times Square. The wind blew over the Hudson and brought fresh air from across America. A pretzel vendor fired up his charcoal burner on a corner across from the terminal. The smoke made me think of my childhood, when my father and I used to go to football games in the fall. A few homeless people were pushing their worldly shopping carts around the corner of the bus terminal to set up shelter for the night.

I had gotten to Manhattan early because the trains were actually on time. I had an hour or so to kill before going to a dinner meeting. Crossing 42nd Street, I headed to a corner kiosk to pick up *Baseball Weekly.* I bought the paper, glanced at the headlines, and checked inside on the Yankees.

As I walked up toward Broadway, a kid carrying several large bags of takeout food caught my eye. He was stocky and powerfully built. His head bobbed over the crowd of businessmen and other pedestrians shuffling through the theater district.

Something clicked inside me. I shouted at the top of my lungs, "Darren!" There was a lot of traffic. No response. I broke into a trot to catch up. I got closer and after about five excuse me's on the way and a couple of nasty New York comments and glares, I was within ten feet and shouted again, "Darren!" The kid in front of me slowed, turned, and smiled.

Darren stopped and waited while I came up to him. We both were laughing. He held up three enormous sacks of food and said, "Don't damage the merchandise."

I said, "You or the food?"

He laughed, "Same ol' Yehudah."

I was like a kid seeing a long-lost friend. I shot out my questions: "Where'd you go? Where've you been? What are you doing here? How come you didn't leave word? Shoot, man, I was worried about you." I've never been very adept at being detached.

"Yehudah, I've got to make this delivery and take the receipts back to the restaurant. Then I'm finished for the day. I've got a little time before I catch a train uptown to class. So we can talk then."

He emphasized the word *class*. His eyes gleamed with a mischievous sparkle.

"Class?" I said, "What class?"

"I'm getting my GED." He said it with a big smile and a chest full of pride.

I felt a rush of goodness run up through my heart. I was about to get sloppy. Instead, I put my arm around his shoulder and said what I tell my own kids. "I'm proud of you. You're something. I knew you could do it."

And that was the truth. He had the courage to go after his dreams. My job was to be in his court and challenge him to have enough confidence to achieve them. There might be a lot of theories on acquiring self-esteem, but one key to believing in yourself is having someone say, *I believe in you.*

I waited for him outside the restaurant, then we walked over to a smoke shop that also sold coffee and soda. We took our drinks and headed over to the lobby of a nearby building to stand and talk. "So, get me up to speed. What's been happening?" I knew we had little time together. While our meeting was serendipitous, my sense was that he was moving on with his life. I fit into the past, but wasn't at this point part of the future.

"A lot's happened," he said.

"Well, that's obvious," I said.

"I'm gonna try to explain it. I figure I owe it to you. You were the one that kept kicking me in the butt."

I laughed and said, "I'm pretty good at that. Kinda like a pit bull, just chewing away."

"Yeah a pit bull with a preacher's mouth." We both laughed.

"No, really. All that talking we did. I don't know—it changed my thinking. You remember when you talked about forgiveness? About my father and that I had to accept all the things that happened and forgive myself? Well, at first I didn't know what you were talking about. You said I could stay stuck and end up screwing up my own kids someday. That's what you told me, remember?"

I quietly answered, "I sure do remember."

"Well, for sure I was real angry at my dad. I had my reasons and still do, but you were right. That anger was putting me down. It was putting me in the face of people like Tony and making me waste my life. Then I thought, *Here's my momma working and I'm just chillin'*. Why was I doing that? To get back at my dad? Then I had this thought that really scared me. I saw what could happen to me: I'd do nothing for a couple more years, knock up a girlfriend, and still be angry at my dad, but I'd be ending up just like him. Bang! I saw it.

"Yeah, my dad screwed up and hurt me and things went wrong, but I thought, *What good is it going around thinking* I *got to hurt him?* He did a lot of bad things, but I saw real clear that it ain't happening now. It's only happening if I let it. So, I decided, I'm not gonna let it.

"Then I got it. I had to forgive myself for being angry and screwing up, and for all the fighting and not helping my mom. Then I could forget it all and get on with other stuff. You know, forgive and forget.

"So I did it. First thing was to get out of that old life that was leading me nowhere. Just like Angel did. He got out of a dead end, and I did too. I just split all the old scenes. I wanted to talk to you, but I wasn't about to go back to any of those places you'd be or talk to any of the people you'd talk to. I knew you'd somehow figure it out. Then I took that list you gave me, found a GED program, got a job, and that's it. Here I am."

He looked at me. It was a rite of passage. In this old lobby in Manhattan, we were experiencing a celestial moment.

"Darren, you got it. Just like Angel got it. You've got perspective. You're seeing the truth of how things are for you and you're living your forgiveness. Let me tell you something deep. In Hebrew the word for *truth* is *Emes.* It's got three letters. You spell it with the first, middle, and last letters of the Hebrew alphabet. You've got to have all three letters to spell the truth. Take off the first letter and you've got no truth. In fact, it spells the word *Mais*, which is the word for death. To be alive and truthful you need your beginning, middle, and end. You need all your life. Never forget that, my friend. I'm so proud of you. You've got strength and courage. Forgiving yourself makes you brave and gives you peace because it's a soulful thing. A blessing from God."

Darren didn't say anything. He just reached over and gave me a big hug in his big arms.

He then tossed me a smile and said, "I gotta go now."

"Of course." I felt like I was in a movie with a great ending. I wanted to say something profound like, *May the force be with you,* but instead I said, "You're doing good, Darren. Go get your dream."

A year later I got a letter postmarked from Midtown Manhattan. I opened it. Inside was a picture of Darren, smiling with his arms around his mother and sister. It was taken in a city park. On the back it read, "I graduated. I'm starting community college in the fall. Thanks, Darren."

STEP EIGHT

Falling in Love with Life

LAURIE'S STORY

Everything has its season,
and there is a time for everything
under the heaven:

A time to love and a time of peace
Koheles; Chapter 3

The one who serves God out of Love . . . and walks in the pathway of wisdom—not because of anything in this world; not because of fear that evil will happen; not in order to get something good from it; but rather the person does what is true because it is true—in the end, goodness will come from it. . . . What is the proper amount of love? A person should love God with a great and powerful love until that person's soul is bound up in the love of God. . . . One cannot love God except through the knowledge that one knows God. According to the amount of one's knowledge will be the amount of one's love.

(MAIMONIDES, *Hilchos Teshuvah*, Chapter Ten, Sections Two, Three, and Six)

Eavesdropping and Inspiration

The New York subway system between 4:30 and 6:00 P.M. is crowded, stuffy, and confrontational. After a hard day's work, it's frustrating to join the thousands of other straphangers riding the train tunnels home. So some of the regulars from Sunday Night Class came up with the bright idea of holding class in Manhattan right after work. This way, they could leave the office and catch a nice talk that finished up at 6:30 before hitting the trains. They'd get home maybe half an hour or forty-five minutes later than usual—plus they'd also get a little nourishment for the soul. Not a bad way to finish up a tough day. The class was held Thursday afternoons in a board room at the company where one of my students worked.

Word of mouth traveled and the class turned into a lecture series titled "Opening the Gates of the Heart"—an eight-step approach to Teshuvah. Naturally, I always brought plenty of copies of the eight steps.

After one of the lectures, a few people wanted to get a cup of coffee in the Village and continue the discussion. I thought it sounded like a good idea and headed out with them into the late spring sun that cast just enough warmth to assure you that summer was coming. Winter coats had been traded in for trendy sweaters. The Rollerbladers had come out of hibernation.

I suggested a coffeehouse that specialized in exotic brews. It was on a side street near Broadway and Houston. On nice days, the owner put some tables and chairs out on the sidewalk. Inside, there were a dozen or so tables tastefully arranged in a rustic West Coast setting. The walls were covered with strips of weathered-gray barn siding, and the front windows sported an impressive array of cacti and exotic leafy plants. Interestingly, the place was run by an Indian, but the decor, down to the music, was unquestionably Californian.

When the owner saw me walk in, he asked, "The usual?"

I smiled and said, "Let's try something exotic today, say, something from Africa." Turning to the group, I said, "It's my treat on the first one."

We grabbed a corner table and they placed their orders. The conversation became animated as I fielded questions about personal growth. Everybody was holding their eight-step sheets from the lecture and firing questions. About a half hour in, I noticed two girls sitting next to us. One of them was eavesdropping. I couldn't blame her, considering the liveliness of the conversation. I turned to her and smiled, "Enjoying the talk?"

She giggled and said, "Was I that obvious?"

I said, "No, if you were, you'd have been falling out of the chair. And by the way, you're eavesdropping on the tail end of a lecture I just gave."

"A lecture?"

"Yeah, my name's Yehudah. I'm a rabbi, and I hang out a lot in the Village." Motioning to the others at my table I said, "These folks wanted to talk some more about it, so we decided to come here. Things are winding down. They're all about to head home, but I've got a few more minutes. If you have any questions, I'd be glad to answer them."

She extended her hand and introduced herself. "My name's Laurie, and this is my good friend, June."

Looking at her watch, she said, "I think we have some more time, and I am interested, if you've got a few more minutes."

I said, "Good, fine by me." June was staring at the wall—definitely not interested. I filed that, and then handed Laurie an extra copy of the eight steps. After another five minutes, the lecture group said their good-byes and headed home.

I turned my chair, picked up my coffee, and joined Laurie and June. As usual, my curiosity kicked into high gear. I believe there are no accidental meetings in the world.

The Odd Couple

One look at Laurie gave me a rough outline of what she was into. Her black hair flowed down to her shoulders. One side shone with a beautifully conditioned black luster. The other side shined too—purple on the outside layer and black underneath. Her right ear had at least five different colored studs in it. The rest of her outfit was very chic, but not very imaginative. She dressed in black, right down to her shoes. She even wore dark sunglasses. I was nonplussed by her wardrobe. After all, this was the Village. She was in uniform.

I noticed that she carried a big black canvas bag packed with sketch pads, assorted charcoals, and other colored drawing sticks that stuck out on one side. She was an artist, and hip. The bag, though, was too easy to snatch. I suspected she was from out of town. New Yorkers, after all, get an early education in basic street smarts. Her smile also didn't fit. It was too warm, kind, and engaging. People from New York simply don't smile that openly to strangers. She reminded me a bit of my sister, who is definitely *not* from New York.

June was another story. Her eyes were heavy and lidded. She dressed hard and punk. Her spiked hair was tinged green. She wore two leather wrist bracelets laced with steel spikes that would make a mess out of anyone's face.

June had slid herself into a pair of jeans and cinched them up with what looked like a bicycle chain. Her boots were army/navy surplus regulation. When she smiled, she looked like an iguana sunning itself on a rock on a warm afternoon. No doubt, June was from New York. She looked right at home in the Village. Don't get me wrong, underneath all that chain might be a fiercely loyal friend, but my first reaction was that June and Laurie made quite an unusual pair.

I took the lead and stepped right in. Turning to Laurie I said, "I see you paint. How long have you been in the city?"

Laurie looked at me quizzically and asked, "How'd you know I wasn't from around here?"

I smiled and said, "I suppose you could call it a lucky guess. But the truth is, your bag was a dead giveaway. Anybody could snatch it or cut the straps easily with a razor. You obviously still have it, but that's just because you've been lucky to not run into any purse snatchers. When you do, you'll switch bags and I won't be able to figure you for an out-of-towner."

She laughed, "Well, for a rabbi, you give quite a lecture in street safety."

June chimed in. "You don't talk like a rabbi. What are you doing out here?"

There was a certain wariness in June's voice. Giving her the benefit of the doubt, I interpreted her tone as one of distrust, rather than what it was tinged with—nastiness.

Keeping focused on Laurie, I replied, "Now, June is from the city. She wants to interrogate me. She's being careful and suspicious—a time-honored New York tradition." Laurie laughed an easy laugh and June just stared off toward the window.

I went on, talking to Laurie. "The truth is that I *am* a rabbi. Part of my work is in street outreach, and part of what I do is teach classes. I also have a weekly spiritual gathering at my home in Brooklyn called Sunday Night Class."

Laurie seemed interested in everything I was saying. I finished with, "So that's what I'm doing here, and what about you?"

"Well, I am an artist. I moved to New York about eight months ago. I've got a loft with some other artists here in the Village, and I'm working in a record store to support myself."

"Where are you from?"

"Cleveland."

For a moment, I felt out of place asking this complete stranger personal questions and developing a profile. But I couldn't help it. It's a habit from all the street counseling. No matter who a kid or young adult seems to be, I've got to determine if he or she could be a runaway, throwaway, or just plain in trouble. I kept up the questioning.

"So, you decided to come here straight from your high school graduation?"

"Gosh, no. I mean, I graduated and even took some art courses last year at a community college. It's just that New York has so many opportunities."

I groaned inside. How many kids hit the trail to New York or Hollywood seeking fame and fortune because *There are so many opportunities?*

"Bet your folks weren't thrilled at your departure."

For the first time, I saw a shadow pass over Laurie's eyes. Poof, the sparkle went out. "My parents are another story. Sure, they didn't want me to come to New York. They thought it was a stupid idea. They're very into their careers. They said it was a dumb move and that my artwork was a waste of time. But the truth is, they didn't fight it. They were, as always, too busy. I mean, they just didn't care." She then politely and firmly added, "Let's leave it at that."

I learned later that Laurie's parents had adopted the attitude of, *when you're eighteen, you're on your own.* They were so busy with their own lives that they didn't have time for her. They had cut her loose, lacking the emotional resources to care about her. Laurie had figured out their disinterest at an early age, so she spent her childhood nourishing herself through art. When the first opportunity presented itself, she split. Her parents hardly even noticed. Out of sight, out of mind.

We talked for another ten minutes until I could see from June's signals that I was running out of time. June said, "We got to go—get ready for tonight." Laurie turned her eyes up a bit at June's comment. She didn't seem to like being ordered around.

I said, "You ladies going out partying?"

June half-closed her eyes and glared, clearly brushing me off. "What of it?"

I saw we were at a crossroads. I smiled at June and said,

"Well, I'm not against partying, but let's not kid ourselves—there are edges to everything. And the club scene can be rough."

June shook her head, purposely failed to look me in the eye, and said, "So?"

I didn't want to get into an argument, so I backed away, but not before adding a final cautionary note. "Like I said, there are edges—and those edges can be drugs. Partying is cool, but getting stoned on weird designer cocktails isn't. You know what I'm saying?"

Laurie's eyes shifted away. She glanced at June and then, with a guilty smile, she told me, "Yeah, we know all about it."

I almost shook my head because there it was, clear as day. They partied with more than just music. I wasn't happy. When I see someone who could be in trouble, I can't just turn away. I sensed danger, so I made a decision to try and do something about it.

I pulled out a piece of paper, jotted down my address and phone number, and said to both girls, "Why don't you take the D train over some Sunday night and come to Sunday Night Class? It's a wonderful gathering. A great place to meet people. You probably won't get a place to sit unless you come early. But if you don't mind old carpets with holes and lumpy furniture, you'll fit in fine."

At that time, we lived in a second-story walk-up apartment on Avenue J in Brooklyn. The place had two bedrooms, a small living room, and a dining room. You could barely squeeze two people into the stand-up kitchen. My wife would always laugh and say, "That kitchen? I think there are closets that are bigger than that kitchen."

We loved that apartment. Our three children were born there. It was a magical place filled with constant visitors—a place for people to stay who were trying to get their lives together. Out the kitchen window we could see tall majestic maple trees growing nearby. On snowy winter days, we would stare out that window and dream we were in the country.

I slid the paper across the table and started to get up.

"Ladies, it's been a pleasure. It's time for me to go back to work."

Laurie took the paper, folded it, and slipped it into her bag. "Is it Rabbi or is it Yehudah?"

"Best to call me Yehudah. Everybody else does."

"Okay, Yehudah. Maybe I'll come. I've never been to a rabbi's house before."

I said, "It's a different kind of party and it would be a pleasure to have you visit. Don't let me down."

I got up. Laurie smiled and June snorted. Not everybody likes me.

Just as I was stepping away, two guys walked over to the table. One of them gave June a kiss. I thought, *At least she's on friendly terms with someone.* I paused and took in the elements of this new scene. Laurie's effervescence seemed to have evaporated with their arrival. In fact, she squirmed a bit in her seat and was working on acting cool. She seemed embarrassed by their arrival, as if she didn't want me to see her with these guys.

I made the guys out right away. One of them may have been June's boyfriend, but I certainly knew how they made their living. They were drug dealers—in the business. They weren't the kind of guys who dealt dime bags on some street corner, but I'd been around enough clubs to recognize their kind.

While I've made my share of mistakes and misjudged people and situations over the years, I've still managed to learn. I now can recognize hustlers, pimps, and drug dealers. Both of these guys were packing. I could see bulges under their jackets, and it wasn't just the way they eyeballed me and checked me over that made me suspicious. It was also the way they divided and swept the room with their eyes. Their every move was wary. While the boyfriend gave June a kiss, his partner kept his eyes on the street. They looked cool, dressed cool, but under that veneer I could smell the paranoia. They were so cool they were jumpy. Drug dealers are like that. I didn't want to hang around.

I have a rule. I will socialize with hookers, transvestites, hustlers, runaways, throwaways, and assorted street kids and the like. I don't socialize with pimps, drug dealers, and the johns who prey on kids. While it's true that I believe everyone has a heart and can make peace with God, there *is* a difference between good and evil. I've got to draw the line somewhere.

I immediately left without introductions, saying to Laurie, "I'm looking forward to seeing you Sunday night. No kidding, I think you'll really like it."

Consequences

As I made my way over to Christopher Street, I wondered if I would get a chance to really engage Laurie. She was like so many young people I've met—naive and on the edge of trouble. From the look of her friends and lifestyle, my gut feeling told me she was heading into dangerous water.

A lot of kids don't think about consequences—about cause and effect. When people ask them, *How could you have done that? What were you thinking?* the confused stare they get back is due precisely to the fact that the kids *weren't* thinking about what they were doing. It wasn't even in the equation.

When I was in high school, back in 1964, I liked fast cars. I drove a '64 289 four-barrel Comet Cyclone. It had a raked front end and chrome wheels. I fitted the exhaust with 'glass packs. You could hear me coming a block away. I never watched the speedometer, just the tachometer to make sure I didn't blow the engine when I shifted through the gears. My best friend cruised with a '64 yellow tri-power 389 GTO. It had two three-barrel carburetors and Hurst linkage. When he punched it, you got flattened to the seat by the force. We liked to drag race. We never thought about the consequences.

Then one night a friend of mine who had a Triumph Bonneville motorcycle took it right over the edge of a cliff. He died the next day in the hospital. That's when I learned about consequences. I was lucky though. I was raised with enough inner resources to slap myself awake.

Kids I meet on the street have no idea what's going on until it's too late. They don't just walk out there and start selling their bodies. They don't simply get up in the morning, head down to the street corner, and become crack addicts. It starts long before. When kids are growing up, they put their trust in the adults around them. They trust the fact that someone is going to be there for them. That trust is what is supposed to build their character. Take that away in varying degrees and you get varying degrees of trouble. The bottom end of the equation gives you both the perpetrators and the victims. But before the dark blossoms of trouble flowered in their lives, they all started out like deer caught in a spotlight—sweet and innocent, stepping unsuspectingly into trouble. I saw Laurie in that spotlight.

Children like Laurie, who grow up with absentee parents, are left to fend for themselves. The parents have opted out of taking any responsibility for raising their kids, other than providing a roof over their heads. No one is looking out for the emotional welfare of these children. Kids like Laurie are keenly aware that their parents aren't interested in them. Anyone familiar with family systems knows that these parents likely received little parenting themselves, but that doesn't make it any easier for the Lauries of the world. Kids need love, attention, and warmth; not distance, disinterest, and the cold shoulder.

Although I didn't know Laurie's life story, I'd been around enough people living on the edge to know that trouble was knocking on her door. I hoped she would show up Sunday night.

Sunday Night Class

Sunday night arrived. As usual, the living room was packed. The furniture was occupied, and there was hardly a space available on the floor to sit. Ten minutes into the class, I saw Laurie squeeze herself through the hallway door. Her eyes bugged as she surveyed the crowd. She saw me sitting in one corner of the room. I waved to her and smiled.

The basic theme of every class was that each of us can make a difference in our own lives and in the world. I said, "The class tonight is about falling in love with life. The question is, how do you do that?" I would pose questions to get the discussion rolling. "If our goal is to unabashedly fall in love with life, what do we do with our lackings, pain, and imperfections? If love is to be our motivator, how do we use it to find the courage to face our everyday struggles?"

The discussions were always profound. The comments that night were filled with incredible wisdom. One person said: "It comes down to experiencing gratitude that you are simply alive. Once you have gratitude for your life, you have courage to face your struggles and enough sense to accept your imperfections." Another commented: "I think the key to truly being in love with life is discovered by giving to others. By giving to others, you discover the love you have in your own life. Otherwise, why would you give?" Another profound comment was: "Doesn't it really all come down to recognition of faith? Isn't the expression of our love on the deepest level a statement that if not for God's gracious love, we would not have found life again, but despair?"

Laurie was drawn to this. Perhaps she felt a compelling need to fill the emptiness that dominated her childhood and cast her adrift, to find what she missed in her childhood—love. The parties, the drugs, the move to New York were all part of her attempt to free her spirit to become who she needed to be.

In a world filled with so much alienation and so many failed relationships, Sunday Night Class was a healing place for many people over the years. I used to read my students a page from Leo Buscaglia's book *Loving Each Other,* which speaks to people who are seeking, as Leo says, "Love, tenderness, compassion, caring, sharing and relating." He writes,

> *If you love, you are considered naive. If happy, you are considered frivolous and simple. If generous and altruistic, you are considered suspect. If forgiving, you are considered weak. If trusting, you are considered a fool. If you try to be all of these things, people are sure you are phony.*[1]

The class was out to make a difference in our lives. Each week I'd give out a life assignment to the group. It was always about making the world a better place, about specifically doing things that brought more goodness into the world. The question always was, "What can I do right now, in spite of my imperfections, that can bring me closer to being a servant of God?" What can I do to turn the corner and ultimately fall in love with life?

I'd open up the Bible and read about what Joseph said when he confronted his brothers:

> *And now, don't feel sad or guilty because you sold me. Behold, God has sent me ahead of you to save lives.*
>
> (Genesis 45:5)

I'd ask, "What's the message here? What's this passage telling us to do with our lives?" I'd frame the discussion by adding insights on a biblical passage from great rabbinical sages, such as the Hassidic master Rabbi Shlomo HaKohen Rabinowitz of Radonisk, who commented:

> *Behold, contained in the word* ve'ata, *which means* and now, *is the expression of the language of teshuvah. Even though you must do teshuvah over the misdeeds you committed, don't let that be a source of sadness. The way of teshuvah is not done in a state of sorrow . . . as it is written,* Serve the Lord with joy *(Psalm 100:2). Therefore,* ve'ata, *and now, when you do teshuvah, you are saying* ve'ata, *and now I am committed to teshuvah. I am doing teshuvah. I am not dwelling on my past follies. I am* now *in the present and I am blessed.*[2]

I would then ask, "In light of what I just translated, what does it take to be happy with our lives?"

One class, I asked everyone to spend the week finding ways of telling others that they love them. In class the following week, we reported what happened. Another time, we spent the week looking for ways to specifically compliment others in our personal and professional lives. Then again, we reported what happened. We also did things that encouraged the expression of our feelings and thoughts toward one another, like giving a gift or a card, or calling someone on the phone simply to ask, "How's your day?" It was powerful stuff designed to focus everyone on the importance of living each day in fullness. We discovered that even if we didn't grow up in families filled with warmth, doing concrete loving actions allowed us to cross a threshold to a new perspective where we could say, "I'm in love with my life."

That was the scene Laurie walked into. And like the rest of the group, she joined in and became a regular.

Futile Warnings

As time went on, Laurie began showing up at our home on the Sabbath. She enjoyed the talking that would go on and loved playing with my kids. We got to know each other. That was the upside. The downside was that she was still hanging out with June and doing a lot of partying.

I'd often bring it up when she'd be getting ready to leave. Once I came right out and said, "Still hitting the clubs and partying? Not that I have anything against partying necessarily, it's just, you know, it's that you're hanging with dopers."

She shot back, "Yehudah, I don't do drugs. You know that."

I just shook my head and said, "That's what a million other users say before they take their first hit. I don't mean to come down on you, but the scene can get out of control. Things happen. And it takes a long time to clean up once it does. So, why *do* you hang out with June?"

She gasped. "Gosh, she's my closest friend!"

I winced, "How long have you been closest friends?"

Laurie lifted up her eyebrows, thought for a moment, and said, "Maybe a few months. We hang out a lot and do things together."

"So you know her for a while, spend most of your time together partying hard, and now you're like sisters?"

She looked at me defensively and asked, "What are you getting at?"

"Laurie, it takes a long time to build true friendships. It takes a lot of work to know, love, and trust someone in your heart. Please don't take offense, but from what I've seen of June, she may be 'closest' to you when hitting the clubs, but it seems to me you live very different lives."

"What do you mean by that?" she asked.

"Well, you work in a record store and support yourself. You're working on your art. And June—do you even know what she does? How she supports herself?"

Laurie quickly answered, "She just gets so defensive whenever I ask her anything about herself, and I figure, why do I need to know? It's her business."

I tipped my head forward and stared over my glasses, "Maybe it's time you realize she may be involved in things you're better off staying away from."

Laurie took in a deep breath and said, "Hmm."

That "hmm" told me she'd had her doubts too. I hoped she'd reconsider hanging out with June.

When people are lonely and desperate for true affection, they cover up their feelings by dancing with words of love and friendship. I constantly hear kids say things like, "This here is my best friend in the world," or, "She's my number-one girl." It's not that they don't want close, lasting relationships, they simply don't have the tools to cultivate them. How could they? They never have seen it.

What they *have* seen is abandonment by those whose duty it was to protect, love, and care for them. That kind of upbringing has driven countless kids out of their homes to become part of the underbelly of the urban landscape. Yet given half a chance, some kids can make it. They can fall in love with their lives.

Laurie came back a bit tough. "I appreciate your concern, but I can take care of myself."

"Well, you can't blame me for trying." After she left, I felt that my efforts had been a bit futile.

Designer Cocktail

Several months later, I was coming through the door on a Friday morning loaded down with groceries. I had just gone shopping for the Sabbath on Avenue J. The apartment was bathed in the spiritual fragrance of roast chicken, carrots, and gefilte fish.

The phone rang. I picked it up. It was one of Laurie's club friends. She told me Laurie was in the hospital. The night before, she had been partying and someone had slipped something into her drink—some kind of hallucinogen spiked with Meth or who knows what else. I remember back in the sixties, some warped chemist laced LSD with a bit of strychnine to help balance out the trip. The Open Door Clinic where I volunteered at the time got pretty busy with people who dropped that and went right over the edge. I used to sit there and manage the phone from midnight to 6:00 A.M., talking folks down off bad trips.

What I didn't know back then was that I was an apprentice in training for life in *The Way Beyond.* When I think back to my life then at twenty-one years old, I shudder. I shudder when I remember my peers who had to be restrained in straitjackets because of bad trips. I shudder at the scary rides I took with them to the hospital; I shudder at their psychic pain. It was an extraordinary time to come of age. It was a world of body bags from 'Nam filled with shattered dreams and of flower children soaring on their exalted message of fading hope.

Laurie's friend reported that Laurie had completely freaked after drinking the concoction. Someone, thank God, had enough presence of mind to get her to the emergency room. She had been alternating between crying uncontrollably and screaming out in pain. At the hospital, she started coming down in the wee hours of the morning. She wanted to see me. Her friend gave me the phone number of the hospital and I immediately called.

The phone rang into the nurses' station. I was told by a nurse that Laurie wasn't allowed visitors until Sunday. Hospital policy. They wanted to make certain she rested and was stabilized. I extracted a promise from the nurse to tell Laurie I had called and that I would be there Sunday morning. Not being too trusting, I asked the nurse if Laurie could get a message back to me through her. She said, "That's not policy. I'm not in the message delivery business."

I knew I had to get through to Laurie. There was no way for me to be sure that this nurse would give her the message. If she *didn't* tell Laurie that I had called, what would Laurie think? I decided to use the persuasion of the cloth. "I don't want to bend any rules, but I'm her rabbi and she doesn't have any family in New York. I'm pretty sure it will make a big difference to her if you would ask if there's anyone she wants me to contact."

The nurse was silent at first. Then she said, "I'll take care of it. Don't worry."

I thanked her and hung up.

I headed out the door to pick up my kids from school. As I drove by the Avenue M train station, I saw that someone had spray painted *Speed Kills* in red on the gray metal support of the subway platform. I hoped the rest of the day would be more promising.

Spiritual Bank Account

Sunday morning came quickly, and I drove to the hospital. I met Laurie in the big visitor's room. It was actually divided up quite nicely, and we were able to find a spot where we could get some privacy. There were other people wandering around. Laurie wasn't the only one who'd had a rough night with chemical concoctions. Many of the patients were being tended by saints—their mothers and fathers. I saw great lessons in unconditional love.

Laurie looked weak—wiped out. She probably had lost five pounds and could have used a long shower. She had a faraway, dull look to her eyes from the medication she had been given to bring her down.

After sitting quietly for a moment she said, "Thanks for coming."

I immediately said, "Well, you look like you've had an interesting weekend. From the looks of things, the party wasn't too successful." Humor is a healing force when someone looks as depressed and down on themselves as Laurie did.

She almost cracked a smile. "You were right, Yehudah. I didn't see it coming. I've been partying too much and not thinking about me, about what I want and why I came to New York. I mean, I didn't come here to get messed up. I came here for my art. You know, to get my life together."

I got more serious. "I didn't tell you all that stuff so I could sit high and mighty and say *I told you so.*" I took her hand. "Kid, I was worried about you. It's easy to slip over the edge. Hanging with people like June and her friends makes it too easy for crazy stuff to happen."

She got weakly defensive for a moment. "They didn't give me anything. I don't know who did, but . . ." She sighed and then went on. "It was frightening. At least I'm sort of feeling better."

"So, what did happen?"

"I'm not sure. This is what I've been able to piece together. We were out partying. It was hot. You know how it gets. I got so thirsty and kept having guys get me drinks. One of those times, somebody put something in my drink. I don't know who and I don't know when, but when it hit me I felt totally lost. It was like my insides—like my feelings were being sucked down this black hole. I couldn't hold onto anything emotionally. It was terrifying. I couldn't function. All I could do was cry. I couldn't think. I felt like I was dying inside, but couldn't die. It was like I was drowning inside myself. I started yelling for someone to save me. The more I yelled, the more scared I got. I thought it would never end. It was a nightmare."

I let her unload. She needed someone to listen. The more she talked about it, the more she'd get perspective. Affirming someone by your gift of silence is often the best way to help that person work out his or her problems and spiritual dilemmas.

She sat quietly for a few moments, digesting her words. Then, as tears welled up in her eyes, she began, "You know, it's all very surreal. It's like all this stuff has happened and I'm talking about it in the past tense and feeling like that wasn't even me. It's like I had to go through this to turn over a new page in my life. It sounds weird, but I feel relieved. It seems almost spiritual even though it's real embarrassing being in the hospital. I feel like, I don't know . . . this is going to sound strange . . . but it's like God woke me up. From one point of view, I feel ashamed, but in another way I feel lucky to get a chance to see myself."

It felt really good to hear her talk like that. There was a spiritual transformation afoot. It's an exciting moment when a new door opens in your heart, but it takes work to keep it open. I decided to say something affirming and different—something I hoped she wouldn't forget. "Laurie, you just opened a spiritual bank account."

She looked at me. "What do you mean?"

"Well, it goes like this. When something profound happens, we get a rush of feeling and new understanding. The big question is, how do we stay open and remember how profound life is? It's pretty easy to do when we're feeling inspired. But what about the times when we feel closed and out of touch with our feelings and inspiration? It's not so easy to remember then. So what we do is open a spiritual bank account. Any time we are spiritually inspired and in a very thankful place, we ask God to help us remember that moment, to deposit some of that goodness for other times when we need to call on it. It goes along with a beautiful teaching in the Song of Songs that says, *I am asleep, but my heart is awake* (Chapter 5, Verse 2). Even when my conscious mind is asleep, my heart is awake to do the right thing. So even when I'm feeling down, uninspired, out of touch, I can ask God to help me remember that my heart is awake. I can take comfort in it. I can bank on it."

Laurie smiled. "I like that. It's like depositing a positive reminder in my heart for a rainy day when I'm for sure going to need it."

"I couldn't have said it any better. You've got it. So, what happens next?"

"I'm getting out of here tomorrow. I spoke with a doctor

yesterday morning and today. He told me I was okay, but that I should be careful who I hang out with—or, as he said, *who my associates are.* He also thought it might be a good idea if I got some therapy."

I nodded to myself. At least someone else was affirming me in all this. It was time for Laurie to move past the angry Junes and the desperate part of the club scene. The Talmud says, *The way you walk is the way you are led.* I put it another way: *Pick a new direction and pick a new life.* That's what Laurie needed.

She looked at me with a smile. "I suppose you can recommend somebody for me?"

"I can. I know a woman who works with people who have waltzed into problems and dilemmas like this. What do you say I make the referral? You can also run it by the doctor before you check out of this hotel."

Laurie got serious. "I really can't be the person I was. I mean, things have changed."

I gently answered, "Yes. Unless you want to dance with all this again."

Letting the words sink in, she stared across the room and said, "I understand."

We talked for another couple of hours. I asked her if she had called her parents. She said, "What, are you kidding? It would ruin their Sunday afternoon."

I said, "Well, I've still got to ask."

"Thanks, now you've got the answer." But she added, "You know, I've been thinking about them. I think a lot of why everything's happened is because of how I was brought up. Living there in that house with them, I felt really empty—like I wasn't even really there. Nothing mattered to them except what they were doing for themselves—like I was always behind them where they couldn't see me. Most of the time it was like they didn't even hear me when I told them about things I was doing. They said they cared but they never connected with me. They never once did anything really with me. I'd spend time at other people's houses and feel the warmth. Then I'd go home, and I'd literally feel cold. I felt that same cold when I

OD'ed. I tell you, Yehudah, I see a connection in all this. It's like if I'd grown up with different kinds of parents, things would have been different. And now, after all of this, I've got to make things different for me."

Sometimes things can't get straightened out in families. There's just too much difficult history. Estrangement and antipathy don't arrive at the doorstep of someone's heart and mind overnight. While Laurie, like every kid, needed her parents, she saw no benefit in reaching out to them, at least not yet. They wouldn't be there for her. Why call up to get lectures and recrimination or, even worse, disinterest and silence? There is a time and place for everything. It was Laurie's time and place to straighten out her life.

I left around midafternoon. On my way out, I dropped in on the resident on duty and gave him my name and number. We compared notes, and I told him I'd make the referral for therapy. His only comment was, "She's a good kid who tangled with a nasty drug cocktail." He had that right. He was glad she was going to have some follow-up. As I drove home, I thought that all in all, this might turn out okay.

I got home and went for a walk with my kids. Around the corner from our apartment was a house that had lion statues in the front yard. My kids loved to be scared by them. Later that evening, my wife and I baked some cookies, or I should say, she baked and I watched. I picked up a novel and zoned out for the night. I had done enough thinking for the day.

Falling in Love with Life

Therapy was a positive experience for Laurie. I didn't ask her much about it. It was none of my business. Therapy needs the benefit of confidentiality.

When she first shared some of what she had learned she said, "When I began my work, I discovered that I had massive chunks of my inner emotional life that needed to be developed."

I laughed and said, "Good job. The way you remember your therapist's words, maybe when you're finished you'll head back to college and major in psychology."

That got a chuckle out of her. "I'll let you in on a little secret, though," she said. "I *am* thinking about going back to school and majoring in art therapy."

Another time, Laurie said, "I've spent a lot of time talking about the whole scene I've been in, you know, with June and the clubs. It's not who I am anymore. What do you think of that?"

I said, "You know what I think. I think it's terrific."

Laurie continued as a regular at Sunday Night Class. She carried a journal in which she kept track of her inner work. She took a keen interest in studying a wide variety of spiritual texts. She built up a small library of the writings of Hassidic rabbis that had been translated into English. She drifted out of the club scene and out of June's life. She devoted more time to her art.

One evening after Sunday Night Class, Laurie and I sat on the living room couch. It was around 11:00. The crowd had left. My kids were asleep. Raindrops tapped lightly on the living room window. The drops beaded together to form tiny rivulets that broke free and made iridescent designs on the panes.

I looked out onto Avenue J. The streets were black and wet. An occasional car came by and emptied the puddles onto the sidewalk. I drifted for a moment back to my childhood. When I was a little boy, my mother, sister, and I would sit on the floor by the big picture window in the dining room on rainy nights. My mother would open the curtains and turn off the lights. The streetlight would light up the night in shades of yellow-black shadows. We used to sit there and talk, as we waited for my father to come home from his rounds at the hospital. We played a game—who could spot him first? Recalling these images, I felt how much I missed him. I felt a warm emptiness in my heart.

I hadn't spoken for a couple of minutes. I swallowed and turned to see Laurie staring at me. She had an inquisitive look on her face. I simply said, "The rain reminded me of when I was a little kid. I miss my father."

She nodded her head and said, "I wish I had feelings like

that about growing up. I wish I could miss somebody that strongly." After another moment she said, "I wanted to share something with you. Run it by you. Something I've been rethinking the last several months. I've been putting together some important things that I think I've learned."

I took a deep breath and settled back into the couch until I felt comfortable. I said, "This seems like a good time."

"Okay. Here goes." She rolled her eyes toward the ceiling and stared as if she were looking into the memories of her mind. Then, she closed her eyes, pursed her lips, and began. "When I OD'ed and was getting my head back together in the hospital, I had what I can only describe as a two-track experience. There was all the regular medical stuff going on, you know, figuring out what happened—if I was okay, when I could go home, and all the other embarrassing stuff of being where I was and feeling foolish. Then there was another track going on inside me. It took me by surprise. It was like all the stuff that was happening to me became extremely significant. I don't know how to describe it, but I saw for the first time real spiritual meaning to my life. It shocked and inspired me and it continues to inspire me. Do you know what I'm saying?"

I chuckled, "I suspect you know that I do. After all, you've been coming and hanging out here quite a while. I guess the themes and subject matter rubbed right off into your reality."

She nodded. "No kidding. It was like when we were working on the concept of falling in love with life. When we first talked about it in Sunday Night Class, I thought it was kind of superficial. Cute, but superficial. Then when I was in the hospital and I took out my notebook and read stuff like, *We have to take great chances in confronting our suffering,* I was knocked over. Or when I read, *There comes a time when we choose to face our problems head on,* I had a different take on what was happening to me. While I didn't choose to OD, it did make me face my problems. It motivated me. Way inside, I felt moved. My life suddenly meant something. It was like you said at class, 'Sooner or later it would be a good idea to fall in love with your life.' That just made sense; you know what I mean? It was important. What I did counted. For the first time in my life, I felt a kind of inner peace. I felt I really did care about myself. I don't know how to say this, but I felt like God had touched my life. I have no other explanation for that depth of feeling and insight. Now I just wake up in the morning and it's the first thing I think about every day."

I smiled. "There's a statement in the Talmud that says, *All beginnings are difficult.* But when people encounter great difficulties in the beginning, they often tragically let their fears overwhelm them, making them opt out of the struggle. You pushed right past any fears you may have had. It's like God gave you the strength to accept what happened to you and now you've got a small taste of what lies beyond all that. Beyond it is the love in your heart. Well, it doesn't get better than that."

From Art to L.A.

Several months later, I got a letter in the mail from Laurie. I opened it, wondering what she possibly could have sent me. Inside was a flyer advertising her first art show in the Village. She and her art friends had taken the initiative to rent a small exhibit room in a loft to display their work. One of the dates on the flyer was a Sunday night, so I decided to cancel class that Sunday and bring a group of about fifteen of the regulars with me to Laurie's show.

David, a friend who was visiting from Los Angeles for the week, also wanted to come. He was a doctor who had just finished his first year in private practice. We had been friends for five or six years. We met at a lecture I gave at a synagogue on the Upper West Side of Manhattan. He was completing his residency at that time and we hit it off right away. He had a great sense of humor, a keen interest in working on himself, and a love for baseball. At that time he began studying with me once a week. When he moved back home to Los Angeles, our study sessions switched to weekly phone calls.

The evening of Laurie's art show was warm and humid. A thunderstorm had passed through the city an hour earlier, and its drenching rain made even the gutter smell fresh. The loft

Laurie and her friends had chosen was tastefully appointed with sweeping white ceilings and walls that were framed by the original foundation bricks. A string quartet of Laurie's friends played quietly in one section of the loft. I had to hand it to her, she certainly had made the rounds in the Village. When we arrived, there were at least fifty people inside enjoying the art and ambiance.

Laurie looked elegant. She wore a black evening dress highlighted by a short white jacket edged with gold and black brocade. Her purple hair had been dyed back to its natural black, but was still highlighted with small purple strands. She made a terrific hostess and was a unique artist. I introduced her to my friend David, and after the three of us spent a few minutes talking, I wandered off to view all the paintings on display.

As the evening wore on, David and Laurie ended up in a corner, lost in conversation. During the following week, they went out on several long dates. A month later Laurie flew out to Los Angeles for the weekend.

I gave David a call and asked, "Is this serious or what?"

He said, "Well, you introduced her to me. What does it look like?"

Six months later, they were engaged. They were married within the year. At the wedding I thought about all the kids I knew on the street. When I thought of them, it almost stopped my heart. The paradox between the wedding and the street stretched my mind taut. My hands got cold and clammy. I shut my eyes. They stung. It's true—there are great mysteries in life, things we can feel but not understand and see.

Today, David and Laurie live on the West Coast. They have three beautiful children, and Laurie continues with her art. We're still terrific friends.

Conclusion

Had I not fallen, I would not have risen,
had I not sat in darkness,
God would not have been a light for me.
Midrash Tehillim Socher Tov, Psalm 5

In the world I walk I've been a witness to the intimate connection between the darkness and our ability to discover the light. It is a wondrous revelation to experience that our daily struggles have at their core a transcendent meaning. There is a teaching that says Teshuvah was created before the world came into being. I think it means that, built into who we are is the ability to find great meaning in our existence, even when confronted with great trials and tribulations. God gives us the ability to turn, and in that turning we discover the light of our lives.

Perhaps the deepest insight we can understand from these kids' stories is that we truly are never alone. Not only is that a comforting thought, but having the courage to turn and face our darkness and pain can unlock a wellspring of love and enthusiasm for life that we never knew we possessed. Crisis and suffering can lead directly to understanding the uniqueness of each of our lives. The path of Teshuvah inevitably turns life into a wonder that can become the door to unlocking the great mystery and sacredness of each of our lives. The eight steps are designed to be signposts on the road to reawakening the inspiration locked in each of our hearts.

If you had a chance to meet the many kids I've been privileged to work with, I trust they all would tell you pretty much the same thing—they still struggle. They would tell you that Teshuvah is a continual process of accepting who they are while knowing it's possible to always be a better person. They would tell you that they are committed to that process in their daily lives and in their personal relationships. I have no doubt you would hear this from those who went on to become schoolteachers, homemakers, musicians, attorneys, therapists, nurses, doctors, salespeople, and business professionals. The message reflects the depth of their commitment to their lives and the discoveries they have made in the midst of their struggles. It is my hope that the stories and steps in this book will provide courage for others to persevere in the face of the difficulties we all inevitably encounter.

It is no accident that the eighth step is Falling in Love with Life. It has been my experience that once we are engaged in the process of Teshuvah, our appreciation for being alive grows. With it comes the recognition that we all need each other's help. No matter how difficult the circumstances, we all have the ability to understand that love, caring, wisdom, understanding, kindness, and compassion are part of the sacred trust God imparts to each of us in our lifetime. And these gifts are attained if we are willing to give them and humble enough to receive them.

Notes

STEP 1

1. "Playing for Keeps," *Sporting News,* 18 August 1973.

2. Bernie Siegal, "The Diagnosis Is In," *Life's Good Stuff* 1, no. 1 (1992): 14.

STEP 2

1. Frank S. Pittman, *Turning Points: Treating Families in Transition and Crisis* (New York: Norton, 1987), 176–77. (Partial paraphrase.)

2. Pittman, *Turning Points,* 177.

STEP 3

1. A. TH. Phillips, "Daily Prayers," chap. 2, sect. 20 in *Pirkei Avos* (New York: Hebrew Publishing, 1923), 462–63.

STEP 4

1. A. TH. Phillips, "Daily Prayers," chap. 2, sect. 21 in *Pirkei Avos* (New York: Hebrew Publishing, 1923), 464.

2. Leo Buscaglia, *Loving Each Other: The Challenge of Human Relationships* (New York: Ballantine Books, Fawcett Columbine, 1984), 65.

STEP 5

1. David Plant, ed., "The Green Fields of the Mind," in *Speaking of Baseball: Quotes and Notes on the National Pastime* (Philadelphia: Running Press, 1993), 395.

STEP 6

1. Rabbi Simcha Zissel Ziv, *Chochmah Umassar,* vol. 2 (Jerusalem, Israel: Aber Press, 1924), 218.

2. A. TH. Phillips, "Daily Prayers," chap. 3, sect. A in *Pirkei Avos* (New York: Hebrew Publishing, 1923), 464.

STEP 7

1. Tommy Lasorda, *New York Mets broadcast, WOR,* 31 July 1996.

2. Rabbi Uri of Strelsik, *Sefer Hassidut* (Tel Aviv, Israel: Azioni Publishing, 1961), 227.

STEP 8

1. Leo Buscaglia, *Loving Each Other: The Challenge of Human Relationships* (New York: Ballantine Books, Fawcett Columbine, 1984), 11.

2. Rabbi Shlomo Hakohen Rabinowitz of Rodonisk, *Tiferes Shlomo* (n.p., Israel: Books Export Enterprises, n.d.), 45.

Index

About the Author

YEHUDAH FINE is the director of the Jewish Family Institute. For the past twenty-five years, he has worked with families and kids in crisis. Prior to coming to New York, he ran a unique secondary school program for migrant farmworkers in the Sacramento Valley of California, and later founded and directed an award-winning alternative high school in northern California. In New York he completed his rabinical studies and trained as a family therapist at the Ackerman Institute of Family Therapy.

Because of Fine's extensive background in education and outreach, people from all walks of life began to seek him out for advice. Runaway and homeless kids found their way to his door. As a result he began to actively provide outreach to kids on the streets of Manhattan and the other boroughs of New York City. Currently, he is a member of the counseling staff at Yeshiva University and his work with kids continues. He recently moved, with his wife and three children, to the Catskill Mountains to begin building the next phase of his work in outreach.

Rabbi Fine can be reached at
www.timessquarerabbi.com—the site of The Hope Forum.

HAZELDEN PUBLISHING AND EDUCATION is a division of the Hazelden Foundation, a not-for-profit organization. Since 1949, Hazelden has been a leader in promoting the dignity and treatment of people afflicted with the disease of chemical dependency.

The mission of the foundation is to improve the quality of life for individuals, families, and communities by providing a national continuum of information, education, and recovery services that are widely accessible; to advance the field through research and training; and to improve our quality and effectiveness through continuous improvement and innovation.

Stemming from that, the mission of the publishing division is to provide quality information and support to people wherever they may be in their personal journey—from education and early intervention, through treatment and recovery, to personal and spiritual growth.

Although our treatment programs do not necessarily use everything Hazelden publishes, our bibliotherapeutic materials support our mission and the Twelve Step philosophy upon which it is based. We encourage your comments and feedback. The headquarters of the Hazelden Foundation are in Center City, Minnesota. Additional treatment facilities are located in Chicago, Illinois; New York, New York; Plymouth, Minnesota; St. Paul, Minnesota; and West Palm Beach, Florida. At these sites, we provide a continuum of care for men and women of all ages. Our Plymouth facility is designed specifically for youth and families.

FOR MORE INFORMATION ON HAZELDEN, please call **1-800-257-7800.** Or, you may access our World Wide Web site on the Internet at **http://www.hazelden.org**.